THE
SECRET
ARMY

THE
SECRET
ARMY

BY GEOFFREY BOCCA

Prentice-Hall, Inc., Englewood Cliffs, N.J.

Turning and turning in the widening gyre
The falcon cannot hear the falconer;
Things fall apart; the centre cannot hold;
Mere anarchy is loosed upon the world,
The blood-dimmed tide is loosed, and everywhere
The ceremony of innocence is drowned;
The best lack all conviction, while the worst
Are full of passionate intensity.

W. B. YEATS

FOREWORD

❖❖❖

Any reader embarking cold on the history of the French Secret Army can be excused for confusion caused by the coincidental fact that several of the leaders of that band had similar, sometimes almost identical names. For that reason a brief dramatis personae of some of the principal members is included here for easier reference should the reader get lost.

ARGOUD: Colonel Antoine.

Educated Polytechnique. Served in the Battle of France, 1940. Landed with Free French Forces in Provence in 1944 with the 3rd African Chasseurs. Expert on armored warfare and the youngest colonel in the French Army. Served at Suez in 1956, and later as Chief of Staff to General Massu in Algeria. Implicated in the Affair of the Barricades, January, 1960. Took part in the Generals' revolt, April, 1961, and escaped to Spain. Married, two children.

BROIZAT: Colonel Joseph.

Studied Gregorian University, Rome. Joined the Army as 2nd Lieutenant from l'Ecole de Saint Maixent. Served in Second World War. in Tunisia, France and Germany with the 3rd Regiment of Algerian Tirailleurs. Parachutist in Indochina and Algeria. Implicated in the Affair of the Barricades, and joined Generals' revolt. Went underground, but declined to join the Secret Army itself. Edited its newspaper, "The Centurions." Married.

BIDAULT: Georges.

Born October 5th, 1899. Professor at the Rheims Lycée and elsewhere. Editorialist on L'Aube. Resistance leader, elected President of the National Resistance Council in 1943. Foreign Minister in the government of General de Gaulle in 1944. Twice Prime Minister and nine times Foreign Minister of France in Fourth Republic. Designated by General Salan his successor in March, 1962.

CHATEAU-JOBERT: Colonel Pierre.

Born Morlaix, February 3, 1912. Wounded Battle of France, 1940. Joined Free French later the same year. Parachute brigade commander in Indochina from 1947 to 1952. Fought at Suez, 1956. Put under house arrest for his sympathy with Generals' revolt, escaped and went underground in January, 1962.

DEGUELDRE: Lieutenant Roger.

Born 1925, Louvroil (Nord). Served as a boy in the Resistance. Joined the Foreign Legion at the end of the war, and served in Indochina. Wounded and taken prisoner at Dien Bien Phu. Commissioned 2nd Lieutenant in 1958, he took part in the Generals' revolt with the 1st Foreign Legion Parachutists, and then went underground. Twice married.

DOVECAR: Sergeant Albert.

Born July 19, 1937, in Tezno, Yugoslavia, of Austrian parents. Enlisted in Foreign Legion 1957, wounded in Algeria. Joined Generals' revolt with 1st Foreign Legion Parachutists, and then went underground. Engaged.

GARDES: Colonel Roger.

Born October 4, 1914, in Paris. Graduated from Saint Cyr in 1937, fought in Battle of France, 1940, and in Italy, France and Germany from 1943 to 1945. Commanded Algerian Tirailleurs in Europe and Indochina, and later press information officer in Hanoi. In Algeria he specialized in psychological warfare. Was implicated in the Affair of the Barricades in January, 1960. Took part in the Generals' revolt, 1961, and went underground. Married, six children.

GARDY: General Paul.

Born August 11, 1901, in Paris. Graduated from Saint Cyr. Served in Morocco and the Middle East before the Second World War. Fought in the Battle of France in 1940, and with the Free French after 1943. Named Brigadier in 1956, and Inspector of the Foreign Legion in 1958. A leader in the Generals' revolt, he then went underground. One son in Legion. Two daughters married to Legion officers.

GODARD: *Colonel Yves.*

Born December 21, 1911, in Saint Maixent. Graduated from Saint Cyr in 1932. Taken prisoner by the Germans in 1940, he escaped from a prison camp in Poland and joined the French Resistance in Savoy. Commanded the 11th Parachute Battalion in Indochina. Served under General Massu in Algeria, and appointed head of the Algerian police in May, 1958. Implicated in the Affair of the Barricades, he joined Generals' revolt in 1961, and went underground. Bachelor.

JOUHAUD: *General André*

Born Bou Sfer, Oran, April 2, 1905. Graduated Saint Cyr, 1926. Joined Air Force. Commanded an air reconnaissance group in 1940. Joined Resistance in 1942, and the Free French in 1943. Appointed Brigadier in 1949. Commander of the French Air Force in Germany in 1952. Appointed Chief of Staff of the Air Force in October, 1958. Joined Generals' revolt in 1961, went underground and appointed second in command to General Salan as head of the French Secret Army.

LAGAILLARDE: *Pierre.*

Born May 15, 1931, in Coubevoie. President of the Algerian Students' Association in 1957. Called to the bar at Blida. Elected deputy in 1958. Took part in all Algerian political manifestations, and, with Joseph Ortiz, directed the Affair of the Barricades in January, 1960. Imprisoned for nine months, he jumped bail, fled to Madrid, where he formed, in January, 1961, the French Secret Army. Married.

SALAN: *General Raoul.*

Born Roquecourbe, Tarn, June 10, 1899. Served in trenches from 1917, in Syria in 1921-1922, and then in Indochina from 1924 to 1936. Fought in 1939-40 as head of a battalion of Senegalese Tirailleurs. Head of French Intelligence in Dakar from 1940 to 1942 when he joined the Free French. Fought in campaigns in Africa, France and Germany from 1943 to 1945. Aide de Campe to General Leclerc in Indochina in 1946. Commander in Chief of the French Army in Indochina after the departure of General de Lattre de Tassigny. Left Indochina in 1953. Commander in Chief of the French Army in Algeria from November, 1956. One of the principal figures in the restoration of General de Gaulle to power after the demonstrations in Algiers on May 13, 1958. Appointed Inspector General of the French Army in November, 1958. Retired in 1960 as the most decorated and most wounded soldier in the Army. Joined conspiracy against General de Gaulle in Madrid. Flew to Algiers to lead the Generals' revolt in April, 1961, and became commander of the Secret Army. Married, one son (by an Indochinese mistress).

SOUSTELLE: Jacques.

Born in 1912, in Montpellier. Educated Ecole Normale Supèrieure. Joined General de Gaulle in London in 1940, and served as Minister of Information to the Free French. Appointed Governor General of Algeria in 1955. Leader of the movement to restore General de Gaulle to power in 1958. Minister of Information in first government of General de Gaulle, then Minister for Sahara Affairs in 1959-60. Left Government in 1960 over objection to Algerian policy, fled France after the Generals' revolt of April, 1961, and went underground.

SERGENT: Captain Pierre.

Born 1927. Fought as a boy in the Resistance then graduated from Saint Cyr. Fought in Indochina and Algeria in the Foreign Legion. Took part in the Generals' revolt, then sent by General Salan to lead the Secret Army in Paris.

SUSINI: Jean-Jacques.

Born July 30, 1933, in Algiers. Studied medicine in Strasbourg and Lyon. In 1959 elected President of the General Association of Algeria Students. One of the instigators of the Affair of the Barricades in January, 1960, imprisoned for nine months, and then joined the French conspirators in Spain. Flew to Algiers with General Salan in April, 1961, to join the Generals' revolt, and became the intellectual leader of the organization. Married once.

CONTENTS

PART ONE: THE ORIGINS

PART TWO: THE HAPPENING

PART THREE: THE FRENZY

INTRODUCTION

❖❖❖

The Algerian war began in November 1954 with attacks by Moslem nationalists on French Army outposts in the Aurès mountains. The Prime Minister of France at the time, Pierre Mendès-France, called the attacks "an act of terrorism" and told the National Assembly on November 12 that "the criminal designs of a few men will be broken by a repression without weakness." The Assembly demonstrated its approval when Mendès-France declared: "The departments of Algeria are part of the French Republic. Never will France, never will any Government yield on this fundamental principle."

The rebellion spread through the Department of Constantine and into Kabylia. It inflamed the nervous and polyglot city of Algiers but spared for a long time the more homogeneous city of Oran. Only a few hundred rebels were involved at first, and the revolt attracted little popular support, the Algerian Moslem being noted for his sobriety and patience. This pattern is usual in revolutionary movements, in which the tail usually wags the dog. Revolutions tend to start quietly and unexpectedly against sleeping garrisons. The Algerian insurrection was different in one vital respect. The rebels, misreading history, saw, in the defeat of the French Army at Dien Bien Phu earlier that year, an opportunity to revolt against a demoralized force. They ran instead into the angriest, most battle-hardened and most professional army in the world. When the war ended in the summer of 1962, it was conservatively estimated that 150,000 Moslems and 17,000 Frenchmen had been killed. Tens of thousands of noncombatants died violently or from starvation. One-sixth of the population was uprooted and displaced. An entire European population of a million, whose roots in the country stretched back 130 years, was made homeless. The war was responsible for the overthrow of the Fourth Republic, and the successor Fifth Republic came close to collapse and civil war.

Out of this gradually accumulating bitterness was distilled a tragic and lethal brew called *"l' Organisation de l'Armée Secrète,"* the Secret Army Organization, better known as the "O.A.S.," a band of men and women committed to keeping the French flag flying, come what may, over a country of 9 million Moslems and 1 million Europeans. It received a poor press. It was called "fascist" and "racist," whereas, of all the criticisms that could be legitimately brought against it, these two were the least relevant. Many of its members saw themselves in a context as simple as did their detractors. They considered themselves centurions. When Rome abandoned the Empire, the centurions turned on Rome because they had sworn to protect the Empire with their blood. They assumed power in the provinces and waited for the capital to fall of its own weakness. The O.A.S. hoped to emulate them. When Paris decided that it had had enough of the Algerian war, the O.A.S. took over in Algeria and waited for Paris to fall. Paris staggered, stunned by bloody riots and deafened by the explosions of plastic bombs. It walled itself in with roadblocks, sandbagged the police stations, posted squadrons of tanks on the main boulevards and watched the skies for rebel parachutes—but it did not fall.

What kind of force could commit atrocities, could murder and maim and could bring one of the major capitals of the world to such a point of desperation—and at a time of unparalleled prosperity? A clandestine organization aimed primarily at maintaining the French presence on an African shore, at whatever cost, found itself able to recruit thousands of people from every social class and all age groups; from students, professors and scholars; from generals and sergeants, former Cabinet ministers, shopkeepers, religious mystics and even communists. Of the four generals who led the Army revolt against General de Gaulle in April 1961, the incident that spawned the O.A.S., three were men of the political Left. At least one O.A.S. commando was led by an armed Catholic priest, and many of the most fanatical and ruthless fighters were Jews and Moslems.

The O.A.S. was not a table with four legs, as its critics might have liked to define it. It was a nest table, a *gigogne*; when one table was removed there was another one underneath. The O.A.S. was many people; the O.A.S. was a handful of people. The O.A.S. was a force of two hundred professional soldiers in revolt; the O.A.S. was an army of a thousand or two thousand or three thousand. The O.A.S. comprised the entire Christian and Jewish population of Algeria; the O.A.S. was a foreign body left at the point of the needle by a quack doctor into the flesh of Algeria. The O.A.S. was also one man, Lieutenant Roger Degueldre; when he departed all the heart and high hopes went out of the Organization. The O.A.S. was a philosophy and a state of mind, a beautiful dream and a nightmare.

And after all the blood was shed, the atrocities committed and the crises just barely survived, the simple, bitter fact was that the Algerian war in the end did not matter very much neither in the context of history nor in the fortune of most of its participants. Most of the Europeans of Algeria make more money in France today than they did before in Algeria. Algeria did not, as the French generals and the O.A.S. warned, become a French Cuba, a communist bastion bringing Paris within the range of medium missiles. Less inflamed observers could see in advance that such a situation was impossible. Algeria is physically separate from areas where it might otherwise have influence. It lies west of the striking power of the American 6th Fleet, which lies between it and the faraway Arab peninsula, and, on the one occasion that its army, the best in the Arab world, was needed—against Israel in 1967—it found itself impotent to move.

The plight of the Europeans in Algeria in the 1950s and the early 1960s was not a unique one. It was part of the price the West has had to pay for its past. The tide of events ran over those Europeans as it is running over the Rhodesian farmers and colonials everywhere. There is no one to speak up for them, no UNESCO to help them, but they are people too. What set the Algerian war apart from the other colonial wars was the diversity of interests involved. The French Army, the O.A.S., the *colons,* the Jews, the Moslems, the Metropolitan French all saw the war quite differently. Their aims were not only different; they were also often completely unrelated, and the result was chaos, desperation and revolt.

Revolt is nothing new and, in the French Army, not necessarily dishonorable. When General de Gaulle refused to accept the armistice in June 1940, he was being true to his own stated opinions. In *Le Fil et l'Épée,* written in 1932, he said, "Those who accomplish something great must often go beyond the appearance of a false discipline." He quoted what Lord Fisher had said about Admiral Jellicoe in the First World War, "He had all Nelson's qualities except one; he did not know how to disobey."

At the end of the Second World War, Colonel Jacques Weygand, discussing the merits of obedience and revolt in the French Army, mentioned the problems of the Pétainist officers:

> Some shaped their thinking around a symbolic abandonment of personality. They accorded a mystical value to the complete abnegation demanded in a tragic circumstance by the First among them [Pétain], and denied themselves the right of exercising their free minds. Some were even enthusiastic about a submission whose very excess seemed to contain the germ of the future revival of our humiliated arms. The return to reality was all the more powerful for these generous spirits in that they had to descend from these spiritual summits to learn that, in the army, to have served without reserve was no longer a safe-conduct; it was a fault.

In 1945 those who had revolted were promoted and loaded with honors; those who had obeyed finished in Fresnes prison. The French officers in Algeria were gorged with obedience, and what, they asked themselves, had it brought them but a drip-drip water torture of endless humiliation, not only in the Second World War and in Indochina, but also in Morocco, in Tunisia and at Suez? They had changed directions so many times on orders from above that, in the end, some came to believe in the one direction they had not tried—revolt. Lieutenant Daniel Godot, one of the leaders of the O.A.S., expressed at his trial the full agony of the Algerian officer: "We—the O.A.S.—did not fight to win, but to prove a point; that we did not order our men to their deaths, nor even did we kill the enemy, for nothing."

Lieutenant Jacques Favreau, son of the French military attaché in London, did not join the O.A.S. but testified at the trial of General Challe. "What Paris could not understand," he said, "was that in the bled, in the field, we lieutenants were desperate."

THE
SECRET
ARMY

PART ONE:
THE ORIGINS

1
TOWN AND COUNTRY
1830–1958

When the Europeans quit Algeria in the tormented, panic-stricken summer exodus of 1962, the French Government, fearing the emergence of a political bloc, tried to force them north by refusing compensation to those who settled along the Mediterranean. What a hope! To pull a European Algerian from the Mediterranean shores was like pulling a fish from water. When the sun is hot and sharp and dry, so that one can feel it almost like fresh, new banknotes, to be rubbed between finger and thumb—and in Nice and Alicante, Marseilles and Málaga it often *is* like that—the exiled European looks out of the taxi he is driving, straightens from his labor or gazes through prison bars. "Ah," he says. "Today it is like Algeria." Had he not believed in the O.A.S. he might still be in his homeland today, but the history of the Algerian war is a history of people— civilian and military, European and Arab—who made the mistake of believing in promises, including their own.

"Algeria" is a beautiful word that could scarcely sound more Arabic. It is like "Allah" and "algebra" and "inshallah." In fact *Algérie* is French, from the Arabic *el ejezair,* meaning island. The French annexed it in 1830, ostensibly to suppress Barbary pirates who hid in islands that were later filled in to create the city of Algiers. Until then Algeria was a sparsely populated land of nomadic Berber tribes and Arabic-speaking Sephardic Jews. The European settlement of Algeria began before that of most of the United States. When France claimed Algeria, only 24 states had been admitted to the Union.

3

The Europeans are all gone now, but, wherever they have settled, until a new generation grows up unshackled by memories, their
horizons will continue to be dominated by the great empty stretches
of Kabylia and the naked yellow mountains of the Aurès, whose
stark towers and volcanic shelves turned from molten lava into stone
in a single moment of prehistory, so that the convulsions of the
dawning world seem to have happened only yesterday. All these
memories of endless perspectives in the harsh sunlight, the smell of
anisette, the colors and odors of the Arab markets, the taste of purple Mascara wine and mutton couscous, are the inheritance of the
man known as the *pied noir*.

He was called "black foot" by derisive administrators because he
arrived in Algeria from Spain, Italy, Malta and Corsica, as well as
from France, so poor that he had barely soles on his shoes; and he
accepted the term not as an insult but as a statement of fact. The
pied noir is basically a simple fellow with few attachments either to
work or to family. Meursault, hero of Camus' *The Stranger* is a
pied noir employed as a clerk, but neither his office nor his relatives
touch him much. "Mother died today." the book begins. "Or, maybe,
yesterday."

Albert Camus was perhaps the most distinguished of all the *pieds
noirs*. His father was killed on the Marne in 1914 when he was
eleven months old. His mother, a pious and illiterate woman, supported Camus, his elder brother, his grandmother and his half-
witted uncle on her earnings as a charwoman in a little flat in Belcourt,
a working-class suburb of Algiers. Although desperately poor as a
youth, Camus said later that he "envied for almost nothing. Poverty
was never a misfortune to me, for it was flooded with light." He
claimed that his first lessons in ethics he learned playing soccer.
Christianity had for him, as for many *pieds noirs*, little effect because
exaltation came simply from the state of being alive.

It became fashionable, even in the early days, for Metropolitan
Frenchmen to sneer at the *pied noir* as a lazy mongrel whose
blood was mixed with Arab blood, whose accent was an affront to
the language, whose standard of living was abysmal and whose
taste for anisette defied slaking. Marshal Bugeaud, Governor-General from 1840 to 1847, called the *pieds noirs* "the agricultural
scum of the European countries." The *pied noir,* looking into the
mirror, combing his dense mop of shiny black hair and regarding

his swarthy Mediterranean features and brilliant brown eyes, might recognize and even acknowledge himself in such descriptions. Yet it can be argued that he was an engaging fellow with a rough sense of humor, a kind of physically stunted Australian or American cowboy. He alternated, like the Australian, between bursts of backbreaking labor and a languor that often approached total immobility. Like the American cowboy, he had little respect for pretention, pomposity and snobbery.

As an artisan, the *pied noir* learned efficiency. His great achievement was the draining of the Mitidja swamps outside Algiers and the conversion of the area into one of the most fertile plains in the Maghreb. Toward the Moslem the *pied noir* could be cheerful and paternal or mean and vicious, depending usually on how the Moslem behaved toward him. Being at the foot of the French social ladder he needed someone to kick around, and that someone was usually the Moslem. One of his common expressions for the Moslem was *raton*, "little rat." In certain country districts the *pied noir* who killed a Moslem was expected to leave money for the dead man's dependents or risk losing his cattle or having his windows stoned. The Moslem who killed another Moslem went to prison for a year or two. The Moslem who killed a *pied noir* was publicly executed on a guillotine transported in an open truck from Algiers. Elections were ruthlessly rigged to make sure that no Moslem achieved a position of power. John Phillips, a *pied noir* of British origin, recalls how his local mayor used to declare a smudged ballot void and kept a piece of lard under the table to smudge the Moslem ballots himself. The relationship sounds not unlike the old relationship between white and Negro in the American south, but in fact it was quite different. The *pied noir* was often physically indistinguishable from the Moslem, and he had acquired the Moslem's fatalism and inertia. The difference was not one of color but of irreconcilable religious beliefs. The European owned the property and the political power, and his livelihood and prosperity depended on his holding it, whereas the Moslem lacked even the energy and the education of the *pied noir*, poor though it was, to try seriously to take it away.

The *pied noir* learned in time that the easiest way to untangle incomprehensible political problems was to kill those obstructing his understanding, as was done in the United States in the days of the frontier—and he was not necessarily wrong. Admiral Darlan was

assassinated in Algiers in 1942 after the Allied landings in North
Africa. One of the most notorious of the Vichy leaders, he was
captured by the Allies and agreed to cooperate with them. General
Eisenhower's acceptance of Darlan's offer created a political hubbub;
the *pieds noirs* shot him, and even Allied leaders had to admit that it
simplified matters considerably.

The *pied noir* woman was usually more estimable in character
than was her mate, accepting as her lot the need to have energy for
two. She was tempestuous, emotional, intellectually honest and fearless. A brilliant example of the *pied noir* woman was Geneviève
Salasc, who will be mentioned many times in this book. At one
moment the fate of the O.A.S. hinged upon her courage. Had she
exhibited the slightest weakness in that moment, the Secret Army
would have been crushed in a matter of hours.

The fundamental problem of the educated Moslem in Algeria was
that of his national identity. History had never known an Algerian
nation. The Moroccans and Tunisians on either side possessed ancient dynasties, hereditary aristocracies, written history, architec-
ture and universities. Moslems who were born in or moved into
Algeria could be only Frenchmen, third-class Frenchmen—second-
class being reserved for the *pieds noirs* themselves—but Frenchmen
nonetheless. The educated Moslem who had studied his history
books found his nearest counterpart in the American Indian, which
tended to make him grateful to the French, who at least allowed him
to live and occasionally to prosper instead of wiping him out. The
absence of an Algerian national identity and the ineluctable link-
ing of Algerian destiny with that of France were the basic themes of
Moslem intellectuals' philosophy. In 1937, the Sétif chemist, Ferhat
Abbas, published his "Algerian Manifesto" in an article that was to
become famous as *La France, c'est moi*:

> If I had discovered an "Algerian nation" I would have be-
> come a nationalist and would not have blushed. . . . I did
> not find it. I consulted history. I looked for it in the ceme-
> teries. But no answer came. You cannot build on air. We
> have driven away the clouds and chimeras in order, once
> and for all, to bind our future to the French work of con-
> struction in this country. Six million Moslems live on this
> soil which has been French for a hundred years. They live
> in hovels, go barefoot, without clothing and often without

bread. Out of this hungry mass we will make a modern society . . . elevate them to human dignity so they may be
worthy of the name of Frenchmen. . . .

As a compliment to the French it was double-edged, but Frenchmen in Algeria liked to quote it. More percipient Frenchmen, however,
also recalled a statement made by Marshal Lyautey, the great French
imperialist, as long ago as April 1925 in Rabat, Morocco:

It is to be foreseen, and indeed I regard it as a historic truth
that in the more or less distant future, North Africa, mod-
ernized, civilized, living its own autonomous life, will detach itself from Metropolitan France. When this occurs,
and it must be our supreme political goal, the parting must
occur without pain and the nations must be able to continue to view France without fear. The African peoples
must not turn against her. For this reason, we must, as from
today, as a starting point, make ourselves loved.

The Europeans of Algeria took Ferhat Abbas' words for the
fundamental Moslem position. Lyautey's words were forgotten. But
in 1954 the Moslems of Algeria rose to fight for the independence
of their country. A national identity had been found, and it expressed itself in the *Front de Libération Nationale,* the National
Liberation Front, or F.L.N.

And it was at that point that the French Army came in strength
to Algeria from its defeat at Dien Bien Phu, climaxing years of repeated frustration. Fourteen years earlier it had been beaten by
the Germans before it could catch its breath. For the next three
years it was stabled by the Vichy Government while other armies,
even that of the Italians, were fighting and dying. Its victory of 1945
was only a token granted by the Americans and the British. When
other armies were exhausted, the French were still hungry. Germany's defeat was for the French army only a canapé to whet its
appetite for a victory of its own. Even while Ho Chi Minh was
negotiating in Paris, Admiral Georges Thierry d'Argenlieu was
ordering an attack on the Vietminh in Haiphong, and the Indochinese war began. Thierry d'Argenlieu died a monk in 1966, but the
war he started lives on.

The French war in Indochina lasted eight years. Sometimes it
was waged with considerable success, but it ended in disaster at

Dien Bien Phu. It was another twelve years before the French (and Algerian and German) veterans of Indochina could take consolation from the fact that they came closer to victory over Ho Chi Minh than the United States could, and with a fraction of the power. The army that left Indochina for Algeria was not, however, the same band of ardent amateurs that had occupied the Rhine and Berlin in 1945. Not a single conscript had fought in the Indochinese campaign. The French Army, was all professional, with an unequaled corps of combat colonels, including Bigeard, Langlais, Jeanpierre, Godard, Château-Jobert, Trinquier, Broizat, Guiraud and Gardes, men who combined intellect and enterprise with physical courage. Their most traumatic memories from Indochina were not of the defeat at Dien Bien Phu but of the hundreds of thousands of Vietnamese men, women and children fleeing south after the division of the country, people who had believed in French offers of protection and had therefore collaborated. French officers have high self-esteem. Most of the refugees had simply backed the wrong horse and were fleeing from vengeance, but the officers preferred to think that the refugees loved the French and fretted at the thought that they had let the natives down. They searched for a solution in the thoughts of Mao Tse-tung and especially in such terse maxims as "power comes from the mouth of the gun" and "the people are the sea in which the guerilla swims." They came to believe that the way to prevent another Indochina was to win the native population to their side by a combination of example, persuasion and force.

Scarcely had they arrived in Algeria than the rebellion began, giving the soldiers the golden opportunity to put their theories into practice on what they considered an ideal testing ground. Most had commanded Algerian troops or fought side by side with Algerian officers, whom they admired, respected and—they thought —understood. But the educated Moslem, in his relationship with the Army as in his relationship with the *pieds noirs* was still subject to the essence of his religion. Despite himself, despite his diplomas and his major's or colonel's bars, he still looked to Islam in a way that no Christian could understand. Paris gave him his education and opportunities, but Islam sustained his spirit, and in that period of change and rebellion the man who spoke with the voice of Islam was Gamal Abdel Nasser. It should have been an easy problem to solve. In fact it became more insoluble the more it became understood.

2
MAY DAY
May 13, 1958

✣✣✣

On the morning of May 9, 1958, amid rumors circulating in Algiers that French diplomats were offering negotiations to the rebel F.L.N., General Raoul Salan, Commander in Chief of the French forces in Algeria, sent a telegram to his superior officer in Paris. It stated that

> the French Army unanimously considers it outrageous to abandon the patrimony that is Algeria. One cannot forecast how it will react to its own despair. I beg you to call the attention of the President of the Republic to our anguish, which can be effaced only by a Government firmly committed to keeping our flag in Algeria.

This tacit threat of military rebellion after three and a half years of war in Algeria seemed a world away from the mood of spiritual dedication and psychological exuberance that had moved the Indochinese veterans when the war began, when proseletyzing French officers still believed that they could turn the peaceful Moslem population away from the rebels and toward an integrated French Algeria. To some extent they had succeeded. The F.L.N. survived as a military force only because of its sanctuary in Tunisia. Ten times as many Moslems served in the French Army as in the F.L.N. Most of the country had been pacified, by rough means and smooth, but pacification had left a legacy—at worst of bitterness, at best of apathy—that the officers seriously underestimated. What the officers had not counted on was the collapse of the Fourth Republic itself. Once again a government had fallen, as so often in the past, but this time the task of forming a new one was proving hopeless. The

9

French public was sick of the Algerian war and wanted it ended, but the majority also wanted Algeria to remain French. Inevitably, and at last hopefully, the country was turning to the one man who could achieve both peace *and* a French Algeria, General Charles de Gaulle. Aside from that, Paris was politically stagnant, drained of ideas. But Algiers, numerically and politically the second city of France, was neither.

Algiers, like most cities built on hills, is beautiful, with a gorgeous bay and unexpected vistas of mountains above and sea below; it rises and dips at every street corner. By day it is a Naples; seen from the hills by night, it is an inverted bowl of stars. In the old days it was a little New York, with its European population from all over the continent. Its Brooklyn was the working-class district of Bab-el-Oued, its Harlem the Casbah.

Algiers, even more than most political cities, was a paradise for plotters. By 1958 there existed within the city networks of conspirators to satisfy all tastes. There were conspiracies of Poujadists, communists, socialists, innumerable veterans' groups and a full spectrum of religious mystics. There were a conspiracy of streetcar operators and a conspiracy of railway workers. The university was so feverish with conspiracy that one could be excused for wondering when the students found time for their homework. There were a Corsican underground and a Jewish underground. There was even a conspiracy of Algerian liberals, two of whom—Pierre Popie and William Lévy—were later murdered.

The Army had a finger in all the conspiracies, which was why the combat officers detested the city. They found themselves intellectually suffocated, unable to breathe for the back stabbing and plotting of the intelligence and staff officers. A few days of comfort at the Hotel Saint George or the Aletti were enough. After that they could not wait to go back to the bled, the country, where their men in visored caps and leopard-man camouflage suits waited to resume pursuit of the rebels, the fellagha, whom they called "fels" and sometimes *gibier*, or game.

But after Salan's telegram, Algiers moved out of the league of petty conspiracy and into history. The day after it was sent, the French prisoners held by the F.L.N. in Tunisia were shot as a reprisal for the execution of three terrorists. Demonstrations were called for May 13 by the French Algerians. They were planned to take place simultaneously in Paris and Algiers, but Paris was too exhausted by political crisis. Only the helmeted policemen massed outside the Palais Bourbon and the trucks blocking the bridge from the Place de la Concorde revealed that trouble had been expected. It did not matter. Algiers was providing all the action necessary.

By midmorning a great horde of Europeans and Moslems had gathered around the Government palace. They had overflowed the Champ de Manoeuvre and had flocked through the public gardens, around the atrocious Monument to the Dead and up the 189 steps to the Forum. They sang the *Marseillaise* and chanted their slogan, *Al-gé-rie fran-çaise*. The confusion was without venom. There were children in the crowd, and lovers went hand in hand. The riot policemen threw a few tear-gas grenades, but their hearts were not in the job, and apart from a few smarting eyes they caused little damage. After this ritual gesture of devotion to duty, they retired to play cards in the anterooms of the palace; their places were taken by the 3rd Colonial Paratroops, who were warmly received. Algiers adored its paras.

There were shouts of "Massu to power," and when General Jacques Massu, the idol of the Europeans, appeared on the balcony there was pandemonium. Massu announced that he would put himself at the head of the committee of public safety. At 9:35 P.M. a secret telegram arrived from Paris. It was from the outgoing Prime Minister, who was still serving because no successor had yet been found, and it read:

> From the President of the Council of Ministers to General Salan, Commander in Chief, Algeria; General Salan is authorized to take all measures for the maintenance of order, protection of property and persons until further notice.

With this cable from a prime minister without office, Algeria was given to the Army. The Fourth Republic was packing up, and the date, May 13, was to prove the turning point of the war and one of the turning points of the twentieth century, because it brought General de Gaulle to real power at last.

Two days later, General Raoul Salan also appeared on the balcony, barearmed, bareheaded, a dying khamsin riffling his sparse gray hair; he was also given an ovation. Eighteen months earlier a *pied noir* terrorist group, regarding Salan as a socialist (which he was), had tried to kill him with a bazooka. Today the *pieds noirs* shouted "Long live Salan," hoping that he had forgotten the incident, which he had not. He cordially detested the lot of them, but he was smelling power and liked it.

On May 17, Jacques Soustelle arrived at Maison Blanche Airport in Algiers. Former Governor of Algeria, Soustelle had, like Salan, been distrusted by the *pieds noirs*; they had rioted against his appointment. Later he became another of their idols, an ardent spokesman for French Algeria and the presence of the French Army, their two most popular themes. It was Soustelle who coined the dramatic phrase, "France, from Dunkirk to Tamanrasset," which meant from the northern tip of Metropolitan France to the southern tip of the French Sahara.

To say that Soustelle simply "arrived" at the airport, however, does not do justice to the man's personality. A Gaullist since the first days of the Free French in London in 1940, he had a passion for dramatics. Because of the explosive atmosphere in Algeria, an atmosphere Soustelle's presence certainly did little to calm, the French police had ordered him not to leave Metropolitan France. He was not under arrest, they assured him, but merely being "protected." Soustelle smuggled himself out in four different cars, hiding under suitcases and, in one instance, in the trunk of a new Simca, whose makers were advertising its extra luggage space. By these means he reached Switzerland and flew to Rome and Algiers.

An anthropologist turned statesman, he had been called "the most dangerous man in France," "Jacques the Wrecker," *le gros matou* ("the fat cat"), "the Molotov of Gaullism" and "a born secret policeman." He had earlier said, "I have no other ambition than to remake national unity on both shores of the Mediterranean." But one political commentator claimed that "Soustelle has ambitions far beyond French-Algerian unity; that he is primarily interested in the advancement of Jacques Soustelle."

He appeared in his familiar dark glasses, the customary cigarette between his fingers. General Salan, sniffing stolen thunder in the air, rushed to block his way and divert him, but it was too late. Algiers heard of his arrival immediately, and the crowds made their way in thousands to the Forum, chanting "Sous-telle! Sous-telle! Sous-telle!" Soustelle made a rousing speech, concluding with the words: "Long live the Republic! Long live Algeria! Long live France! Long live de Gaulle!"

General de Gaulle duly accepted the call to power. Not a drop of blood was shed. Whereas two World Wars had been necessary to pull down the supposedly weak Third Republic, the Fourth was overthrown after a day of jovial demonstrations in Algiers. It was like a miracle, like the walls of Jericho falling at the trumpet blast. Accept a condition of total fantasy, a claustrophobic isolation from international opinion and the realities of world politics. Assume that it was possible for one million Europeans to shape not only the destiny but also the nationality of nine million Moslems. Recognize these factors and it is indisputable that the victory won by the crowds in the Forum, including several thousand Moslems on May 13, 1958, was one of the most dramatic political-military upsets of the century.

A novice who shoots a hole-in-one in his first game of golf tends to believe that the game is easy. The citizens of Algiers were now conditioned to believe that if anything went wrong they simply had to demonstrate at the Forum and everything would be all right. They later learned that life was not that easy. Nevertheless, the situation in Algeria was crudely susceptible to a simple equation, namely that Algeria plus the French Army plus General de Gaulle add up to the O.A.S. Until May 13 the necessary element for the fusion was missing. After it was fitted into place in the person of General de Gaulle, catastrophe was inevitable.

But the euphoria that followed the evening of May 13 was no encouragement to forebodings. From that moment until the truth was revealed, the Europeans of Algeria believed that no problem could not be solved by French generals addressing crowds from the Forum in Algiers.

❖❖❖

Some months earlier, an event had taken place in Algeria that found no place in the newspapers save for a formal line in the *Journal Officiel,* but it had a painful impact on Algeria's destiny. Chief Sergeant Roger Degueldre had been commissioned a second lieutenant.

Degueldre was a huge man with a blurred face like a squash, lacking in protuberances. It was an ugly face, yet at the same time haunting and appealing, not a face to forget. In repose it was morose and pessimistic, but when he was happy his smile was like a wolf cub's, showing teeth so long and vulpine that they seemed almost to drip. He was born in 1925 in Louvroil in the Department of Nord, near Belgium. As a boy he served in the Resistance, and, his appetite for war unappeased, afterwards enrolled in the Foreign Legion. He was wounded several times in Indochina and Algeria.

Not all good soldiers look the part. Many are fat and short, wear spectacles and suffer from ulcers. But Degueldre could have been nothing else but a soldier. When he stood at attention he tipped forward slightly, as if the ground below were a trampoline responsive to the slightest pressure on the balls of his feet. Except on parade no one ever saw him without an unfiltered Gitane bobbing up and down at the corner of his mouth or between his fingers, and chain-smoking seemed to have put sand dunes into his voice.

By a process of elimination and logic, one could argue that Degueldre was the best soldier in the French Army. The basic assumption is that the Foreign Legion, the most decorated force in the Army, was also the best, which would be disputed, and properly so, by the Colonial and Marine paratroops. What is undoubtedly true of any army is that it is as good as its N.C.O.s, and the N.C.O.s of the Foreign Legion enjoyed far greater power and prestige than those of any other section in the French Army or, for that matter, of any other army in the world. Also indisputable to detached observers was that the 1st Régiment Étrangère Parachutiste, the 1st R.E.P., or Premier Repp, was the elite force of the Legion. Roger Degueldre was acknowledged as the outstanding N.C.O. in the best battalion in the best regiment of the most decorated force in the French Army. He was most certainly an impressive man. To both his superiors and his men his behavior was correct, taking and permitting no liberties. He had the gift of making both men and women adore him, and, unlike many men who find the love of other people easy to take, he never abused or slighted it. As a result the people who knew him dreaded his anger, for they knew that the fault must be theirs, and grave. Degueldre, more even than most Legionnaires, was a man who wholly rejected his own past. He lived for his regiment, his commanding officer, and the present. He almost never allowed a photograph to be taken of him. He never answered letters, and he tore up those he received. When friends and comrades remonstrated at this antisocial attitude, he replied, "*Pas de photos. Pas de lettres. Pas de souvenirs*".

On the night of his promotion, an uproarious party was given in

the field. De Gaulle, accompanied by General Salan, stood beside the coffin, saluted and, speaking "both as a soldier and the new head of the state," made a short address on the military virtues. Lieutenant Degueldre was among the officers who listened. Dovecar, by then a corporal, was not present. He had been wounded in the same action as that in which Colonel Jeanpierre had been killed.

In Paris de Gaulle described Algeria as "forever the body and soul of France." The September referendum gave him the overwhelming vote of confidence he had demanded, 80 percent of the electorate, both European and Moslem.

But, perhaps to his own surprise, the war went on, and the new President began to think again. On January 8, 1959, he referred to "the choice place" of tomorrow's Algeria and of Algeria's "developing her personality herself and tightly associated with France." This "association" was not quite the same thing as a French Algeria. In September of the same year he said flatly that he preferred "a government of Algerians by Algerians." At the same time he arranged that officers of dubious loyalty to the Fifth Republic be transferred to France and Germany. General Salan was given a phantom post as Inspector General of the Army and removed from Algeria. His place was taken by General Maurice Challe, an Air Force man and a Gaullist.

General de Gaulle was, of course, merely facing disagreeable facts. He realized that the Army had to put down the rebellion or get out. The more complete the French victories over the F.L.N. in the field, the more hostile the Moslem population became. To win the war required an effort that Metropolitan France was more and more reluctant to take. De Gaulle, however unhappily, was drawing the obvious conclusion from this fact.

But the *pieds noirs* heard the words and watched the change with anxiety mixed with panic. The old nightmare had ended, only to be revived in ever more hideous visions than before. They had pulled down the Fourth Republic, which at least was weak enough to manipulate, and replaced it with a man who, unburdened with gratitude or consistency, was showing himself an enemy of their cause and, what was worse, too strong to budge. In November there were anti-de Gaulle riots in Algiers and Oran.

The Army was as bewildered as were the *pieds noirs* and found itself breaking up into factions. There were not only the old Pétainist and Gaullist factions and the "Indochina Mafia" of colonels but also the considerable, liberal Mendès-France faction, which was larger than was generally believed and, though opposed to de Gaulle, believed fatalistically that Algeria could not be kept. General Challe was a de Gaulle appointment, but the presence of General André Zeller, an avowed anti-Gaullist, as Chief of Staff was an important weapon in the hands of the *pieds noirs* and the supporters of French Algeria. Other factors increased the confusion. New colonels associated with neither Pétain, de Gaulle nor Mendès-France, were arriving to introduce fresh ideas into the French Army. The two most important at that period were Colonel Antoine Argoud and Colonel Roger Gardes, both of whom were to influence the O.A.S. profoundly.

Argoud was a small man, scarcely 5 feet 4 inches tall, slender and taut, with a brilliant, calculating mind. Although he was born at Darmey near Metz in Lorraine, his northern blood was tempered by that of a Spanish grandmother, who endowed him with the narrow face of a Greco painting. Throughout his career his Spanish blood stirred him to rash, adventurous and quixotic acts. His mother was severe and beat him, but her methods abundantly justified the old axiom for he was admitted to the Polytechnique, which ensured him a place in the nation's technical and scientific elite.

A serious and very religious young man, given to occasional morbid depressions, he was also capable of enormous, seductive charm. His ambition was consuming which was not unusual and rarely unjustified in a Polytechnician, and beside ambition he had a feverish hunger for women, who were both his victims and his scourge.

He was graduated with honors, but his instructors were not wholly sorry to see him go. He was considered an eccentric, a maverick. His fingernails were always dirty, and he was a compulsive crotch-scratcher. It was assumed that no matter what Antoine Argoud undertook to do, it would be quite the reverse of what was expected of him, and he predictably demonstrated his unpredicability by joining the cavalry. He quickly mastered the cavalry horse and became a fine, but insanely reckless, horseman. He learned to speak Russian, less fashionable then than today, and to play the piano. During the war he served as a tank commander with General Leclerc's Free French, and afterward he was singled out by General de

Lattre de Tassigny and General Juin as a young man destined for the highest honors the Army could offer.

This recognition suited Argoud's temperament to a degree, but he was scandalized at the realization that he was considered too valuable a technical officer to risk death in Indochina. Despite anguished appeals to de Lattre, his mentor, he remained in France.

His disappointment did not interfere with his womanizing, which was as impetuous and unpredictable as everything else he did. One colleague in an advanced military course recalled seeing him hunched mournfully over a drink in the bar.

"Seven times I asked her to marry me," he said apropos of nothing, "and seven times she refused."

"Who?"

She turned out to be the girl at the cash desk in the officers' mess.

In 1950, his life veered again, in a direction that would have been appropriate in a romance by Pierre Loti. He met a rich and beautiful Moslem princess from Tehran, Fourrough Lighvani, known to her friends as "Fourry." She was fully two inches taller than he, but, swept away in the torrent of his personality, she agreed to marry him and even became a Catholic for his sake. The marriage sent his ambitions soaring even higher. Like many small men, he took Napoleon as his idol, and his favorite episode in history was 18 Brumaire. Unlike most men, however, he found that his education and his prospects entitled him to make comparisons not too disadvantageous to himself. He became the youngest colonel in the French Army, and after the Indochinese campaign he was one of the officers assigned to launch the Javelot Brigade, the armored division designed for the atomic warfare of the future. To this degree it could be said that Argoud was one of the principal creators of the modern French Army.

In front of his two small daughters, Marie-Claire and Catherine, Argoud would pose with his tricorne from the Polytechnique sideways on his head and his hand in his jacket. Nothing seemed beyond his grasp. His name would have been on the short list of any officer who wanted to predict a future Commander in Chief of the French Army. But even the overall command was not the limit of his ambitions. More than once he told his wife, "You will walk by my side in the Élysée."

Yet the aberrations in his character continued to work against him. Women pursued him, and he pursued them. There were threats of suicide and hairbreadth escapes from irate husbands. One woman loved him with such insane jealousy that she sent a poison-pen letter, made up of words clipped from newspapers, to her own husband alleging that she was having an affair with Argoud. Such compulsions ultimately led to divorce proceedings between the Argouds.

Algeria seemed a healthier place for Argoud. Transferred in 1957, he set about the problem of combating the F.L.N. with the same violent energy with which he approached everything else. "The Army has not understood the Algerian problem," he said. "It is making war and cannot see the wood for the trees. Instead of concerning itself with the population, which is the key to the problem, it is feverishly chasing rebels, who are only a secondary aspect."

Argoud's concern with the population was direct and ruthless. He moved into the Arbat area, where, between August 1956 and February 1957, there had been a killing or an ambush on an average of every three and a half days. He established his headquarters at an Arab farm, interrogated suspects or prisoners and, like cunning old Fury in *Alice in Wonderland,* appointed himself the court of first and last appeal. Those he found innocent he released. Those he found guilty were taken out and shot in the square; the bodies were left lying for 24 hours as an example. Argoud spent five months in the area, during which time all violence, including finally his own, ceased. When he left, he declared the area "pacified," thanks, he said with reason, "to my kind of justice." It remained pacified.

Later, at a secret inquiry, Argoud insisted that he had acted under orders, not only from Algiers but also from Paris, and Argoud is not a man to lie. Nevertheless, the Army authorities, embarrassed by newspaper stories of atrocities in Algeria, transferred him to Germany. There boredom added extra edge to his tongue. Like many Frenchmen he came to have only one preoccupation, one topic of conversation—Algeria. And he could discuss it only with people who agreed with him. He was incapable of detached argument and roundly insulted the wife of a senior officer at a cocktail party when she suggested that France should give up the whole Algerian nonsense.

"You, Madam," Argoud shouted in her face, "are an insult to French womanhood," and stormed out. The Army decided that he was better off in Algeria after all and sent him back as Chief of Staff to General Massu, to whom he presented no problems at all. They admired each other.

The situation, as Argoud saw it on his return, had seriously deteriorated in his absence. Success had always come easily to him, and, viewing the retention of Algeria as a personal trust as well as an intellectual exercise, he was outraged to see it slipping away from French control. He felt as if his valuable time had been wasted and his intelligence insulted. The fault, of course, lay not in Algeria but in Paris. Every soldier knew that. Argoud was thus drawn—or rather he plunged—into the conspiratorial world of Algiers.

So much for Argoud for the time being. The other influential colonel, Roger Gardes, was an unusual combination of soldier, journalist and political theorist. He was a small man also, with an attractive, open and rather apologetic face. He was born in southwest France in 1914. His mother went on to run a restaurant, Les Ministères, in the Rue du Bac, Paris, favored by politicians of the Third Republic, and Gardes grew up in a Radical-Socialist atmosphere. He was graduated from Saint-Cyr, then fought in Tunisia and Italy; some senior officers said that he was the best combat lieutenant in the Army. He was given a command of Algerian tirailleurs, from whom he acquired a great love of the Moslems. In Indochina he directed the Press Information Service for foreign correspondents and showed an understanding of press needs unusual in a professional officer—especially a French officer, usually the most obscurantist of fellows in his dealings with newspapermen.

The adaptable Gardes—"little Gardes" as his fellow officers affectionately called him—was what Americans would call a "joiner." When Gardes undertook something he committed himself utterly. Not for him the impersonality so common in his métier; and he was incapable of cynicism. He liked to quote Lyautey: "He who is only a soldier is a bad soldier." On marrying he proceeded to have six children. He took the French defeat in Indochina as a personal blow and, on hearing the news of Dien Bien Phu, he had a nervous breakdown, though the defeat was scarcely his fault. As a propagandist and newspaperman, he was one of the most avid students of Mao Tse-tung, seeking to learn how peasants on bicycles, each with only a bag of rice and a rifle, could defeat a modern army of paratroops.

The Algerian war began almost immediately afterward and gave him the chance to commit his pent-up emotion again, this time to a French Algeria in which the Moslems he loved could live in peace under the benign protection of the French Army. Indochina, he resolved, would never be repeated in Algeria. He was placed in charge of psychological warfare in Algiers, which gave him automatic entrée into the conspiratorial worlds of Pierre Lagaillarde and Joseph Ortiz.

So the team of colonels began to form, a team that was to dictate to—and ignore—the generals. The future leaders of the O.A.S. emerged from the gimcrack edifice of the defeat in victory of May 13. Colonels Argoud and Gardes were followed by Colonels Godard and Broizat, Colonels Lacheroy, Vaudrey, Château-Jobert and Dufour. And like uncorked champagne a fountain of majors, captains, lieutenants and second lieutenants—even more violent, even more committed and, as it turned out, even more able and resolute—erupted after them.

In January 1960, Algerian nerves snapped again. General de Gaulle had replaced the officers who had brought him to power with others whom he knew were loyal to him personally rather than to the French Algeria myth he had once seemed to represent. His trump card was General Massu, Commander of the Army Corps of the Department of Algiers. This massive officer, with his cowboy strut, his Cyrano de Bergerac nose, his face like one carved out of Mount Rushmore, was an unquestioning Gaullist and, paradoxically the idol of the *pieds noirs*. Massu's toughness and tolerance for pain were so legendary as to be scarcely believable. During the Second World War, while serving under General Leclerc, he had been hit by a German bullet, which went through his leg. He cauterized the wound by jabbing his burning cigarette into the hole. Still more incredible, after accusations had been published that his paratroops were torturing suspects, it was revealed by correspondents of the responsible conservative press that Massu had tried all the same tortures on himself first to see how much they hurt.

Extraordinary though this practice was, Massu's apologists could scarcely use it to justify an appalling and inhuman policy. The difference between Massu's submission to the *gégène*—French Army slang for the field telephone, which could be adapted to send electric shocks through a suspect's genitals—and that of a prisoner was that, when Massu said "stop," the torture stopped.

But above all, Massu was the hero of "the Battle of Algiers" of 1957. Until then the city had lived under a reign of F.L.N. terror, with plastic-bomb explosions, abductions and throat slittings as facts of daily life. Thanks to a brilliant exploit by his intelligence chief, Colonel Yves Godard, Massu learned where the F.L.N. headquarters were and where its arms, ammunition and archives were stored. The 1st R.E.P. under Colonel Jeanpierre put a ring around the Casbah, killed or captured all the leaders and broke the F.L.N. in the city. After that Algiers was a city at peace.

Massu was an inarticulate man, who could utter little more than orders. Not that he was without views or that those views lacked intelligence. He knew what he thought about de Gaulle, Algeria, France, the Army. But, when asked about them, he was unable to select his phrases in any kind of orderly manner and could only gush forth, at machine-gun speed, an almost incomprehensible mumble of disjointed thoughts and unconnected sentences in obscure Army slang. His speeches, when he had to make them, were agony for himself and his listeners.

A correspondent from *Süddeutsche Zeitung* of Munich visited him, and Massu grumbled. He regretted that de Gaulle did not come out unequivocally for "French Algeria." He said that the Army was in a state of near revolt and that the officers found themselves increasingly hamstrung in their campaign to stamp out terrorism.

It was all in the good French military tradition. The *grognard* was the heart and sinew of Napoleon's armies. He grumbled about the food, the officers, the choice of terrain, the marshals. "Follow me you swine," cried Marshal Murat. "My arse is as round as an apple." The soldiers grumbled and followed him to win battles like Austerlitz and Jena for the Emperor. The *grognards* of the First World War were wiped out at Verdun; it was the whitefaced and silent masses that mutinied. Perhaps Massu was thinking of Argoud, his Chief of Staff, who had once been transferred to Germany because he had obeyed orders that Paris regretted having issued. Or of intellectual Parisiennes like Simone de Beauvoir, Simone Signoret, Françoise Sagan and—of all people—Brigitte Bardot, who supported the F.L.N. and encouraged French conscripts to desert, seeking, it seemed to Massu, to impose their own refined consciences on farm boys and students in uniform. Perhaps he was thinking of all the officers who had been loaded with honors and shelved in military sinecures in Metropolitan France. He was soon to join the club himself.

In the conspiratorial atmosphere of Algiers in January 1960, it was later affirmed, the German correspondent Kempski was part of a frame-up to trap the unsophisticated general into expressing just such thoughts. It was said that General de Gaulle resented Massu's popularity with the *pieds noirs* and wanted to get rid of him. The evidence offered was that Massu, who knew his oral weaknesses, never gave interviews unless he was ordered to, and that Kempski's bill at the Hotel Aletti was picked up by the French Government. It was an unlikely story and irrelevant. The point was that Massu was unwavering in his basic loyalty to de Gaulle as long as he served him. When the story of the interview was picked up in the French press, de Gaulle immediately ordered him back to France. In Algeria, the *pieds noirs* and soldiers, without Massu, felt themselves allied on the precipice of disaster. Only one thing saved them from despair, and that thing was the magic that never failed, action in the Forum of Algiers.

4
A JOB FOR THE COLONELS
January 1960

✢✢✢

All day January 24, the crowds had been assembling at the foot of the steps of the Forum, and by 5:00 P.M., as dusk descended, they were in a state of high excitement. But there was still little indication of the horror that was to come; mobs intent on violence don't bring their wives and children. Many of the demonstrators were armed and wore the uniforms of their territorial units; they were part-time soldiers who formed a kind of urban reserve. Although they were nominally under Army orders, many of the units had become semiautonomous and did not willingly respond to discipline. The wives and children were there, but this time, ominously, there were almost no Moslems.

Roadworks were in process, and gangs of demonstrators began to rip up paving stones with pickaxes and pneumatic drills. One man even climbed aboard a parked bulldozer and started its motor. Although the demonstrations had been inspired by the dismissal of Massu, they were not, in fact, spontaneous. For months various rightwing groups had been gathering stocks of arms for a new rising that would force Paris to reverse its policies. These groups even maintained liaison with the Army, through Colonel Argoud and Colonel Gardes. Two main groups dominated the city that evening, one led by Pierre Lagaillarde, the other by Joseph Ortiz.

As far as Lagaillarde was concerned, it seemed that the gods had been almost too generous with the gifts they bestowed on him. Oddly enough he was not a *pied noir*. He was born in 1931 at Courbevoie near Paris and was taken to Algeria as a child. He was graduated from the University of Algiers and became head of the Students' Union. He was called to the bar at Blida at a precocious age and elected to the National Assembly in Paris. He was as handsome as a film star, 6 feet tall, with slender flanks, lime-green eyes and high cheekbones. His even good looks were enhanced rather than marred by a small gap in the upper teeth, which is supposed to mean "money" or "luck," or both. He was highly intelligent, sensitive, and imaginative, a good dinner-table conversationalist. His voice was mellow, like that of a classical actor, and he could have declaimed Shakespeare or Racine. It was, alas, his fate to declaim political ideology instead.

Little of his political oratory is worth quoting. He was of the Poujadist Right fashionable in Algeria at the time, and he had a flamboyant, rabble-rousing delivery that went well with his masterly appearance.

Lagaillarde, like many vigorous young Europeans of Algeria, was a frustrated Legionnaire. He wore a red beard, and he used a lieutenancy in the Army reserve as an excuse to wear paratroop battle dress on all possible occasions. He was always armed, as he was dressed, to kill. The man who created the O.A.S. and was then destroyed by his own Frankenstein's monster first stepped to the center of the Algiers stage that he loved in order to fill the fearful gap left by the departure of General Massu.

Pierre Lagaillarde, by his personality, charm and influence among Algerian students, outclassed and dominated all the other leaders, save one. Joseph Ortiz, a café proprietor and sometime pimp, ran an organization called the Front National Français, an independent semimilitary group with headquarters in a building at the foot of the steps to the Forum. "The Affair of the Barricades," which began with the uprising of January 24, 1960, has gone down in history as the joint work of Lagaillarde and Ortiz, which is ironic, for the two men loathed each other and saw as little of each other as they could. Their very entourages were sufficient indication of their incompatibility. Lagaillarde was always followed by admiring groups of students and pretty girls, the young intellectuals of the Algiers Right, the city's debutantes, the Algerian equivalent of the "jet set," Ortiz' men, in contrast, were the rowdies and tough artisans of Bab-el-Oued and Belcourt; they called their boss "Uncle Joe" and themselves occasionally "communists."

The demonstration had been expected by the authorities for some days, and counteraction had been prepared. Fifteen squads of Gardes Mobiles, a thousand men in all under the command of Colonel Pierre Debrosse, were waiting in the Government Building. The Gardes Mobiles, a shock force from Metropolitan France, were known to the population as "the Reds" because of the red bands on their caps, which distinguished them from "the Whites," the ordinary police. The Reds were regarded by the *pieds noirs* as a hostile "occupying" force.

The agreed plan was for the police to march down the steps and chest the demonstrators back. At the same time the 1st R.E.P., under the command of Colonel Henri Dufour, would close in from the Avenue Pasteur, on the right, while the 1st Colonial Paratroops, under Colonel Joseph Broizat, would close in from the left. With the police serving as a piston, the crowds would have nowhere to go but back and, presumably, home. The plan depended on efficient coordination, but three elite groups, military and police, were involved, and all were briefed and ready.

Colonel Debrosse was an affable man with a sense of humor. His hair was mown like a lawn, to match his name, and fleshiness at chin and jowls showed a true Frenchman's enthusiasm for good food. He had disposed nine of his platoons to descend the steps by the right of the Monument to the Dead and the other six by the left. At 6:00 "H Hour," the gendarmes, in black riot helmets and with tommy guns in hand, received the order to march. The tommy guns were empty, so that no nervous gendarme might squeeze a trigger and start a riot. Their only weapons were teargas grenades and the small arms in their holsters. Unlike the Light Brigade at Balaklava they had a descent to make, not heights to storm, but otherwise the battle that took place in the next hideous half-hour was not dissimilar. From the top of the steps, one can see the Mediterranean straight ahead. Looking down, the gendarmes saw thousands of people breathing hatred at them, an ugly-sounding mass filling the huge Boulevard Laferrière.

The policemen began their descent, with Debrosse at their head, as a loudspeaker called on the crowds to disperse. Those gendarmes who took their eyes from their objective looked left and right for the arrival of the paratroops. Stones and beer bottles rained on them. The police replied with tear gas. Suddenly, from what direction is not known, shots were fired, and a policeman fell. The crowd screamed and became a mob. The policemen quickened their pace and drew their revolvers. But men, some in uniform, were now firing steadily from the windows. Policemen tumbled and rolled down the steps dead or clutched their bodies, screaming. For the first time in the Algerian war, Frenchmen were firing on Frenchmen, and nobody knew why.

The police plunged into the milling, panic-stricken crowd. Five times, six times, Debrosse, among the collapsing policemen, sounded the withdrawal on his whistle. Those gendarmes who could extricate themselves from the mob fled up the steps, some carrying their wounded. Some were captured by civilians, stripped and beaten. The scene was one of indescribable confusion and mob hysteria, growing more macabre as night fell and all the street lights went on automatically, shining hazily through the smoke from tear-gas grenades and gunfire. The clang of ambulance and police alarms added to the deafening clamor.

By 6:30 most of the policemen had managed to detach themselves and withdraw into the Government Building.

At 6:45 the paratroops made an unhurried appearance from either side, notifying headquarters by walkie-talkie that they had been delayed by barricades. They were greeted with cheers and kisses by the crowds. Colonel Debrosse stood among his shocked and dying gendarmes and watched, with incredulous bitterness, the fraternization at the foot of the bloodied steps. One of his fatally wounded men, Lieutenant Éjarque was groaning. "For two years I have been fighting the fellagha," he gasped. "And now I am dying at the hands of men who are shouting 'Algérie française.'"

Debrosse said nothing. He lit a cigarette with hands shaking so that he could scarcely strike the match, not so much from fear as from grief and an indescribable resentment at injustice. Fourteen gendarmes were dead and 135 wounded. Among the demonstrators 8 were dead and 24 wounded. Most of the latter had been hit in the crossfire, and it was noted in the hospital that their wounds were from guns that were not of police caliber.

History has blamed Lagaillarde and Ortiz for this atrocious massacre, but no one ever found out who fired the first shots, and it was equally impossible in the confusion to see if the men firing on the police were doing so under orders or spontaneously. Both Ortiz and Lagaillarde later denied giving orders to fire. One cannot see

Georges Scapini, Vichy Ambassador to Berlin, and General Bridoux, Pétain's Minister of Defense (who proved singularly reluctant to defend anyone from anything, especially if the "anything" was German), had also made their homes in Madrid, and Bridoux had died there.

These men of another generation, another lost cause, showed little interest in the new arrivals from the Barricades, but one man at least considered it his spiritual and moral duty to bridge the social gap between the old and the new. Father Grasset was a priest in the French *maison de retraite* of the *Pères de Chabeuil* at Pozuelo de Alarcón outside Madrid. There are several old peoples' retreats dotted throughout the world under the same aegis. One is in Buenos Aires, and one of its more important functions after the Second World War was to hide French war criminals. During the war Father Grasset had served as an officer in the French Milice, a paramilitary organization formed in 1943 after Hitler had ordered the French Army to disband. The original conception of the Milice was as an elite force, like the German Army after the 1918 armistice. In practice there was nothing left in France that could be fashioned into anything approaching an elite. All able-bodied males were in either prison camps, the Free French or the Resistance. The Milice became a security force that hunted, tortured and executed members of the Resistance; it is not well remembered. Its leader, Joseph Darnand, was executed as soon as the war was over, and most militiamen were also executed in one way or another.

Grasset hid his uniform and took holy orders in Spain, the monk's cowl replacing the sword, rather as in the case of Aramis. In the French religious community of Spain he formed a right-wing religious-mystical movement of his own, called "Cité Catholique." Grasset took an immediate interest in the *pieds noirs,* an interest that wiser men saw could lead only to trouble, for the religious mystic had nothing in common with the earthy, lecherous, practical Algerian Frenchmen now arriving in Madrid. Grasset became the confessor of Lagaillarde, who was not, of course, a *pied noir,* and he was soon the confidant of nearly all except the suspicious, antireligious Jean-Jacques Susini.

If Grasset was Aramis, he had a splendid D'Artagnan in the godlike Lagaillarde and a suitably porky Porthos in Joseph Ortiz who occasionally visited the city. What was needed to complete the brigade of Musketeers was Athos, and, in October, he appeared in the person of General Raoul Salan. Salan had, in fact, preceded the others, but he had finally decided to make Spain his home. He had been forbidden to return to Algeria after uttering some inflammatory remarks to the press. The interdiction did not include Spain, but it pleased Salan to make a mystery of his destination. He booked a sleeping car to Bordeaux, then took a train in the opposite direction to Nîmes, where his brother was a doctor. He then quietly crossed the border at Le Perthus, having successfully thrown nonexistent shadowers off the track; the French and Spanish immigration officials passed him through without interest or comment.

Salan had enjoyed a long, honorable and orthodox career, which, despite many endearing eccentricities, was strangely lacking in panache. Born on June 10, 1899, at Roquebrune (Tarn), he went into the trenches after only one year at Saint-Cyr. He was wounded several times and won the Croix de Guerre. After the war he served in the French Empire—against the Druses in Syria and Lebanon and then in Indochina, where he added to his collection of war wounds. In the Far East he enriched the lonely evenings with a study of Oriental mysticism, which earned him the nickname of the "Mandarin," used by friends and critics alike. It pleased him and he frequently used the term when speaking about himself. In Indochina he developed a taste for opium and a passion for astrology in the writings of Confucius and Buddha. This interest gave him a reputation as a mystic, which was justified only up to a point. Salan had an endless curiosity about exotic or esoteric experiments, and at a later date he would no doubt have tried an LSD trip. But his interests were catholic, and he enjoyed a circle of friends unusual for a professional officer. It included, among many others, Graham Greene. Despite spending more time away from his native land than had General MacArthur, his political views remained unusually rational. Within the military hierarchy, he was considered a republican and a socialist. His political hero was Georges Mandel, the Jewish liberal, who had been murdered by the Nazis. Like many French soldiers, he had taken an Indochinese mistress and had had a child by her. Unlike most soldiers, however, he accepted his paternity, brought the boy up and entered him in the French Army, where he serves today as an officer.

Many of the years abroad were spent in Special Services, the underground branch of Army Intelligence, and it was in this service that he

observed the Italo-Abyssinian War of 1936, although according to
his documents he was covering it as a war correspondent for *Le
Temps* (now *Le Monde*). Those years gave him a voracious appetite,
not unusual in a French officer, for plotting.

Five months before the outbreak of the 1939 war, when he was
forty years old, he married Lucienne Bourgnin, known to her friends
as "Bibiche," a beautiful young woman of great mental tenacity, who
immediately became a dominant influence in his life. After the fall of
France Salan supported Marshal Pétain and did not join Free French
until 1944, when he was given a brigade by General de Lattre. He
commanded competently but without bravado. During the French
war in Indochina he again served under de Lattre and, on the latter's
death in 1952, was appointed to his place. Again he served well, maintaining his predecessor's momentum but leaving in time to avoid all
but minor responsibility for the disaster of Dien Bien Phu. By then he
had become the most decorated officer in the French Army.

At some time during the war in Indochina Salan seemed suddenly
to age. Earlier pictures revealed a handsome man of evident dyna-
mism, with dark hair and a humorous mouth. The man who left Indochina did not look like that at all. The mouth had become acrid and
pursed, the eyes hollow and haunted. The hair had turned white, thin
and brittle. He reminded one of Richard Watson Dixon's chilling
"Ode to Advancing Age":

> Emptier the weary face; like to the shore,
> Far ruined and the desolate billow white.

Although he was as responsible as any man for bringing General
de Gaulle to power, indeed he claimed to have done it single-handed,
he had been a confirmed anti-Gaullist since the days of Vichy. His
wife Bibiche was even more fanatical on the subject. After de Gaulle
had assumed the Presidency, Salan wondered how to receive him.
Bibiche is reported to have said, "If you receive him at all it will be
over my dead body," and lay down in the doorway, compelling Salan
and his embarrassed staff officers to step over her.

Bibiche remained in Algiers when her husband went to Madrid,
and he was accompanied by his aide, Captain Ferrandi. Ferrandi was
Salan's most loyal friend and helper, praised and admired by those
who admired Salan, sneered at as a Sam Weller or *porte-serviette* by
those who didn't. These latter did Ferrandi an injustice. Ferrandi had

won many decorations in the field, and possessed a great deal of common sense which enabled him to assess situations with clarity and without illusion when most of the conspirators of Algiers and Madrid were allowing their heady illusions to carry them away. The Salans were, in fact, a foursome. Staying with Madame Salan was Captain Noëlle Lucchetti, a round, jolly, middle-aged Corsican lady who held a commission in the P.F.A.T. (*Personnel Féminin de l'Armée de Terre*); in uniform, her breast, ample though it was, was solid with decorations. Captain Lucchetti had been with the Salan family since 1950, sometimes as aide to the General and at other times as secretary and companion to Madame Salan. At any rate, any reference by friends to "the Salans" automatically meant, not only the General and Madame General, but also Captain Ferrandi and Captain Lucchetti.

Salan's presence in Madrid gave the French-Algerian colony a special prestige, and various members were introduced to him as though he were a visiting potentate. This attention Salan liked. He had little interest in actually wielding power, but he loved its trappings; the rodomontade, parades and display; the general's flag on the bonnet of his car, and the outriders who flanked him. This love of pomp, together with his mandarin's temperament, made his subsequent career all the more remarkable; he became the leader and symbol of clandestineness and secret warfare.

Lagaillarde's charm did not work on him. Salan distrusted him. Perhaps the real soldier recognized the toy soldier, or perhaps he saw in him a younger rival enjoying the airs, the bands and the trappings of the military. Ortiz, the café proprietor, Salan considered it beneath his dignity to meet at all.

One man who impressed him was Father Grasset. In a way both Grasset and he belonged to the same school and to the dreamlike, twilight world of Vichy, which both understood and which no one who had not experienced it could ever understand. Salan, like most Pétainists, found it hard to condemn the Milice as the sadistic brutes portrayed by adherents of the Resistance in such works as Sartre's *Dead Without Sepulchres* and Genêt's *Journal of a Thief*. Salan, like Grasset, could recall the high principles of its conception and liked to think of what it was intended to be rather than of the band of rascals it became. Grasset had joined the Milice when it was first formed, which made him respectable in the Mandarin's eyes. Salan made his confession regularly before this rum prelate.

But most of all, Salan was impressed by Jean-Jacques Susini. Susini's father was Corsican and had worked on the railroad, but his mother was Alsatian, and from her he had inherited his blond coloring and his withdrawn temperament. No one could have been less like a *pied noir* than this *pied noir*. He was small, with pale eyes. He inspired the adjectives one associates with very weak people, yet the impression from the first grip of his handshake was just the opposite. He walked like a cat, silently, and spoke little until he had something to say—and that something usually had a beginning, a middle and an end. One could see why a man like Salan, with his curious, questing mind was attracted to Susini. Susini was unlike anyone a soldier is likely to encounter in the course of a tidy military career. He was intelligent, persuasive, a stylish writer, and he looked even younger than his 29 years. He had the air of the eternal student. He had passed his baccalaureat at the formidable age of fifteen, three years ahead of standard. He was an iconoclast, despised the military arts, laughed at high rank and, among military men, affected a dirty raincoat like that of the early Hitler.

Susini was so lucid and had such care for language that, when he described himself as a "fascist," which he did endlessly, one sensed that he did so out of contempt for hearers who could think only in such meaningless, catchall terms—like colonels and the like. Later on he would describe himself equally blandly as a "socialist." One of Susini's uncles had had his throat slit by the fellagha, not deeply enough to cause instant death but deeply enough to kill before help could arrive. This uncle was propped against the door of his home, the bell was pushed and he was left to be found by his wife. Susini, despite his light and retiring manner, felt no revulsion when he saw blood spilled, provided that it was not his own. He was one of the few *pieds noirs* who disdained the myth about "our Moslem brothers," supposed by the *pieds noirs* to constitute the overwhelming mass of the population. Susini considered the sons of the Prophet an unwashed, uncivilized, illiterate mob without art and with the most sterile religion ever conceived. Nor did he ever bother to hide his feelings, and many *pieds noirs* found this shocking.

There remained his sex life. He had been married briefly to a German girl, and he philandered, not always subtly. A pretty American girl, Logan Bentley, was working at the time as a researcher in the Madrid office of *Time* and had to interview Susini. She recalled escaping only narrowly with her virtue—she lumped Susini with Lagaillarde and the other Madrid *pieds noirs* as "an unsavory lot." But the only important female influence in Susini's life was his sister, Virginie, who was, unlike her brother, a complete *pied noir* in temperament—determined, energetic and ardent. Susini loved her and was strongly influenced by her, even in political matters.

Susini, in short, was in love with the darker elements of life, with fascism, intrigue, rape; he loved manipulation—politics that could be fingered and molded; men like Salan who, though bigger and stronger, could be guided intellectually; girls whom he could feel and enjoy; intrigues and plots with the sensual spice of risk and danger. And all these tastes were masked by a shy, aloof manner.

Susini was surprised at the influence he could exert on the Mandarin and immediately began to ponder how to exploit it. He had always been under the shadow of Lagaillarde and secretly hated him. Lagaillarde was, to a degree, what Susini would have liked to be. He would have liked to be irresistible to women as Lagaillarde was. He would have loved to have Lagaillarde's gift of inflaming a mob from a balcony. Susini could dazzle a small dinner party with his mastery of dialectic, but his public speeches were cold and metallic.

Susini was aware that what French Algeria needed was a symbol. It already had one in Pierre Lagaillarde, but Susini wanted a different one, someone whom he himself could influence. He had thought of Massu and Colonel Bigeard, the hero of Dien Bien Phu and creator of the Leopard-men paratroops. Now, quite suddenly, he was like a player in American football who has received a pass and finds the ball in his hands. The ball was Salan, and there was no one between Susini and a touchdown. He could streak for the goal line, leaving everyone else—Lagaillarde included—far behind. Susini was not the young man to miss an opportunity like that.

Recusant generals, colonels and *pieds noirs* were thus coming from divers directions and widely different motives, to the decision to revolt against General de Gaulle. Apart from hatred of de Gaulle, they were united by a vague, incoherent kind of anticommunism. The military men especially had been isolated for so long in their exclusive world in Indochina and Algeria that, when they uttered the word "communism," they believed that all argument stopped. They had no conception of the ferment in the socialist world, the Pandora's box opened by Nikita Khrushchev in his speech to the Twentieth Congress, the consequences of the Poznan riots and the Hungarian Revolution, the falling out of Russia and China or the bleeding ulcer of West Berlin, which was still open to East German refugees. Communism to these officers was what it had seemed to be when they last saw it in Germany just after the war. They still thought of Russian soldiers as they had been in Berlin—hordes of Mongols in padded jackets with bandoleros over their shoulders. The generals could not imagine that the new breed wore white gloves and learned the correct dances in the Soviet military academies. For the colonels it was still "international communism" and sometimes even "Godless communism." When they talked about it, they tended to remind one of Hearst newspaper editorials circa 1947.

One military revolt in Algeria had already been planned and abandoned. It was to have taken place on All Saints' Day, and the general in command, it was agreed, would be General Edmond Jouhaud, Commander of the Air Force in Algeria, who had the political merit of being a *pied noir,* and the reputation of being a socialist. The real leader was to have been Pierre Lagaillarde. In fact it was specifically to lead this revolt that Lagaillarde had jumped bail in Paris and escaped to Spain. Plans for the revolt were far advanced, but they were interrupted by a savage Moslem riot in Algiers, the first time that "the patient Moslem masses" had demonstrated in force against the French, and the Army was so busy suppressing it that it had no energy left for plots.

That was in December 1960. The following month Lagaillarde called fifty or so *pieds noirs,* representing a score of right-wing organizations, to a series of meetings. He sought to end the waste of effort in quibbling and nit picking and to form an organization for coordination of strategy and tactics. He gave the coordinating group its name: "l'Organisation de l'Armée Secrète." Despite the martial title, the organization was overwhelmingly civilian. Salan gave the group his blessing and met some of the leaders. There were some pretty odd characters among them, and they made weird bedfellows, none weirder than Salan himself and one Philippe Castille. Castille was the *pied noir* who, a few years earlier, had fired a bazooka at Salan in Algiers and had missed. Castille now apologized with tears streaming down his cheeks, and what one startled observer called the "bazooker" and the "bazookee" embraced emotionally. Another arrival was André Canal, a veteran conspirator from Algeria, who was sometimes

called "the Monocle" because he wore one and "the Colonel" for no
reason that was apparent. Canal was an important name in monarchist
circles in France. He pined for the recapture of what he called "the old
fortress of monarchic absolutism." Although he had lived in Algeria
for nearly twenty years, he claimed to be in close touch with "public
opinion" in France. The O.A.S. was an Algerian conception, a
strictly practical grouping designed to keep Algeria French, but
nevertheless Canal promised to introduce it into Metropolitan France,
presumably as a movement to restore the monarchy, which had abso-
lutely nothing to do with the original idea. But nobody told him not
to. And no one, then or afterward, questioned the fact that the O.A.S.
was the creation of Pierre Lagaillarde. He had conceived it, and he
had summoned the others to announce its birth.

The birth of the O.A.S. was given no publicity. Only a few people
knew of its existence. One morning in the same January, Madame
Salan, leaving her house in Algiers to go shopping, saw that someone
had painted "O.A.S." in black on her white wall. Later that day she
telephoned her husband in Madrid to ask if he knew what it meant.
Like the man who did not know much about art but knew what he
liked, Salan replied that he knew what it meant but found it awfully
hard to explain.

In the meantime, however, political killings of Europeans in Algeria had already begun. On January 25, Maître Pierre Popie, a young
liberal lawyer, was murdered in his office by two former Legionnaires,
Claude Peintre and Léo Dauvergue, who had served their military
contracts and settled in Algiers. Popie had been advocating Algerian
independence, a courageous thing to do in a country where murder
comes so easily. Dauvergue and Peintre were only two of thousands of
ex-servicemen who, though not *pieds noirs,* loved the climate of Algiers. These men, even more than the *pieds noirs,* later formed the
nucleus of the fighting forces of the O.A.S.

On April 9 a melodramatic and vilely phrased text issued "by the
O.A.S." was found in the letter boxes of prominent Algerian government officials and police chiefs. It is scarcely worth quoting, save for
the fact that it was one of the first tracts to be issued under the O.A.S.
imprimatur. It said:

> The national resistance is victoriously directed against
> the authorities in Metropolitan France itself. Everywhere,
> traitors are beginning to tremble. They know that the blows

of the patriots will not spare them. Coffins are waiting for them in Paris as well as in Algiers. Policemen! Members of the Compagnies Républicaines de Sécurité! All you who belong to the forces of order, know that the time of decision is at hand. Remember the fate of the Milice! Ten thousand of them were shot because they believed they could bargain with the nation! Today, while there is still time, take sides. Sabotage the orders of this infamous Government. Send false intelligence to your superiors. Organize your cells of Resistance. Hold yourself ready to join the national Army when you are called for.

The document's authorship is mercifully unknown, but it is undoubtedly *pied noir*. The reference to coffins is sufficient proof of that. The coffin appears frequently in Algerian conversation, as casually as food and drink and love. In a world where living is easy, death poses fewer fears, and a coffin is merely of wood.

On April 11, two days after the O.A.S. circular had been distributed, General de Gaulle held a devastating press conference and declared almost in as many words that France was giving up Algeria, that she was tired of pouring money into the country and that, if other countries wished to take France's place, "I wish them joy of it." His declaration was an infinity away from his words to the *pieds noirs* less than three years before: "I have understood you" and "France from Dunkirk to Tamanrasset," uttered at Mostaganem. To the generals and colonels, satisfied that they had all but won their war in the bled, the shock was indescribable. Why, they said, had they ordered soldiers to their death? Why, if Algeria was to become independent, had French officers killed the flower of Moslem youth, young men brave enough to stand and fight for their ideals? They were the very men who should have lived to rule a new Algeria, and their blood was on the hands of every French soldier. What was the point of the death of Colonel Jeanpierre, who could have served his country for another ten years? To the officers, with their adolescent interpretation of forces like "communism," de Gaulle's statement could mean only one thing. He was delivering Algeria to Khrushchev and the commissars or to Mao Tse-tung and his thoughts.

Even before the speech, plans for a second military revolt were well advanced, but this time there was better talent available. Colonels like Argoud, Gardes, Broizat and Godard were in touch with Generals

Salan, Faure, Mirambeau, Challe, Zeller and, of course Jouhaud. Challe, who had been transferred to France, indicated that he was ready to lead the generals in Algiers. General Faure would lead the revolt that would follow in Paris. It was agreed, however, that the success of any coming revolt would depend on the key regiment of Algeria, the 1st R.E.P., which was camped at Zéralda on the western outskirts of Algiers. As has already been mentioned, the Premier Repp, the regiment of Colonel Jeanpierre, of Colonel Henri Dufour and of Lieutenant Roger Degueldre, occupied a special place in the hearts of the *pieds noirs*. Not another regiment in Algeria could match its record, 1,600 fellagha killed, wounded or captured in a period of four months; 1,200 rifles and 112 Czech machine guns captured. Losses too had been heavy. 160 young Legionnaires from all over Europe, but mostly from Germany, had been killed. More than any other regiment, the 1st R.E.P. had sunk its roots into Algeria. *Pied noir* girls had married N.C.O.s, and their sisters and cousins had married their comrades. When the men quit the Legion they found jobs, as had the killers of Maître Popie, in the businesses of their fathers-in-law. "The 1st R.E.P.," said Colonel Brothier, one of its former commanding officers, "is not a regiment. It's a bloc." It was even more. It was a family. Portraits of the officers hung in the bedrooms of *pied noir* children, as other children slept with portraits of film stars, footballers, pop singers or racing cyclists. The death of Colonal Jeanpierre caused an outpouring of grief in the small world of Algiers as if it were the untimely death of a son. Jeanpierre's successor, Colonel Henri Dufour, was, like Jeanpierre, a flamboyant man. If one respects the military arts, one must admire a man who could succeed a commander so legendary and command thunderers like Colonel Guiraud, Major Denoix de Saint Marc, Captain Antoine Ysquierdo, Captain Pierre Sergent, Lieutenants Roger Degueldre, René Coatalem and Roger Bernard. These men were professionals to the utmost degree, with penetrating eyes for anything short of military perfection.

For a while Dufour kept the 1st R.E.P. running on Jeanpierre's momentum, but little by little morale sagged. Some of the best of the regiment's officers were transferred to stiffen other outfits, and the mood at Zéralda became restive and ugly, which suited the conspirators perfectly. Contact was made with Dufour, who pledged that the 1st R.E.P. would join the revolt, and if the 1st moved, the 2nd R.E.P. would follow. Other commanders, notably Gouraud in Constantine, had sent word that they would join.

Alibis were ostentatiously prepared. Colonel Yves Godard applied for a job as military attaché in Poland. Colonel Broizat talked loudly to Colonel Trinquier about resigning their commissions to go to the Congo as mercenaries—a bluff aimed at the military Establishment, but one that backfired, for Trinquier took him seriously and went, a severe blow to the rebels. Trinquier, the Army's principal intellectual advocate of physical torture as a legitimate weapon, would have been a valuable man. Several colonels were assigned to the problem of gathering all the major protagonists in one spot at one time. Most of them were scattered around garrisons in France, playing golf in retirement or sitting in cafés looking at girls.

Then Colonel Dufour, who throughout his career had shown certain psychopathic tendencies, upset things by going berserk. Judged politically unreliable, he received a notice from the Ministry of National Defense ordering him back to France. Without informing anyone, Dufour then disappeared, taking with him, for some reason, the regimental flag. Some days later, he resurfaced with the colors but broke, gave himself up and was sent to France under house arrest.

This blow was followed at the beginning of February by a disaster even more unexpected: The regiment woke up to find that Roger Degueldre had also gone. Some days earlier he had been ordered to transfer to the 4th R.E.I, the 4th Legion Infantry; rather than obey, he had taken the classic Legion way out and had deserted.

The disappearance of the 1st R.E.P.'s finest soldier was the subject of much soul-searching discussion in the messes of both the officers and the N.C.O.s. Degueldre, they knew, had been depressed for a long time, but he was not a man who confided freely in others, and it was not easy to define or analyze the roots of his gloom with confidence.

"It began at the Barricades," said one.

"No," said another. "After. He was depressed after he left hospital last October."

"I can give you the reason in six letters," said a third, and, like a parent talking over a child's head, spelled out "N-i-c-o-l-e."

The others looked uneasily over their shoulders and changed the subject. As the days lengthened into weeks, Degueldre was gradually forgotten.

The transfer of Dufour at first seemed a death blow to the plotters, for his second-in-command and successor, Colonel Guiraud, was an uncompromising Gaullist. Although Guiraud might complain, he would never disobey; he was another Massu. The sunlight emanating from Charles de Gaulle had shown Guiraud the true path ever since 1940. In that year he had elected to die rather than to surrender, and he was one of the first professionals to join the Free French. He had fought at Bir Hakeim, and at Dien Bien Phu he had commanded the 1st B.E.P. before it was expanded into the 1st R.E.P.

But in a city like Algiers solutions can usually be found for problems like Guiraud; not the easy solution of death, for in Algerian society killing soldiers was considered bad form. It was discreetly arranged that Guiraud be given a few weeks of deserved leave in France, leaving temporary command of the troubled 1st R.E.P. to Major Denoix de Saint Marc, who was committed to the revolt.

By the middle of April, most though not all of the leaders knew their roles. Unfortunately, one of those who did not was the titular commander, General Challe.

Degueldre was hiding with friends in a villa in Bouzarea. He badly needed time and space to think. The bouts of depression that had been assailing him for more than a year had been increasing in length and intensity so that he could scarcely endure any longer the presence of his comrades. A more refined society would have called for an analyst. Instead, as quietly as he could, he reflected on the events of his life and realized that the fundament of his personal crisis was love, a simple word but one that in his own personal context represented something infinitely complex and ill starred.

Women had always played an explosive and usually unlucky part in his life. He was first married at nineteen in his native Louvroil in 1944. He had been serving in the Resistance, but the Germans were in retreat and the Allies in pursuit, and it was time to cast aside the cover of the Maquis and put on uniform. To his bride of three days he said, "Now I am going to fight," and left. He did not see her again for twelve years, when, to his surprise, he received a writ in Zéralda ordering him to return to northern France and answer a claim by his wife for nonsupport. Colonel Jeanpierre, who loved Degueldre almost as a son, gave him permission to fly back to France, and he appeared in court in his uniform of chief sergeant, carrying with him a flight bag that contained little more than a toothbrush. He found himself standing next to a strange young woman whom he scarcely recognized. They shook hands, smiling nervously, and addressed each other as *vous, Monsieur* and *Madame.*

The judge reminded Degueldre of the last words he had uttered to his wife: "I am going to fight." Degueldre gave his great wolf's grin, pointed to his decorations, raised his flight bag and said, "I haven't finished." Divorce was granted later.

Later in that same year, he fell in love with a beautiful *pied noir* girl in Algiers and proposed marriage. It was the first time, he realized, that he had been truly in love. Almost immediately she fell ill. Cancer was diagnosed, and she died four months later in hospital, in Degueldre's arms. It was then that the depressions began. With the death of Colonel Jeanpierre in 1958, they became more frequent.

In between depressions, he was still capable of boisterous humor, and he was given to flamboyant attitudes. He bought a new Simca and gave a party for his fellow N.C.O.s at an Algiers restaurant to celebrate his new pet. All hands staggered out dead drunk, and Degueldre, accepting a bet, drove the car ten kilometers back to Zéralda—in reverse.

In 1959 he married again, in Bourges, as impulsively as he had the first time, and the effective life of this marriage was little longer. He never brought his wife to Algeria. Then, little by little, the love affair began that was to change his life and plunge his brain into a tumult of conflicting loyalties. The girl's name was Nicole Besineau. On at least two counts this love defied simple solution, for her father was none other than General Gardy, Inspector General of the Foreign Legion, and her husband was a captain in the 1st R.E.P. If ever there were daughters of the regiment, they were the daughters of General Gardy. Two of his three daughters were married to officers in the 1st R.E.P.; the third was still only a child. One son was an officer in the 2nd R.E.C. (*Regiment Étrangère de Cavalrie*).

Nicole's marriage was not a good one, and it was heading for breakdown. She was beautiful, impetuous, well educated, ardent; she was in love with French Algeria, with the 1st R.E.P. and gradually with Roger Degueldre. For Degueldre, a working-class boy and a Foreign Legionnaire, with no ambitions beyond soldiering, Nicole, the daughter of a general, opened a window into a new social world, a world of taste, elegance and politics. He tried for a while to resist a liaison that he considered disloyal, unfair and, knowing himself, doomed to disaster. But he continued to see Nicole, and at the same time he started paying attention to the condition of his fingernails and studying the wine lists instead of simply calling for Mascara as the rest of the Legionnaires did.

In October 1960 he had a physical collapse, a result of the accumulation of war wounds from Europe, Indochina and Algeria, and he went into military hospital. The doctors diagnosed a variety of blood disorders, including phlebitis and varicose veins, which were removed. It was also noticed that he had a slight cardiac condition. That was all Degueldre needed to hear to complete his melancholia. Ever since cancer had claimed the life of the girl he loved, he had had a horror of physical decay. Death in action, in some blazing battle like that of Dien Bien Phu or Budapest, was the only end he could contemplate with equanimity. With a heart condition, his days as a paratrooper and combat officer were over. He knew no other métier but soldiering, and he found no pleasure in contemplating a future career behind a desk at Zéralda barracks, listening to the backbiting of staff officers. Not least, he realized that his prospects for promotion had become almost nonexistent, compromising any hope he may have had for getting General Gardy's permission to marry Nicole. His mind was full of confusion, and his problems seemed infinite, what with pain, physical weakness, Nicole, French Algeria, the Barricades. If only, he kept complaining to his fellow-lieutenants, if only Jeanpierre were still alive. If only he could talk to Colonel de Blignières, his old commander in the 2nd R.E.C. De Blignières always insisted that Degueldre had saved his life in the Plain of Jars in Indochina, which Degueldre insisted was an exaggeration. He briefly wondered if, like de Blignières and Dufour, he could find consolation in the Church. But he couldn't.

He returned to Zéralda from hospital so subdued that his old comrades could scarcely recognize the rough, flashy Degueldre of old. As if he had not problems enough to cope with, he was then informed that he was being transferred to the 4th R.E.I., which for him was literally a legion of strangers. Furthermore, the transfer would isolate him from the military revolt that he knew was coming and in which he fully intended to take part. So he deserted and went away to try and sort things out in his own mind in peace and quiet. Nicole, of course, knew his hiding place and drove out to see him in Bouzarea, bearing good news. General Gardy and Colonel Godard also knew of his whereabouts and transmitted a message, by way of Nicole, asking him to draw up detailed plans by which the 1st R.E.P. could take over in Algiers. This included sealed orders to each officer. The promise of action dispelled his melancholy like a cloud lifting. While cigarette butts made a noisome pyramid in the ashtray at his side, he arranged on paper the disposition of Legionnaires to take over the Government buildings and communication centers. When Nicole informed him that the date had been set, he flung his arms around her, whooped for joy and got his uniform ready.

7
PUTSCH
April 22–26, 1961

❖❖❖

A lost cause is hard to define because there is reason to doubt that such a thing exists. In a declining market one does not lose money if one does not sell, and it may go up again. The British seemed to be fighting a lost cause in the autumn of 1940 and Harry Truman in 1948. Millions of Gaullists fought a "lost cause" between 1946 and 1958. Whether or not detached observation is a good thing is another matter. To believe in such a thing as a lost cause is to believe that the course of history is irreversible, whereas every day history proves that it is anything but.

"The maid's room has been burgled." In the spring of 1961 throughout France, across Algeria and in Madrid, activists and those officers who had pledged themselves awaited this watchword. The operation was optimistically named "Arnat," a combination of "army" and "nation." If it worked—and it had to—the Army would leave its barracks and take over Algeria. What mattered was not the success of the enterprise, for failure was unthinkable, but what would emerge after. According to Challe, it would "end the war in Algeria and hand the country on a plate back to General de Gaulle and the Fifth Republic"; Zeller believed it would "get rid of General de Gaulle *and* the Fifth Republic"; Salan thought it would "reverse the terrible mistake I made on May 13 in bringing de Gaulle back to power"; Jouhaud, the *pied noir,* hoped to "keep Algeria French"; Gardy expected to "save Algeria for the Foreign Legion."

Everywhere in the messes there was stirring and murmuring and a rising excitement. Argoud and Gardes, with false passports, slipped back into Algiers. Degueldre was already there. Challe and Zeller waited at Creil to be picked up and flown to Algeria. The man selected to bring the two leaders in was Joseph Broizat, one of the emerging colonels and, at first sight, an unlikely one. Although he was a fighting soldier and heavily decorated, his education had been religious rather than military; he had been graduated from the Gregorian University of Rome and for a time had worn the monk's habit. He was later persuaded to become a Protestant; then he dabbled with and rejected communism. These permutations suggest the troubled and somewhat fanatical mind common among converts.

In the Second World War Broizat fought in Tunisia, France and Germany with the 3rd Regiment of Algerian Tirailleurs; later he served in Indochina and Algeria as a parachutist. At the Barricades he had been the laggard commander of the 1st Regiment of Colonial Parachutists. In appearance he was anything but soldierly. With his nose disdainfully lifted, the way noses must have been during the Great Plague, and with primly set, steel-rimmed glasses, he had a priestly look but not of the mendicant kind; too many fine stews had entered him for that. A cardinal's hat would not have looked out of place on his shining shaved head. He was as much a loner as Gardes was a joiner, and he was known to his colleagues, usually affectionately, as "the Monk." Inside Broizat's head teemed a multitude of ideas, many of them contradictory, and, despite his decorations and his warlike background, he had an abhorrence of violence and bloodshed that sometimes seemed to amount to dislike for his trade. His wife, Jacqueline, was a *pied noir*. His best friend was Argoud, and intellectually the two towered above the rest of the colonels.

Broizat met Challe and Zeller at Creil. Challe he knew and admired as a successful commander. Usually, the more political the general, the more he denounces politics and politicians; General de Gaulle is the supreme example. Challe was a genuine officer without politics, although such views as he expressed were liberal and toward the Left. He had done a brilliant job in Algeria and wanted to complete it. He was a strange figure to associate with a type like Zeller, who was in every right-wing plot ever mooted. The colonels did not expect Zeller to be of much use once the revolt took place, but his was a good name, for reasons of military prestige, to have on the list. As Chief of Staff of the Army he had a great deal of influence in the military hierarchy. For Zeller it could be said that he was no timeserver, and he had the courage to express his convictions. In 1956 he resigned as Army Chief when the Guy Mollet Government refused to give him the money and troops he asked for to put down the Algerian insurrection. He wrote in a military magazine shortly afterward, "The Army cannot obey words and discipline that it feels are lacking in meaning." At least one knew where Edmond Zeller stood.

With the connivance of an Air Force general, the rebel officers were assigned a military aircraft. Once aloft, they remained silent for a long time, aware of the dramatic nature of their decision. Then Broizat asked Challe his plan of campaign.

Challe removed his pipe and said, "A general strike in Algeria."

Broizat nodded and replied, "And then?"

"That should do it," Challe said.

Broizat was amazed. "That's all?"

"That's all."

Broizat felt his heart sink. On landing at a military airport near Algiers, they were picked up and driven to the Villa des Tagarins on the heights overlooking Bab-el-Oued. This house had been the headquarters of General Massu during the Battle of Algiers; before that it had been a celebrated bordello called "the Nest." There Challe and Zeller met Generals Jouhaud and Gardy. Gardy was older than the other generals and retired; he did not presume to be one of the leaders. Others present were Colonels Godard, Lacheroy, Argoud, Gardes and, of course, Broizat. Several junior officers of the 1st R.E.P. were also there including Degueldre. Poor Colonel Dufour had been unable to slip away from France, but his temporary deputy, Major Denoix de Saint Marc, was there to pledge the participation of the 1st R.E.P.

Coincidentally, for the second time in five years, monumental affairs of violence were to come in pairs, the more trivial in each case distracting attention from the more vital. Just as the Suez invasion occurred at the same time as the Hungarian Revolution, the Bay of Pigs in Cuba coincided with the Generals' revolt.

In Paris, police intelligence was nodding in a way that must have made Fouché and Vidocq turn in their graves, and the capital was deliciously unaware of what was simmering. On the evening of April 21, President de Gaulle attended a performance of *Britannicus* in the company of the President of Senegal and a suite of ministers that included Louis Joxe, Minister for Algerian Affairs. Innocently they heard the words:

De quel nom cependant pouvons-nous appeler
L'attentat que le jour vient de nous révéler?

The General was awakened at 3:00 A.M. in the Élysée Palace and informed that paratroops had taken over Algiers and Oran. The 1st R.E.P. had left its barracks at Zéralda. Paratroopers had entered the residence of Jean Morin, the Delegate General,—a title which had succeeded that of Governor—and had arrested him. Loyal generals and police chiefs had also been arrested, among them Colonel Debrosse. At 2:45 A.M. Colonel Godard, had taken over Army headquarters and assumed command of the Algiers region. The police commissariats, the Post Office and government bureaus were occupied. The gendarmes and the Gardes Mobiles in the city kept quiet and sat on their hands. Responsive as always to discipline, they waited to be given some indication of which authority was the correct one to obey.

Algiers, waking up, went wild, even by that city's spectacular standards. The streets filled with automobiles blasting *Algérie française.* As other paratroop outfits joined the 1st R.E.P., it was not difficult for the citizens of Algiers to believe that the whole Army was in rebellion, in the cities and in the bled. Flowing by the truckload into Algiers from various parts of the country came the 18th Paratroop Division from Philippeville and the 14th Paratroop Division from Djidjelli. Next came units of the 2nd R.E.P., followed by the 8th R.P.I. Ma. *(Régiment Parachutiste d' Infanterie de la Marine).*

This last arrival aroused exciting speculation over whether or not it would be followed by the fabulous 3rd R.P.I. Ma., the men in visored caps first made famous by Bigeard and then Trinquier by their exploits in the bled. The fact that the 3rd had not moved should have given the more sober-minded citizens reason for anxiety. Nor had there been any signs of movement from Sidi-bel-Abbès, headquarters of the Foreign Legion, or from the Navy. Even the 2nd R.E.P. had arrived without its commander, Colonel Darmuzai, who did not forbid his men to move but remained aloof from the revolt himself, a sure way neither to have one's cake nor to eat it. But the *pieds noirs* were too intoxicated with joy to worry about inauspicious auguries for the moment.

Meanwhile General Salan, installed in the comfortable Hotel de Londres in Madrid, had the complicated problem of removing himself and his entourage to Algiers despite police surveillance and official orders that he was not to attempt to leave the country. Fortunately for him, Serrano Suñer, former Foreign Secretary and brother-in-law of General Franco, had been informed of the plot by the French conservative lawyer, Tixier-Vignancourt, and had agreed to cooperate. He provided a private airplane from the Avianca Line, and Susini discovered that the service staircase was not being watched by the police. The party consisted of Salan, Captain Ferrandi and Susini. Madame Salan and Noëlle Lucchetti in Algiers had been apprised of the plans in a secret message. The most prominent absence from the Madrid party was Pierre Lagaillarde. Susini had thought that Lagaillarde was not really necessary, and in any case there was not much room in the plane. Beyond that he would be more useful in Madrid, and apart from that there would be a second plane to pick up Lagaillarde later. Salan agreed with Susini, neither realizing that the two of them had taken the most decisive step in the history of the O.A.S., one whose effects would pursue them to the end.

Suitcases were packed (uniforms and decorations were not forgotten). The little party left through the kitchen quarters and was escorted by an assistant of Serrano Suñer to a large car, who drove them to the airport. A Spanish officer briefed by Serrano Suñer bade them a laconic farewell. "I fear for you, General," he said to Salan, as he shook his hand.

"Why?" asked Salan surprised. "It's not the first time I have faced danger, you know."

"It's not that. I'm afraid you French are too civilized to make a revolution."

"We have made one before," said Salan. "In fact we invented it."

"But we made a more recent one," said the officer. "It started at Tetuán. When we arrived, the headquarters staff refused to a man to follow us."

"So?"

"So, within a few minutes we had shot the lot. Yes, General, we wish you well, but frankly we fear for you."

The party laughed, being in a holiday mood. Spain passed below. Officially the airplane was bound for Majorca, but it continued onward without incident and landed in Algiers. The only casualty was the Spanish pilot, who returned to Spain and, after boasting of the exploit to the wrong people, was put in prison.

The three men were greeted at the airport by a military committee and by Madame Salan and Noëlle Lucchetti. General Salan had changed from a blue suit into a uniform with rows of medals that looked like a page in a stamp album. The four generals appeared at the Forum as a kind of talisman. The appearance of generals had worked on May 13; by the logic of the *pieds noirs* it could not therefore fail now. It was instructive, however, to note that the decibles of applause for each general as he appeared bore little relation to his actual importance in the plot. Salan was vociferously welcomed. He was the man of May 13, and he must have forgiven the *pieds noirs* for trying to kill him with a bazooka, or he wouldn't have been there now. The reception for Jouhaud was deafening, for he was a *pied noir.* Applause for Challe was cool. He had been Commander in Chief when the Barricades were dismantled. Zeller's appearance was greeted with bewilderment. Few people knew who he was.

But if pessimists needed ill omens to feed on, they had ample nourishment in the photographs of the four generals that were circulated to the press immediately afterward. Four less bellicose, less defiant, faces could scarcely have been found. Not one was able to look the camera in the eye. Jouhaud and Challe looked down, as though they had heard bad news. Zeller's head was turned away from the camera, as though it had bad breath, whereas the Mandarin looked into space, his mind apparently far away. Collectively they looked like four schoolboys waiting outside the headmaster's study for a swishing.

The revolt that began with such a bang stalled almost at once. No other important regiments came out to reinforce those in Algiers. Major Julien Camelin, with the aid of Colonel Argoud, had persuaded the 5th R.E.I. to leave the barracks at Géryville, but the troops were intercepted by Camelin's superior officer, Colonel Pfirrman, who ordered them back. Camelin joined the revolt himself, but the conspirators would have been happier had he been able to bring his soldiers along. Even more disappointing was the attitude of Colonel Brothier, Legion commander at Sidi-bel-Abbès, who told Gardy that he did not believe in Foreign Legionnaires' involving themselves in French politics. Brothier had commanded the 1st R.E.P. before Jeanpierre and was considered a member of the family.

But the greatest disappointment of all was the inertia of the great garrisons at Oran and Constantine. General Gouraud in Constantine had promised to join the revolt, but he had begun to have second thoughts and waited to see what would happen next. General (Henri, Marquis) de Pouilly in Oran would have nothing to do with it. Gouraud and de Pouilly telephoned each other hourly, the one distraught and conscience-stricken, the other aloof and disapproving. Meanwhile Algiers, in the middle, looked desperately from one to the other, like a spectator at a tennis match, knowing that the difference between victory and defeat lay with those two unbudging monoliths; in their lack of bellicosity they were reminiscent of the prehistoric Ankylosaurus and Triceratops, heavily armed at all points but strictly vegetarian.

Food supplies in Algiers were dwindling, especially olive oil, without which the citizens scarcely knew how to cook. Zeller had been charged with the task of maintaining food movement, but the conspirators, believing that the revolt would lead to a spontaneous country-wide rising, had not in their hearts believed that the movement of food to the city markets would even be interrupted. And the lack of staying power that the *pieds noirs* had already demonstrated at the Barricades was beginning to show itself once more. The citizens of Algiers stayed home and grumbled.

In Paris, General de Gaulle went on television to denounce the generals as "usurpers, partisan, ambitious and fanatical, who see and comprehend the nation and the world only through the distortion of their frenzy." Prime Minister Michel Debré, in a Kafkaesque midnight broadcast, told the French people to expect a landing by paratroops and "as soon as the air raid sirens sound, go on foot or car to convince the misled soldiers of their grave error." The idea that ordinary citizens could stop an armed invasion was a sure indication that Debré did not dare to leave the task to the Army.

Far from panicking, the people of Metropolitan France generally viewed the revolt as a vast lark, an exciting change from the humdrum events of everyday life. The *métro,* buses and commuter trains were struck by trade unionists opposing the Putsch, but the cafés remained open and crammed with people animatedly discussing what they would do when they saw the parachutes open above them. It was like a Grand Prix race.

Paris was a long way behind the course of actual events. While it looked to the skies for the "paras," the revolt in Algiers was crumbling. The Army in Algeria simply refused to leave its barracks. It was sympathetic, itching to join the revolt, longing for its success but afraid to defy Paris. The Army attitude, indeed, strongly resembled that of the celebrated Italian unit of the First World War, whose officer leaped over the top of the trenches brandishing his sword and shouting *Avanti! Avanti!* while his troops remained under cover crying *Bravo! Bravissimo!*

After four days the revolt collapsed. Challe was the first to realize it and without consulting the other generals, wrote a letter of surrender to General de Gaulle, which he gave to Colonel de Boissieu—the same man who had insulted Debré during the Barricades. He then confided the news to Susini.

"It's finished, Susini," he said. "Yesterday I commanded an entire army. Tonight I won't even have an orderly. I suppose we mustn't despair. We have shaken the régime. I have decided to leave for Paris. A plane is picking me up. I'm going to present myself to de Gaulle and tell him that only one person was responsible for this business, myself."

Susini was shocked. He noticed that Challe's eyes were red as if he had been crying, but he was moved by the youth of the man's face and the gentleness of his smile. He was a fine commander, Susini thought to himself, but not the man to lead a rebellion. Even then his mind began to roam. Who? Where was the man strong enough to lead but pliable enough to be led in turn by him, Susini.

"You can't abandon the whole thing without a fight," he said. "Chances must be taken, and the game played out. Do you think they will shoot you?"

"Perhaps. General de Gaulle will never forgive me."

"Are you scared?" Susini asked brutally.

"No. You know that. The only thing I fear is the legal farce I'm going to have to endure. It's going to be awful."

"Then what does it matter, damn it?" Susini exploded, exasperated at such lack of spirit. "What does it matter if you lose your life a little bit sooner or a little bit later? I mean to say, General, if you are giving yourself up for the purpose of receiving a more lenient sentence, that I could understand. But you won't get it. Let's start all over again with a new resolve, and recover the lost ground. Let's give arms to the thousands of *pieds noirs* who are waiting for the word go, and who won't hesitate to defend heir homes."

It was no use. Challe patted him paternally on the back, and at 4:00 P.M. he called the other generals to a meeting in the General

Government palace to announce to his furious colleagues his personal surrender. Zeller, foaming at the mouth, cursed him, and Salan insulted him with such cold venom that Colonel de la Chapelle, who was present, asked Challe if he should order Salan's arrest. Only Jouhaud, as a fellow Air Force officer, showed a dignified sympathy for his colleague's personal agony.

The scores of officers in the building, left without orders, lounged aimlessly, some sleeping on tables with their heads resting on volumes of the city archives or smoking, hands in pockets, and discussing what they planned to do next. One imagines a defeated army to be forever on the move, frantically issuing orders, but in fact when a battle is lost there are rarely any worthwhile orders to issue except *Sauve qui peut*. Challe lay on his back on a couch, humming *L'Arlésienne*. Jouhaud walked up and down, his hands behind his back, occasionally turning to Challe with a grin to recall some happy adventure that they had enjoyed together in the Air Force. Zeller sat in a chair muttering to himself. Ferrandi sat with Susini in Zeller's office. Bibiche Salan and Noëlle Lucchetti were together in another office. Salan was alone in a separate office, writing orders. One commanded Colonel de la Chapelle to take some Legionnaires to the Orléans Barracks, disarm the Zouaves and hide the arms for future use by the O.A.S. An officer brought the order to de la Chapelle, who refused to receive it.

"I don't obey orders signed Salan," he said. "I am going with Challe."

"So is Salan," he was told.

Outside in the night Algiers resembled a city defeated in war and awaiting the occupation of a barbarous enemy. The population hid behind closed shutters, as parents soothed frightened children and waited for the sound of approaching armor. The streets were deserted, except for military trucks moving out and heading back to barracks. Some of the troops maintained discipline as they waited their turns to board. Others clawed for places in the packed lorries, mouthing foul German curses. Only the dead were missing from a scene that was as old as war itself. The four-day rebellion had ended with only one shot fired—and that by a lieutenant to blow out the tire of a general who was trying to drive through a roadblock.

By midnight, of the regiments that had supported the revolt, only the 1st R.E.P. remained, and an hour later even it had faded away into the darkness.

The same thought occurred to Jean-Jacques Susini that had earlier occurred to Salan, and he approached Colonel Gardes to ask what troops were still obeying orders. Gardes's face was gray with misery. Once again his cause had lost, and he spoke with his head on one side and with the slowness of a man forcing himself to keep self-control. "One company of the 1st R.E.P. and a unit or two of the second Rec," he said.

"Is there any hope?" Susini asked.

"Argoud is supposed to be coming from Oran with two regiments of 'paras,'" said Gardes. His voice rose, and his words though sarcastic were completely without humor. "Argoud is always supposed to be coming from Oran with two regiments of 'paras'."

"Is the second Rec still obeying orders?"

Gardes nodded without speaking.

"I think you should tell them to unlock the arsenal at the Caserne d'Orléans. The O.A.S. is going to need arms when this blows over."

"The what?"

"The O.A.S."

"Oh yes! The O.A.S."

Gardes cheered up. Relieved at the prospect of action, he said "Leave it to me" and left, running.

Susini went back to the main reception salon with its painted ceilings and gilded columns. It smelled of smoke, for "paras" were burning documents in the French Colonial fireplace. Three junior officers of the 1st R.E.P. sat side by side, chatting quietly and occasionally passing a bottle of cognac, which they drank from the lip. They were Major Denoix de Saint Marc, Captain Pierre Sergent and Lieutenant Roger Degueldre. Degueldre, as usual, was lighting one Gitane from the butt of another. A humorless smile hung on his face, the cynical smile that junior officers and N.C.O.s permit themselves when contemplating a foul-up of their betters; it is a smile that washes hands, so to speak, of all responsibility and says, "I knew it would end in a mess, but nobody asked my advice, and since they didn't, I don't give a royal damn."

An officer looked up from a telephone as Challe walked in. "Zouaves are entering the city from El Biar. A company of the 1st *Repp* is facing them. Do they shoot?"

"Ah, no!" Challe exclaimed with animation. "Ah, no! Ah, no!"

"El Biar!" said a junior officer reminiscently. "Great little football team. Remember when they knocked Rheims out of the Cup in 1958?"

"It was 1957," said another.

"1958," insisted the first, and the two began a spirited discussion into which several others joined.

Zeller, Jouhaud and Salan came in to join Challe for a last press conference with the few dozen journalists who had followed the Putsch from the start. Light bulbs flashed. Challe looked exhausted. Zeller and Jouhaud stared into space. Only Salan, with his wife at his side, was bearing up well. A journalist asked him "Are you going to surrender?" Salan smiled and shrugged.

"Not much alternative, is there?"

"I'm not," Zeller snapped.

"How about you?" someone asked Saint Marc, commander of the 1st R.E.P. Saint Marc looked up from the couch. "I go where General Challe goes," he said.

"That goes for me," said Colonel de la Chapelle.

"And you?" a journalist asked Yves Godard.

"I'm going to shoot myself," said Godard and turned his back.

One by one or in little groups they filed out to the square, where a line of lorries waited for them and a bossy lieutenant who had lost his nerve was shouting hysterically: "Only the big ones! Only the big ones! Junior officers and men, you are on your own."

Susini, left almost alone in the great building, went to the balcony and looked out over the Forum, which had seen so much history from May 13 to the Barricades to the Putsch. A thin rain was falling, and it was cold for the time of year when Algiers usually enjoys the glory of its warm spring nights. The city seemed empty. Idly Susini wondered what Lagaillarde would have done had he been there. Faintly he could hear the armored cars of the Gardes Mobiles coming closer, bringing with them all the vengeance and venom of reimposed legitimacy. It was time to fade away. The ghastly, half-hearted, nocturnal revolt was over. When the Army and the security forces reoccupied the city, Susini and the other leaders had gone.

PART TWO:
THE HAPPENING

8
BIRTH
April–May 1961

✤✤✤

We will forget the great hours of Algiers when each lived for everyone. We will snigger when we recall that horrible night of April 23–24; "Order has been restored in Algiers. Salan has committed suicide. The 1st R.E.P. has returned to barracks." That night when so many of us, suddenly turned into toughs, realized for the first time that too much despair is bad for the health. That night when we saw our fathers, our mothers, our officers weeping. The following morning when we had to tell the children who had slept through the night that it had all been a dream, and saw the tears roll down white cheeks. Yes if we want we will forget all that. . . .—Letter from a *pied noir* in Fresnes prison.

✤✤✤

Inside the trucks, which moved in turgid, uneasy lines out of Algiers to Zéralda, most of the Legionnaires joked and laughed with the kind of merriment that is not to be tampered with; the slightest break in its rhythm turns it into uncontrollable rage or fountains of tears and brings the crash of a gun turned impulsively on one's own brain. One N.C.O. sat aloof from the rest, insulated from the crazy melancholia by the intensity of his own thoughts. Chief Sergeant Bobby Dovecar sat near the opening at the back looking outward along cobbled roads streaked with tram lines, shining wet yellow in the rain and dim lights.

The 1st R.E.P. was dying. The most united fighting force in the world had become a clueless German mob. When the apparatus of military discipline tightened the vise, the regiment would be punished and disbanded, the leaders imprisoned and the men transferred to other regiments. Dovecar was only 23, too young to have served in Indochina and thus unmarked in a way uncommon among German Legionnaires; the faces of most bore a "wounded look," even when the owners had emerged unscathed. Four years earlier he had been a waiter in a sidewalk café in Vienna. It had taken him only three and a half years to reach the same rank in the same regiment as Degueldre had just relinquished on the night when Bobby had watched officers and N.C.O.s celebrating. Dovecar's military service had eighteen months to go, and he had intended to re-enlist and go on following Degueldre and the rest—but only in the 1st R.E.P.

As the lorry turned into the Boulevard Bugeaud, Dovecar removed his green beret and thrust it into his pocket to make him less conspicuous. He swung a leg over the rearboard and, without a farewell, without even being noticed by his shouting comrades, landed lithely on the road, his rubber jumping boots soundless; he loped into the shadows before the next truck in line came into view. He moved through street after street, keeping always where the shadows were deepest, until he came to a shuttered boardinghouse, where the bell squealed under his finger tip. It was a long time before there was movement on the other side. It opened an inch, and the concierge, Madame Zambach, recognized him with relief. He was shown to a narrow room little larger than a closet, where he fell on the bed fully dressed, just as dawn broke.

He awoke about 10:00, shaved his chin, leaving the upper lip furry, and from Madame Zambach's cupboard took an old green string-tied cardboard suitcase bought at Monoprix. Inside he had packed all the things he needed to separate himself from the world of the Legion. There was a thick pile of classical sheet music, pictures of his father and mother and letters written to him in the old-fashioned *Deutscheschrift* that is no longer used in Germany and Austria. There was also one complete set of civilian clothes. Dovecar, like many N.C.O.s in Algeria, rented a *pied-à-terre* where he could occasionally sleep and could keep dress for occasions when uniforms were inappropriate. He walked out into the streets with no clear idea of what to do. Self-preservation had led to his abrupt decision to flee. No idealism was involved. The complexities of French Algeria meant nothing to him. He was indifferent to *pieds noirs* and contemptuous of Moslems. General de Gaulle was a name, and France to him, as to most Legionnaires, was a bad word, rarely uttered except in derision. But the basic fact, for Dovecar as for the other Legionnaires who had deserted that night, was that they had lost good jobs. The Foreign Legion, despite its "Legion of Hell" reputation, its toughness and brutalities, had offered a pretty good life to working-class German boys who became N.C.O.s. Pay was ample, comforts and privileges abundant and social status within the regimental hierarchy enormous. Because promotion demands a certain intelligence and an ability to communicate with superiors, these N.C.O.s usually took pride in learning French and often spoke it even among themselves. They had a united contempt for what they called the "new" German Army, with its unmilitary safeguards against Nazism, and they wanted no part of it. Here was the curious paradox of the post-Vietnam Legionnaire—despising France and relishing its language, considering himself a German patriot but with no intention of serving the German Army. If the French lost Algeria the Legion would have no further reason for existence, and for soldiers like Dovecar the alternative would be to go back to serving tables at sidewalk cafés in Vienna. And that is why on this wildly unreal morning, he found himself walking the streets of Algiers as a deserter.

The streets were unexpectedly normal after the trauma of the previous nights and days. Men with briefcases hurried to their offices; with a briefcase one always hurries. Old Arab women cleaned the streets with witches' brooms. But patrols of Zouaves and Gardes Mobiles were everywhere, with tommy guns over their shoulders. Tanks and half-tracks with coiled barbed-wire on their fronts were strategically placed at every corner to form instant roadblocks when required; more discretely in the side streets, lines of Black Marias waited for their clientèle. Dovecar had only military papers. If he was stopped, he had resolved to make a run for it, but in a population of four hundred thousand one anonymous civilian— slight of build and gentle of expression, blessed with the same thick black hair as that of the men of the Midi—stood a good chance of emulating G. K. Chesterton's invisible man, who was not seen because he was not noticed. It would have been difficult for even the most perceptive policeman to guess that this boy, with his indifferent shirt, cheap Tergal suit and pointed imitation-Italian shoes, was one of the most exalted combat N.C.O.s of the 1st R.E.P. He went to a bar and ordered a *pastis* and then another, permitting a little *yaouled* to squat down among the peanut shells and olive pips to shine his shoes. At 1:00 he walked to an Arab café he knew in the Casbah and ate cheuba soup and couscous with a bottle of Mascara. What he needed was time to think. Identification papers were his biggest problem, money his least: He had more than 300,000 Algerian francs in his wallet.

In the afternoon he went to a cinema and saw a funny film with Alberto Sordi and Walter Chiari, but he was so preoccupied with his own thoughts that he could not remember the title and jumped in his seat, startled, at a sudden deafening hubbub of yells and whistles, until he realized that the girl on the screen had taken all her clothes off. When the curfew fell, he returned to his boardinghouse and ate some bread and cheese in his room.

Several days passed in this way. Occasionally he recognized other N.C.O.s of the 1st R.E.P. and 2nd R.E.C., in mufti like himself, and they quietly exchanged addresses, without committing them to paper, promising to stay in touch. This surreptitious passing of messages, this reaching through the unknown, resulted one day in a stranger's addressing Dovecar in a bar in the Rue Joinville. He was a neat young man with a pleasant manner, round face and prematurely receding hair; his dress was adorned with such old-fashioned accouterments as a waistcoat and a fob watch.

"Are you Bobby?" he said.

Dovecar was not alarmed. The stranger, by his carriage, was neither a policeman nor a soldier, and his avoidance of the surname showed a proper discretion. He nodded.

"My name is André Danglade,* " said the young man, and they shook hands. "We heard you were around. Welcome to the O.A.S."

"The what?"

"The O.A.S. Have a drink."

* A fictitious name. See "Notes on Sources"

Dovecar ordered a *pastis* as usual, Danglade a baby whiskey, and they drank in silence. Afterwards the two took a bus to the Boulevard Telelmy. Danglade proffered no information, and Dovecar asked only, "Are you a *pied noir?*" Danglade admitted that he was. They entered a modern apartment building, and Danglade knocked with a code series on the door. It was opened by a pale young man wearing braces over his open-necked shirt.

Danglade introduced them: "Jean-Jacques, this is the celebrated Dovecar. Jean-Jacques Susini."

But Dovecar was looking over Susini's shoulder through the smoke-filled room at a man sprawled on a sofa, with a pretty girl sitting beside him. Instinctively, in spite of his civilian clothes, Dovecar sprang to attention. *"Mon lieutenant,"* he addressed Roger Degueldre.

❖❖❖

Though the escape stories were all different, they were all equally haphazard. No one had really known where he was going. Raoul Salan had fully intended to surrender with Challe; this intention was later affirmed by Ferrandi. Instead, he was literally abducted. A car was waiting outside with a driver to spirit him away to one of the homes of one Robert Martel. Martel was a wealthy and turbulent *pied noir,* a vintner and politician who conspired in and helped to finance every right-wing plot he could find. He lived on his estates in the Mitidja with troops of Moslem servants bound to him by debt and family tradition; there were so many that they constituted almost a private army. Martel was called "sincere" by his friends, "a little mad" by detached observers and "a lunatic" by his enemies. He published at his own expense a clandestine paper called *The Voice of the Maquis*, in which he offered a program called "Defense of Christianity and the West by means of Counter-Revolution." It was a document sufficiently entertaining to be worth quoting, at least briefly. It contained such items as a list of "The Leaders One Should Not Follow;" Such leaders included those who had had their full names printed on the front pages of the Paris newspapers, those who wanted to "assassinate" or "kidnap" and those whom the régime makes respectable by releasing too quickly from prison.

"Liberty," he said, was, first, everything that putrefied the morale of the individual and, second, the art of introducing foreign fifth columnists into the country. Petrol was "the blood of the masses served by freemasonry and synarchy." General de Gaulle was "a pathological specimen that one generally puts away" and "a tool of freemasonry, synarchy." For Debré and Soustelle one was told to "see under Messianism." Bidault was "a bloody drunk." The Assembly in Paris was "an assembly of eunuchs" and Algeria "a springboard for freemasonry, synarchy and the builders of Republics."

Martel, it can be seen, could not abide freemasonry and synarchy. He also indulged in religious mysticism, despite occasional reproofs from his curé. He claimed to have apocalyptic visions, which, of course, delighted General Salan, who had had a few himself. Martel's table and cellar could not be faulted. He had not one but several homes through which he circulated, and Salan was welcome in all, as long as he did not try to escape. Martel put a protective ring around his guest and kept him completely incommunicado. Even Captain Ferrandi was told by a servant not to telephone because "the general was resting." Martel suspected Ferrandi of freemasonry, and he had received a letter from Father Grasset warning him that Grasset suspected poor Ferrandi of possessing the evil spirit. Eventually Martel relented and permitted Ferrandi to visit the General, providing that he wore a medal of the Virgin conspicuously round his neck. It almost seemed as if Martel in his visions saw Salan as a gift from God; more politically, Salan was a hostage whom he could trade for personal advantage. Salan was at first amused, but later he became alarmed.

Ferrandi himself did not at first try to escape at all. On the night of the collapse of the Putsch he drove back to the Hotel Saint George, where he was staying. He was warned by a Moslem concierge that the hall was full of policemen and went to his room by the service elevator. He slept and, when he woke, telephoned various friends until he found refuge in a bungalow on the waterfront.

Madame Salan hid with Noëlle Lucchetti in a villa near Blida and wrote to Martel prescribing how much whiskey should be permitted the General. Godard hid in the apartment of a girl reporter for Écho d'Alger. Colonel Gardes reached the door of a presbytery in a state of collapse and begged asylum. There he enjoyed the amply deserved luxury of a nervous breakdown, just as he had done after Dien Bien Phu. Gardy hid in an apartment in Algiers and boasted later that he had not even attempted a disguise, relying on the honesty of his face to avert suspicion.

General Jouhaud reached his native Oran and went underground among friends. But the heart of the Putsch was in Algiers; with Salan sunning his battle-scarred body in the Mitidja and Jouhaud exchanging reminiscences with childhood friends in Oran, two of the titular heads of the revolt had removed themselves from the hatching site of the Secret Army.

The escape of the leaders was so nearly wholesale that one could suspect either a brilliant prearranged plan or connivance from the police. The facts were quite the opposite. The Putsch had collapsed so suddenly and so unexpectedly that the police had not had time to realize that it was to Paris not to Algiers that it had to look for orders. Paris itself was in a state of utter confusion, still expecting a paratroop drop at an hour when Salan was accepting his first glass of brandy from Martel, and Dovecar was fleeing through the streets of Algiers. The security forces not only worked hard to capture the participants of the Putsch, but they were also extremely disagreeable about it. According to Susini, the police arrested and tortured his sister Virginie, forcing her fiancé to watch. Virginie had been with Susini in the Government-General Building almost to the end, but he had not told her where he intended to hide.

The police caught Major Camelin, Captain Branca, Captain Montagnon and Lieutenant Picot d'Aligny, all of whom returned to the O.A.S. sooner or later, and many others who did not. General Zeller tried to escape but lacked the contacts. He stayed for a few days in the home of a relative. The apartment was raided, and Zeller, unrecognized, showed sufficient sangfroid to help the police ransack the rooms. His host was less amused and asked Zeller to go. Zeller drifted around the city trying to make contact but failed; he gave himself up, penniless and exhausted, after two weeks.

The first meeting of the survivors of the Putsch was held on May 16 in a large new apartment building in the Champ de Manoeuvre. Those who answered this historic roll call included General Gardy, Colonel Godard, Captain Pierre Sergent, Lieutenant Degueldre and Dr. Jean-Claude Pèrez; the last was a popular young physician from Bab-el-Oued who had been arrested at the Barricades. Among the absentees were General Salan in the Mitidja; Jouhaud in Oran;

Gardes who was ill; Argoud in Paris; Jean-Jacques Susini who simply did not turn up and Captain Ferrandi who had set out to attend it but failed to find the address.

Gardy deferred to Yves Godard, who assumed *de facto* leadership. Godard was a big, rough-looking man, whose red face gave the appearance of an English farmer, what the French call, usually in admiration, *bouledogue*. Thick curly hair clustered tightly on his head as on Greek statues, and his nose was battered by a parachute jump that went wrong. All this and a thick bull neck gave promise of hard, bloody fights and furious outbursts. When captured by the Germans in 1940, at the age of 29, he had escaped from a prisoner-of-war camp in Poland, made his way across Europe back to France and joined the Resistance in Savoy. In Indochina he had commanded the 11th Parachute Battalion. He spoke in language that gave final judgment as a matter of course, and his will was as fixed as fate. In fact, his sense of authority was neither as absolute nor as confident as it seemed, but that had not yet become apparent. And, for a man whom his friends described admiringly as "an act of nature," he was capable of unexpected subtlety, as he showed in 1957 during and after the celebrated Battle of Algiers, when he and Massu broke the F.L.N. in the city.

Godard had then been head of the Algiers Sûreté, and he had arrested one Mahmoud. This man was an important prize, but Godard wanted a bigger one, Yacef Saadi, commander of the Algiers terrorists. So Godard decided to *become* Mahmoud. From information he extracted from prisoners, he knew a great deal about Saadi's temperament and opinions. He wrote Saadi letters signed "Mahmoud." Not only was Saadi completely deceived, but also the two men actually came to an intellectual understanding and friendship with each other. "Mahmoud's" good fortune was fantastic. When disaster overtook other key terrorists, Mahmoud always managed to escape unscathed. Finally Saadi put Mahmoud in charge of all military action in the Algiers zone, with these instructions: "I beg you to do the impossible to restore the situation."

Godard instead cordoned off the Casbah and arrested Saadi, his girl friend and every important F.L.N. leader in the city. The long nightmare of urban terrorism had come to an end in Algiers, thanks to Yves Godard. Yet the understanding established in their cor-

respondence was such that the two men remained friends, and Godard often summoned him from prison for a meal and a chat.

At further meetings of the O.A.S. general working procedures
were established. Pseudonyms were distributed, and each had
several to serve various purposes, although the basic pseudonym
generally began with the same letter as the real name. Salan was
"Soleil," "Éléphant" or "Francis." The first could have been either
a reference to Louis XIV, *le roi soleil*, or to a touch of the sun.
Jouhaud was "Soleil bis," "Compagnon" or "Yazid." Jean-Jacques
Susini was "Jeannine." Godard was "Françoise" or "Claude." Argoud was "Albatross." Gardy was "Gulf" or "Guy." Broizat was
"Bravo," a dashing name for such a cautious man. Captain Ferrandi
was "Fayard," "Ferhat" or "Fernandel." Lagaillarde was "Laon,"
and Lacheroy was "Métro." Pèrez was "Papa."

Most of these names became known very quickly to the anti-
O.A.S. forces, but only one became internationally famous as the
symbol of the O.A.S.—the name given to Degueldre. He was called
"Delta," a name that, more than any other, was to connote the violent
reputation of the O.A.S. to the world. So famous did "Delta" become
that Degueldre's other psuedonym was lost, although it might have
given students of Freud an interesting insight into the O.A.S. sub-
conscious. It was "Djamila," already the symbol of the pain, savagery
and brute justice of the Algerian war. As far as Degueldre was
concerned, the man and the occasion was meeting.

Then Gardes signaled Algiers from his presbytery that he had
recovered and was ready for service. He was given the pseudonyms
"Fleur," "Boussouf," and "Hôtel" and assigned by Godard to organize
the O.A.S. in Orléansville and Blida.

It was learned that Lacheroy had escaped to Madrid, disguised as
a priest, complete with breviary, which, according to some accounts,
he studied with an expression of rapture, especially when the police
were near. Lacheroy, although an expert on subversive warfare in
Indochina, was considered something of a lightweight by the other
colonels; but there was consternation in Algiers when it was learned
that Argoud had left Paris and joined Lacheroy in Madrid. The
colonels had been waiting for Argoud to return, for without him the
organization remained in a state of suspended animation. Between
Salan in his gilded cage and Godard the fer de lance, there was too

vast an intellectual and social gap. Colonel Gardes could not help; he still addressed his fellow colonels as *mon colonel*. Argoud would have filled the gap automatically. Some of the leaders had assumed even from the beginning that Argoud would assume formal leadership under Salan, and few would have denied it to him. The disappointment was reflected in a brief, depressed note from General Gardy to Susini. "First Métro and then Albatross as guests of General Franco. Decidedly we don't have a big crowd on the set."

Broizat too remained aloof. Immediately after the Putsch, he had hidden in an apartment and had become a complete recluse for several weeks. Then he saw his priest and discussed the possibility of rejoining holy orders. When he did emerge among his colleagues, he told them that he did not intend to serve in the O.A.S. He would work for it by publishing a clandestine newspaper to express the views of the organization, but he declared himself ineligible for the fighting cadres that Godard was preparing to form.

In spite of disappointments, however, the Secret Army began to find itself and to take shape. It was given a tremendous fillip on May 20, when discussions for a cease-fire began at Évian between representatives of the French Government and of the F.L.N. These discussions were final evidence that the French had decided to abandon Algeria, and the ranks of the *pieds noirs* automatically closed behind the O.A.S. General Salan was formally named Commander in Chief of the O.A.S., then left to his dreams. From that moment on he issued articulate pronunciamentos and made some graceful speeches, but little evidence exists that he gave any important directives or imposed the slightest discipline on the organization.

Little by little, the O.A.S. came under the military leadership of Godard, the tactical guidance of Degueldre and the ideological direction of Susini. According to Susini's analysis, the failure of the Putsch had largely been caused by its confinement to the Army. The civilians had stood on the pavements and cheered. The O.A.S., he said, must unite civilians and military, unite the Europeans of Algeria with the Europeans of Metropolitan France and, in due course, unite the Europeans of Algeria with the Moslems of Algeria. The F.L.N. held every string worth pulling on the Moslem side. It had proved that violence and terrorism *worked* and could force Paris to the conference table. The O.A.S. would demonstrate the same rule but more efficiently, for the men who would apply it were professionals. The peaceful Moslem population must be encouraged to believe that the O.A.S. would protect it against the F.L.N., for it was this population that had been subjected to the bulk of the F.L.N. atrocities.

As Susini saw it, the Achilles' heel of the Paris authorities lay in the *contingent*, the body of conscripts that formed a large part of the French Army in Algeria. The *contingent* did little fighting, but it manned the garrisons. If the violence in Algeria were stepped up, the lives of the conscripts would be placed in greater danger, and there would be a hubbub among their parents in France, which the politicians would find hard to resist. If this hubbub led to the withdrawal of the conscripts from Algeria, the hand of the O.A.S. would be immeasurably strengthened. For it would increase the influence of the professional parachutists, who were largely friendly to the O.A.S. cause. So O.A.S. policy progressively simplified itself: goad the F.L.N. into further violence and worse atrocities, maintain friendships with the Army, frighten the conscripts and, not least, eliminate all Europeans in Algeria who were known to be sympathetic to the F.L.N. or to the cause of an independent Algeria.

The organization of the O.A.S., as set up by Godard, followed closely the lines of the French Resistance, in which he had served so brilliantly. There were two primary branches. One was the Organisation de Masse (O.M.), responsible for raising funds and recruits and providing disguises and false papers. O.M. was also to raise local commando groups to defend residential and business areas and other groups for wider and more ambitious action. O.M. operated on a "horizontal" plan and a "vertical" plan. The former was for raising support and funds house by house and street block by street block; the latter was for raising it through professional groups, from cabdrivers to doctors and lawyers. The Mussulman Bureau was formed under O.M. to maintain liaison with Moslems friendly to France—men like the Bachaga Boualem, Si Cherif, and Si Mohammed, each of whom commanded many thousands of pro-French harkis.

The other branch, operating in equal partnership with O.M., was *Opérations, Renseignements, Organisation* (*O.R.O.*). It dealt with propaganda and direct, violent action. It was through this branch that Roger Degueldre was given the authority to select his men for the Delta commandos. Degueldre was a meticulous chooser and a natural believer in the elite system; his Deltas were composed almost exclusively of ex-Legionnaires of the 1st R.E.P. Operational command was given to Dovecar.

Separate from the Deltas were the Z (for Zone) commandos, which were usually recruited from among local *pieds noirs* and designed for political and fund-raising, as well as military, activity. For this reason they were given to Susini, with Second Lieutenant Bernard Delhomme of the 1st R.E.P. in charge of whatever direct violence was necessary.

Colonel Gardes was placed in command of O.M. and delegated to direct the campaign of psychological warfare. O.R.O. was placed, not too fortunately, under twin military-civilian control and directed by Dr. Pèrez and Degueldre, with Godard in operational command of both O.M. and O.R.O. Susini and General Gardy were given freedom of movement in a largely mythical "political Committee." Gardy was assigned to the Foreign Legion in Oran, with the task of trying to persuade officers to join the organization, either individually or in groups.

The efficiency with which the leaders went about their duties was remarkable, considering the brief time in which they had had to organize and the decimation of their ranks by police arrests. By the end of May Susini and Gardes were issuing manifestos. Bombs began to explode in Moslem quarters; these bombs were designed to warn rather than to kill. The O.A.S. in those early, probing days considered its enemy to be the F.L.N. The ordinary Moslem population was considered a potential ally. O.A.S. graffiti proliferated on the walls of the various Algerian cities, and the original "ti-ti-ti ta-ta" rhythm of *Al-gé-rie fran-çaise* now stood for *l'O.A.S. vain-cra*.

There were the first narrow escapes. Captain Ferrandi, who did not have much to do living in his cottage by the sea at Fort de l'Eau, applied to Degueldre for two liaison officers, specifying Legionnaires. Degueldre assumed that they would be serving General Salan; otherwise it is unlikely that he would have spared valuable Legionnaires, who, within the cadres of the O.A.S., were something of an elite similar to that of English secretaries in New York. Two tipsy Legionnaires appeared at the cabin and, delighted at the lightness of their duties, used their ample leisure to go whoring. The inevitable happened. One started a fight in a bar and was arrested. Fortunately, the accident was reported by an O.A.S. sympathizer at police

bickering and apparently hopelessly divided right-wing groups. Yet not only had Salan and Susini sneaked treacherously back to Algiers without him, but they had even taken his baby, the O.A.S., with them. They had offered the feeble excuse that there was no room on the plane, but they had found room for the expendable Ferrandi. Now the O.A.S. was being formed in Algeria without any reference to its "leader," except for a desultory acknowledgment that he had thought of it first. Lagaillarde tried to keep his temper and wrote friendly letters to Susini beginning "Dear Jean-Jacques" and using *tu;* he suggested that Susini come back to Spain so that they could organize the O.A.S. calmly together in the tranquility of Madrid rather than in the furnace of Algiers, where everyone had to dye his hair and grow a moustache that did not suit him. Susini replied briefly and curtly, sometimes personally, sometimes through his secretary. In conversation Susini referred derisively to his former mentor and guide as "the paladin in the red beard." The pupil had donned the master's robe, and he liked it.

Happily, Lagaillarde, whatever his reasons for grievance and resentment, was adaptable enough to make the best of what he had. There were agreeable aspects to life in Madrid, and he found ways of sweetening his bitterness. He was an enthusiastic frequenter of nightclubs and spent most days by the swimming pool of Santiago Bernabeu, near the Real Madrid football stadium. He was always attended by admirers, of whom he still had many, and girls, who were almost as numerous. The latter he was able to use as an important lever on Argoud.

Argoud was, in fact, thoroughly charmed by Lagaillarde. Like many men who feel deep physical attraction to women, Argoud basically preferred the company of men, and Lagaillarde, by his extraordinary good looks and masculine charm, attracted men as well as women. He also had some useful and entertaining cronies like Michel Fechoz, a veteran of the Barricades and one of the original gang that had tried to kill Salan with a bazooka. Fechoz loved the bullfights and the football matches, and he invariably knew where to find new girls when the available talent had ceased to please. Fechoz preferred to be liked rather than trusted, and he was predictable and punctual only in taking his place on the O.A.S. payroll. Lagaillarde referred to him as "my handyman."

Like most of the others, Argoud was enduring an extremely pain-

ful moral crisis. He had committed himself to the O.A.S. and did
not regret it. He wanted to serve it, but, like his friend Broizat, he
distrusted its incipient violence. He had never met Roger Degueldre,
but what he had heard of Degueldre's cold-blooded efficiency chilled
him. He had received an offer from Latin America for his services
as a Polytechnician, and he had the future of his wife and daughters
to consider. Doing one's duty, as General Weygand once observed,
is easy. Knowing which way duty lies when the signs are pointing in
opposite directions is another matter. As it was with the officers at
Vichy, so it was later with the officers of the O.A.S.

Salan had written to Argoud, asking him to return to Algeria and
offering him command of Oran, nominally under Jouhaud and
Gardy but actually as his own fief. It was a good offer, for Oran
was the most powerful bastion of the O.A.S., more powerful than
Algiers, but as Argoud saw it, it was in Algiers that decisions were
taken and reputations made. The Algiers hierarchy had already
been formed, and he had missed the appointment conferences. An
inferior command was not something for a Polytechnician who had
been Chief of Staff to General Massu.

At the end of May Argoud flew to Paris under the name "Vich-
ard." He was in a depressed mood. He considered the explosion of
plastic bombs juvenile and self-destructive. He would have agreed
with Hilaire Belloc's cautionary tale about "George, who played with
a dangerous toy, and suffered a catastrophe of considerable di-
mensions, and . . .

> The moral is that little boys
> Should not be given dangerous toys."

He would have been even more appalled had he known that the
O.A.S. man in charge of plastic-bomb explosions in Paris was, in
fact, a boy nineteen years old.

In Paris he met Pierre Sergent and Sergent's inseparable friend
and assistant Daniel Godot. The two junior officers had been sent
by Godard to organize "O.A.S.-Métro." They introduced Argoud
in turn to Colonel Barbier de Blignières, who had agreed to assume
military command of the O.A.S. in France. De Blignières corrected
several of Argoud's ideas about Degueldre, and with each meeting
Argoud became more cheerful. These men were real fighting men.
De Blignières was a Catholic intellectual, attractive, fairly wealthy,

witty, with a tendency to let ash drop on his waistcoat while he talked through his cigarette. He was an admirer of Father Grasset and an enthusiast about the priest's political group, Cité Catholique. But de Blignières's participation in the O.A.S. had less to do with his religion or with his wife's Algerian background than with simple comradeship. "You don't leave your friends *dans le merde*" was his soldierly philosophy. When he remembered the Barricades, the Putsch and the O.A.S., he also remembered a certain moment in 1953 in the Plain of Jars in Indochina, where he commanded the 2nd R.E.C.: He lay in a ditch watching his blood flow into the dust. He endured the loneliness that is always more intense amid deafening gunfire, and he made his peace with God. Then he saw a French soldier coming toward him, taking masterly advantage of such cover as there was.

"One of us is enough, Degueldre, for heaven's sake," said de Blignières weakly. "Don't let them get you too. I've had it."

"You are too pessimistic, Colonel," said Degueldre. "It isn't far to go."

Degueldre threw his commanding officer's arm over his shoulders, and the latter, though almost unconscious, could still marvel at the skill with which Degueldre crossed a field of intense fire, by way of dead ground, ditch and hillock, as if it were the Champs Élysées. To de Blignières, the O.A.S. was Roger Degueldre. Before the Putsch Degueldre had often visited the Colonel for dinner at his apartment in the Rue de la Pompe. They would talk Army politics into the night while de Blignières's small daughters in their nighties would peep through the door at *le grand Roger* with adoration. They kept autographed pictures of him by their bedsides.

De Blignières and Pierre Sergent briefed Argoud on the situation in Paris. What impressed Sergent particularly was the number of university students of good family, who were uninvolved with political causes and without sympathy for the Right, yet who were nonetheless trying to make contact with the O.A.S., excited by its romanticism and flaunting of danger.

Argoud next called on a friend, a company director named Maurice Gingembre, who had been in Algiers during the Putsch. Gingembre liked politics and politicians and was a friend of Georges Bidault. He also had a dilettantish liking for dangerous living and the money to indulge such whims. He was not himself a *pied noir,* but his mother had come from one of the oldest *pied noir* families. He owned the Djebel Onk phosphate mines in eastern Algeria and traveled regularly between Algiers and Paris. He was the kind of amusing and intellectually stimulating man for whom Argoud always had a weakness, a weakness that made him unreliable in his choice of friends. Gingembre had many qualities, but discretion was not one of them, and Argoud should have been put on his guard by his friend's compulsive gossiping.

Argoud told Gingembre his problems. "I am going back to Madrid," he said. "There I will decide whether to go on to Latin America or back to Algeria."

Gingembre listened sympathetically. Argoud continued, "Will you keep an eye on my wife and children, until I can send for them?"

"Of course," said Gingembre, and they parted with a handshake.

Paradoxically these expressions of listlessness and uncertainty on Argoud's part had quite the opposite effect on Gingembre himself. Gingembre, as an amateur adventurer, found himself deeply attracted to the romance of the Secret Army. As a businessman he believed that it needed reorganizing on sound business lines. A brain like Argoud's for example, was being unforgivably wasted. When Argoud left, Gingembre began to make notes.

Argoud returned to Madrid, and his disenchantment deepened. Lagaillarde appeared not to have moved from the side of the swimming pool. He continued the monologue about how badly he had been treated. The only differences were that the girls at his side had different faces and that there seemed to be more people in Madrid whom Lagaillarde refused to accept socially. Lacheroy too was full of his usual complaints, the bully aggrieved, the biter bit. Ortiz on his rare trips from Majorca to Madrid was amusing in his earthy innkeeper's way and could make Argoud laugh—for people who slipped on banana peels, appealed to Argoud's sense of humour. But the days seemed endless. Spanish food was oily, and his French liver could not assimilate lunches at 2:30 and dinners at midnight.

Then quite suddenly his decision was made for him, or so it seemed. On June 1 he read in the newspapers that Commissioner Roger Gavoury of the Algiers police had been brutally stabbed to death in his apartment by O.A.S. men. The serious campaign of murder and terrorism, long threatened, had begun. Argoud wrote a furious letter to Godard, stating his refusal to associate his name with political assassination. It was an odd affirmation from an officer who had been the apostle of summary execution in the early days of the Algerian war. As far as Argoud was concerned, it seemed to depend on who did the killing. He packed his bags and prepared to leave for South America.

10
DELTA
May 31–July 1961

✦✦✦

Roger Gavoury had been Commissioner in Algiers for only eight days, having been promoted from assistant, a post he had held for eighteen months. He was fifty years old, a burly, attractive man with a wry, humorous disposition and the inscrutable, piercing eyes of the policeman. Divorced and with three children in Metropolitan France, he lived alone in a one-room apartment in a modern building and paid little attention to his personal security. Even after his fifth-floor apartment had been bombed shortly before the Putsch, he had moved no farther away than to the floor below.

Before coming to Algiers, Gavoury had served for several years in Morocco, where Christian-Moslem relations had always been more affable than in the harsh racial climate of Algeria. In Morocco the women, under the influence of Princess Aïsha, had largely given up the veil. Moroccans and Frenchmen mixed in the cocktail bars and played tennis together. Algeria was not like that.

The night of May 31 had been a night of many explosions, and the Commissioner did not leave his office on the Boulevard Baudin until 11:00 P.M. Plastic explosives, invented in the Second World War, and perfected in technique by the F.L.N., had established themselves as the most suitable form of explosive for terrorism. It is made by mixing hexogen (known as "R.D.X." in the United States) and TNT into a rubbery compound base that feels like putty to the touch. It can be exploded either electrically or by fuse. Among its advantages is that it is so stable that it can be cut into strips of any size. It is light and easily carried, and it will stick to almost any surface—a window sill, the underside of the hood of a car, the inside of a mailbox. *Plastiquer* became a common verb in France towards the end of the Algerian war. It is not a legitimate French word—nor is "to plasticate" good English—but, because it is convenient and appropriate to this brief, bloody period of history, it will be used here nevertheless.

Gavoury's friend, Commissioner Pellefigue, took the wheel and drove through the empty streets of the uneasily sleeping, sandbagged city.

"Listen to the noise," he said. "Yet, when you catch the bastards you'd think they wouldn't hurt a fly."

"They are fly's best friend," said Gavoury. "They leave so many bodies lying around to encourage them."

"You can't trust any *pied noir*," said Pellefigue. "If I had my way . . . well, I'd have only people from France. I wouldn't let a single *pied noir* into the police station."

"Then how would you find your way around? If you figure it out your way, you will finish up hiding behind sandbags and hand the city to the O.A.S. You have to trust your luck."

Pellefigue's car stopped at the door of Gavoury's apartment building in the center of the city, and the two officers shook hands. Gavoury took out his keys, for the building was kept locked at night, and outside keys were confided to each tenant. He did not immediately go to his apartment. He often stopped off at the apartment of a young lady who lived on the ground floor for a glass, a chat and friendly relaxation from the day's endeavors. Afterwards, as usual, he took the elevator to the fourth floor. He was off duty and sleepy, and he did not notice that the door to another apartment was open an inch but closed quickly as he passed. The apartment was occupied by a student called Jacques Malmassari, who crossed to his telephone, which was off the hook, and breathed a signal into it.

Gavoury, entering his apartment, may have noticed that the bathroom and bedroom doors were closed. Confined as he was all day behind the claustrophobic sandbags of the police station, he liked to keep all possible doors open. Without removing his jacket, he opened the bathroom door and looked into the soft brown eyes of Bobby Dovecar, who ran a switchblade into his body. It was not efficiently done, and Gavoury screamed. Three other men—Petri, Tenne and Danglade—burst from the bedroom, and the Commis-

sioner died, as had Julius Caesar, amid a flurry of knife thrusts. The
building was a modern one, with the thin walls favored by specula-
tive builders the world over, and many residents heard the scream,
but they had heard screams before and knew better than to be in-
quisitive in Algiers that particular spring. Nobody reported the incident, and, when Gavoury's Moslem cleaner found him at 7:00
the next morning, his body was completely drained of blood. Malmassari was arrested and admitted to having given keys to a *pied
noir* named Piegts, who had passed them to four other men.

Not only Argoud was appalled by the brutal murder. French
public opinion was outraged. Salan, said the newspapers, had for-
feited whatever sympathy he might once have enjoyed in Metropolitan France. The fact was that Salan, a prisoner on the Mitidja
estates of Robert Martel, knew nothing about it. Nor did Colonel
Godard, who read about it in *Écho d'Alger* and was furious. The
coup had been planned by Susini and Roger Degueldre without discussion with anyone else in the organization. The reason airily given
by Susini was "security." The O.A.S. had become a large organization, and it was wise to presume, from the precedent of the French
Resistance, that, in any secret organization, one of twenty members
is an agent of the enemy. Susini did not trust even the colonels.

Godard declared his refusal to have anything more to do with
Degueldre. The personality of Degueldre already exercised and dominated everybody. The Duke of Wellington's remark about his
troops—"I don't know if they will frighten the enemy, but by God
they frighten me"—could not be better applied than to Degueldre.
Every specialist is impressive when engaged in his métier, and when a
man's specialty is organizing death, as was Degueldre's, the effect is
noticeably heightened. With his great size, physical strength and
ardent temperament, he symbolized everything that was lethal in the
O.A.S., everything that frightened and shocked and at the same
time everything that hypnotized and enticed. His pseudonym, "Delta,"
had become the official title of the O.A.S. killer brigades; Delta 1,
the elite group of all the Deltas, consisted of fifteen men whom
Degueldre had entrusted to Bobby Dovecar.

Among his friends, Degueldre was worshiped as a hero. Frenchmen are much less prone to using first names than are Anglo-Saxons;
one can spend a lifetime with friends and colleagues and still ad-

dress them by their surnames. Yet Degueldre was almost never "Degueldre." When they spoke of him it was always "Roger," and frequently they lowered their voices when they said it, as they might do for a lover. But, face to face, even though they were outlaws together, he was always *mon lieutenant.*

Politically Degueldre was not a complicated man, and he spent little time worrying about "communism." "Listen," he said to Susini. "I have been a soldier for fifteen years. I have tried to be good at my métier. When our colonels began to interest themselves in Algeria, I warned them after the Barricades, 'You say nothing will stop you from keeping Algeria French? Very well, I take the same oath with you. But understand that so far as I am concerned it will be respected. I will go on to the end.' I told Colonel Dufour as much." It was not hard, despite everything, to see Degueldre for what he was, an innocent—a dangerous, a stupendous innocent but an innocent all the same.

Women were unable to resist him. The great, solemn, ugly mug, the heavy sensuous mouth, the huge, sharp-toothed smile, like the sun emerging from storm clouds; the brilliant pale-blue eyes; the ability of the soldier to spring from profound sleep to taut alertness all made him deeply loved. Degueldre was, in short, a star and not a tinsel star like Lagaillarde. Yet it would be difficult to make a film about him, for the only actor who could truly portray him would be Errol Flynn, and Flynn is dead.

Degueldre's main problem, apart from the heart condition that worried him, was a curious one of identity, and it exasperated him. He was constantly accused of being someone else. This false alter ego had pursued him throughout his Legion service, and now it appeared on the Algiers police description, which said that Degueldre was a Belgian who had joined the Foreign Legion after serving in the Walloon Division of the S.S. The person to whom they actually referred was a man named Roger Deguelle, a minor Belgian war criminal who had never been traced. The name and place of birth were similar, and Degueldre had indeed joined the Legion when it was being deluged with S.S. men, so the confusion was understandable. But Deguelle, as police records in Brussels showed, was born in 1914, which would have made him nearly fifty, whereas Degueldre was certainly not.

Degueldre had become the latest to attract the attention of Jean-

Jacques Susini. Seeking as always to manipulate a man more important and stronger than himself, Susini had selected Degueldre as the natural leader of the O.A.S., and he proceeded to give him a short course in the realities of politics. Degueldre admired Susini's intelligence and took a vicarious pleasure in Susini's lack of respect for things that he, Degueldre, revered, such as uniform, rank and military authority.

For Degueldre's killer instincts Susini had nothing but respect. What chilled him was Degueldre's military nihilism. Degueldre's philosophy of life was simple; if you live, you burn. His mind dwelt constantly on Budapest. Algeria as a country meant nothing to him; it was merely a country that he had sworn to keep French. This sense of detachment made it easier for him to organize a war apparatus. If necessary, he told Susini, he would blow up the Casbah without a qualm. He considered that in Algeria he had complete liberty of action, "Like the Russians in Budapest." He said to Susini that if the O.A.S. were to win the war, every city had to be turned into a fortress and defended house by house, so that the Government in Paris would either have to capitulate or, in his own words, "reconquer cemeteries." Susini quickly realized that a Budapest was just what Degueldre wanted to satisfy his personal destiny and cheat the death that might otherwise creep up quietly on him by way of an uneven heartbeat. Degueldre had never had any illusions about his personal longevity. He wanted to die the way he had lived. To die in the blazing rubble of a fortress would be perfect. Ideally, though he never said such a thing, he would be the last to die, like Macbeth at Dunsinane. Whoever else died in the holocaust did not really matter.

Susini, as has already been observed, was quite impervious to the deaths of other people, but he drew the line at a philosophy that included his own demise with that of Degueldre. Vikings were once buried in flaming ships with their dogs at their feet; though Susini could see Degueldre as a Viking, he was reluctant to be cast in the supporting role.

"It won't wash, Roger," he said. "The population of Algeria will accept sacrifices, but only after a long and convincing indoctrination, *and* a certainty of ultimate success."

But the Gavoury affair, which Susini had inspired, had put Degueldre in serious trouble with the colonels. Even before the murder, Godard had disliked him. The man who had accepted the active leadership of the O.A.S. was tormented by forebodings of the future. He sensed that Degueldre was becoming too big. He was the cuckoo in the colonel's nest, growing bigger and pushing them out. He could see the moment coming when Degueldre would be "Mister O.A.S." It was left to poor General Gardy to try and smooth the various sensibilities. Gardy's position could hardly have been more sensitive. Nicole's husband had been arrested after the Putsch and was serving his prison sentence. The General's other son-in-law was in the O.A.S. in Oran. His son had not joined the Putsch and was serving in the Legion. Degueldre had become his de facto son-in-law. He and Nicole had announced their intention to marry as soon as possible. Furthermore, Nicole was pregnant by Degueldre.

Godard knew all this too, but Gardy felt compelled to write him a humble-pie letter that must have been galling for an old man of such pride:

> I know Degueldre is a desperado, but there is a danger that he might abandon the organization altogether and simply take off. He is a major force in the organization. He should be cossetted and placed in the best possible post we can offer him so that we don't lose him. We should use him to the maximum, and fit him into the senior cadre of the O.A.S. In my opinion he should be second-in-command to you. I beg you to concentrate on this problem and I am certain you will find the proper solution. . . .

After a few weeks Godard agreed to forget his rancor, so that Roger was able to emerge from the Coventry to which he had been sent. For one thing, Degueldre stood head and shoulders above the others as an organizer. His Delta 1 commando had become his joy. It was to the O.A.S. what the 1st R.E.P. had been to the Foreign Legion. He barred men who drank too much. He preferred bachelors to married men, and those who he felt had let the Delta down, by, for example, involving themselves in local rackets, he simply ordered shot. Dovecar did the shooting.

Compared with the spruceness and military efficiency of Delta 1, the rest of the O.A.S. stumbled and blundered badly during the early groping months of its existence. One imagines that a band of swashbuckling outlaws would be full of initiative and improvisation, nimble with their wits. But many of the officers were long-service professionals. They had become accustomed to passing the buck and avoiding decisions, and they still showed marked distaste for making decisions.

As for the *pieds noirs*, they were generous with encouragement and promises, but their performance fell short of perfection. The *pieds noirs* shopkeepers who had assumed command of subsections and commandos left their carbines and submachine guns at home, as soon as it was time for anisette and lunch. This attitude put a heavy load on the fighting officers, especially as even among the colonels themselves several, like Broizat, Argoud and Lacheroy, preferred to remain aloof from the dirty world of actual warfare. Susini reported one explosive incident between Godard and an Algiers shopkeeper who commanded a sector in the center of the city. Not only did the exchange reveal the strain under which the officers were living, but also it exposed the shallowness of the alliance between the French military and the *pieds noirs*. Godard had drawn up on paper an "organigramme," a detailed set of instructions for the defense system of the sector, and was explaining it. The *pied noir* protested, "Colonel, it will be very difficult to find as many volunteers as you say I must."

Godard was astonished. "Why?"

The shopkeeper cachinnated. "You know how it is. The *commerçants* here are generous with their sympathy, but how does one get them to give more?"

Godard looked at the shopkeeper and saw a reverse image of himself, an officer who had sacrificed everything for the O.A.S. He flew into a rage, slapped his hand across the sheet of paper he was holding and barked: "The problem is clear. If these fellows, these— Algerians—refuse to fight we have not the slightest reason to sacrifice ourselves. We will take our jackets and quit before Algeria becomes independent."

Money too was short. Millionaires like Martel tended to use their fortunes to pursue their own schemes and dreams. The O.A.S. officially imposed a tax of 2,000 old francs, or $4, every two months on all *pieds noirs* but discovered that the latter preferred sounding *Algérie française* on their auto horns to giving money to the cause. Susini thought up a supremely simple method to change the ideas of nonpaying shopkeepers. The O.A.S. bombed their premises at night. It used only small charges of plastic, but a bombed shop was a social stigma.

The Casbah. "Had it not been for the great Moslem riot of All Saints Day, 1960, the generals' revolt would have happened five months earlier." A.F.P. *from* PICTORIAL

General and Mme. Salan. "She found the inscription 'O.A.S.' painted on the wall outside her home and wondered what it meant." Soon the whole world knew. *Wide World*

Soustelle, Algiers, 1958. Speaking from the Forum. "Long live Algeria! Long live France! Long live French Algeria! Long live General de Gaulle!" *Paris Match*

Colonel Argoud. Distributing arms to loyal harkis, while General Massu looks on. "Their views were so similar they never had to argue."

The 1st R.E.P. "The Premier Repp is not a regiment. It's a family, a bloc." At far right is Major Denoix de Saint Marc who led it into revolt.

Colonel Gardes. "Not for him the impersonality of his metier. He liked to quote Lyautey. 'He who is only a soldier is a bad soldier.'" *Paris Match*

Lagaillarde. With *pieds noirs* in Algiers bar. "He was always surrounded by admirers. He ran a kind of Right-wing Algiers jet set." *Paris Match*

Bastien-Thiry. "Whatever motives he had for wanting to kill General de Gaulle, lack of privilege was not one of them."

Lieutenant Degueldre. "The man and the occasion were meeting . . . he had all the qualities which frightened, and all which enticed. His philosophy was, 'if you live, you burn.'" A.F.P. *from* PICTORIAL

Jouhaud, Salan, Challe, Zeller. "Less bellicose rebels could scarcely be imagined . . . they looked like schoolboys outside the headmaster's study, waiting for a swishing." *Paris Match*

Generals Massu and Challe. There was little conflict in their points of view. They gave different answers to one major question; how far does loyalty go? *Wide World*

Colonel Godard. "A force of nature. He gave promise of hardy bloody fights . . . but found that a colonel without a regiment is just a monsieur." *Paris Match*

Colonel Broizat. " 'The military monk,' he showed an abhorrence of violence that sometimes seemed to amount to a distaste for his vocation."

Jean-Jacques Susini. "A scholar, a man of the night . . . he felt no revulsion at the spilling of blood, providing it was not his own." *Paris Match*

Not all the local cadres were inadequate, of course. Many were formed' of veterans, civilians, students and Moslems. Ex-servicemen were a particularly rich source of manpower. *Pied noir* businessmen had traditionally offered jobs to soldiers when their military service was over, and European families encouraged their daughters to marry soldiers and keep them in Algeria. Many of these men were former Legionnaires, and they were the most fanatical of the ultras.

The civilian commandos also included a fair proportion of delinquents, which the climate of Algiers bred only too freely. A young European coming of age in 1961 had been born in wartime and had known war until he was four and food rationing until he was seven. After nine years of relative peace, watching the colonial regiments and the Foreign Legion leave for Indochina, at the age of thirteen, he endured a new war of the nastiest and most repellent kind. He moved into a world of shadows, where death from throat slitting, castration, evisceration and gouging out of eyes was among the natural hazards of life. As the years went by, he scarcely looked up from his school books at the sound of bombs, machine-gun fire, screams for help or sirens of ambulances and police cars, although he knew subconsciously from the timbre whether the activity was coming from Belcourt, Climat-de-France or Bab-el-Oued. Since 1955 F.L.N. atrocities had been so successful politically, pulling Paris into negotiations, that the European student, who may have seen his parents with their throats cut, could be excused for believing that such violence was the most effective form of political expression.

The bewilderment of the civilian commandos of the O.A.S. increased as they observed that, although in Metropolitan France and at the United Nations, the atrocities of the F.L.N. were passed off indifferently as the products of an inert culture, the atrocities of the Europeans aroused furious indignation. The Europeans of Algeria had become, in the eyes of the world, a mob of fascists and Army deserters, un-French people with names like Fernández, López and Susini. Bab-el-Oued, beloved by generations of its inhabitants, had become, without their realizing it, Nazi Germany distilled into a single suburb. The fact that Algeria's 150,000 Jews were among the most militant commandos of the O.A.S. was dismissed with words like "Stern Gang."

Popular support for the O.A.S. was overwhelming. But the colonels were incapable of accepting the idea that their army was really commanded by a lieutenant and kept searching for what they considered a real leader, one who would relieve them of the supreme decisions. One of the few things they agreed on was that General Salan's leadership left almost everything to be desired. Even his appearance was depressing. Without his uniform and with his hair dyed black as a disguise, all his distinction was gone. His mournful Dalmatian's face seemed molded of putty. Hidden sadness seemed to knit his brows, and anxiety was depicted in his looks. His mouth and eyes were tight with constipation. At one point, if Jean-Jacques Susini is to be believed (which he often is not), there was a serious discussion among the colonels and civilian leaders of the O.A.S. about whether or not to assassinate both Salan and Martel, but they agreed that it would damage rather than help the cause. Nobody had reason to believe that Martel—"Salan's Rasputin," as Susini jovially called him—was doing actual harm to the Mandarin; that is to say, they had no reason to believe the Mandarin would be more effective without Martel. But it was the worst ill luck that Massu languished in northern France, playing tennis at the Montargis Tennis Club, and that Colonel Bigeard, the fitness faddist, spent hours tramping round the outside of Toul Prison looking for glimpses of old comrades, as Blondel had looked for Richard the Lion Heart. These two natural leaders of the O.A.S. were inextricably locked in the straitjacket of memories of Free French glory days. And why didn't Antoine Argoud, the best technical brain in the French Army, abandon the fleshpots and late lunches of Madrid and come to join the fighting? To the activists of Algiers, Argoud seemed a latter-day Saint-Éxupéry, who had lived in New York after the fall of France and wrestled with his conscience while his compatriots were dying in Syria and at Bir Hakeim. Where was such valuable material as Colonel Trinquier, Colonel Château-Jobert and Colonel Dufour? Trinquier was in the Congo. Château-Jobert was in Madrid making contact with Argoud, Lacheroy and Lagaillarde. Dufour was being carefully watched by French security agents.

And if General Salan was unsatisfactory, General Jouhaud scarcely seemed to exist at all. He was happy to vegetate in his native Oran and to issue occasional manifestoes. General Challe and General Faure were in jail and could scarcely take over from General Salan. On June 12, the leaders met at Susini's flat and agreed to approach General Massu yet again, then Generals Mirambeau, Dulac, Gracieux, Valluy, Crèvecoeur, Maison-Rouge and Ducourneau. Some of those generals were interested, but they were followed by French security men and imprisoned.

A week later, Godard addressed a note to the other colonels, in which he stated that he accepted the situation as it stood. "There can be no real question of getting rid of Soleil [Salan]," he wrote. "We have to all intents and purposes recognized his authority. His presence in Algeria, is a symbol, in spite of the reservations his personality provokes in certain quarters. The mass of the population would not understand that he is not the great chief of the O.A.S. and our adversaries would not fail to make capital out of it."

By the end of June the leaders still had little idea of where they were going or of why they were there at all. On June 29 a meeting was held to resolve some of the many problems and ended in such a flaming row that Godard threw his cigarette lighter at Dr. Jean-Claude Perez. Perez was a general practitioner from Bab-el-Oued; he was married to a rich woman whose father manufactured anisette. Perez was an extremist, an ultra, accepted as the dean of O.A.S. doctors, but his generosity of spirit and his devotion to his patients, not least to his Moslem patients in the Casbah, was such that he was known in the district as "Saint Vincent de Paul of Bab-el-Oued," a not inconsiderable accolade. But he was a trouble maker and a gossip, and his hints that he controlled Bab-el-Oued politically and could tender or withhold its support made the military men uneasy. But the soldiers themselves were finding it difficult to come to terms. General Gardy criticized the collegiate system of control based on the French Resistance. He wanted the violence to be stepped up; "We are not a party of academic opposition," he said and proposed a reform by which Colonel Gardes would keep O.M., he himself would command O.R.O. and Susini would direct the political bureau. On July 5 Godard agreed with most of Gardy's ideas: that Gardes, the unquestioned expert on psychological warfare, was the man to control O.M. and that Susini was the best politician around. But he believed that he himself, rather than Gardy, was the man to control O.R.O., or direct action. To Gardy he offered the same kind of job the latter had held in the Foreign Legion—as commander emeritus with no power to give orders or make decisions. "You are the man to command," he wrote conciliatingly. "I insist that you accept the post of *patron* to which you are entitled. With Fleur [Gardes] and myself I am convinced that your command will be possible. Jeannine [Susini] should concentrate his efforts on politics and propaganda and not involve himself in matters that do not concern him."

This last remark touched on Susini's command over the Z commandos. Although most of the military respected Susini, the fact that he was a *pied noir* but a social barrier between him and the officers that was hard to define. As for Perez, the other *pied noir* in the inner circle, nearly everyone wanted to be rid of him but did not dare do anything because of the political popularity he kept insisting that he possessed.

Popularity, especially in Algeria, is ephemeral, however, and the soil of the country was richest in breeding dreams. The story of war is the story of chaos, of squabbles between commanders, of back stabbing, criticism, belittlement, self-justifyication and mass scrambling for authority. The O.A.S. was no exception. But wars are won, as well as lost, by the system. The O.A.S. grew stronger and bigger, so strong that Salan was able to turn the tables on the crazy Martel and walk out. Previously Martel had wielded the unspoken threat of handing him in to the police. But now Salan could threaten Martel —again by implication only; no word was spoken on the subject— with the vengeance of the O.A.S. commandos. Salan appeared to make a show of leadership in Algiers. It was the official administration of Algiers and Oran that was retreating in consternation behind sandbags and barbed wire, and it was the O.A.S. that was emerging into the open.

11
THE MAN CALLED
GINGER (GINGEMBRE)
August–September 1961

❖❖❖

The O.A.S. blossomed because the soil was too fertile for it to wither. The Europeans of Algeria backed it almost to a man, and it grew from a basic, natural impulse. It was supported by the moderates, as well as by the ultras; by those who could foresee ultimate defeat, as well as by those who still lived in dreams of a collapse of the Fifth Republic. It was supported by workmen who called themselves "communists"; by the Marquis Alain de Serigny, publisher of *Écho d'Alger*; by the garage mechanics of Bab-el-Oued and the rich lawyers of Hydra.

Of all the supporters of the O.A.S., the most fanatical were Algeria's 150,000 Jews, for most of whom neither France nor Israel had much appeal as alternative places to live. The O.A.S. even had a special bureau within the organization, the O.A.S.J., to look after the Jews' interests.

In Algerian life the Jew occupied a special place, midway between Christians and Moslems. Whereas Islam and Christianity were mutually incompatible, the Jews could communicate without much difficulty with each side because they could speak both French and Arabic with ease. Before the French arrived the Algerian Jews, who had been there since their expulsion from Spain by Ferdinand and Isabella in 1492, spoke Arabic and Ladino; they were sunk in degradation and squalor. The French occupation galvanized them into commerce and business activity. By the Crémieux decree of 1870, they were made French citizens, whereas the Moslems remained merely French subjects. Crémieux, it has been pointed out many times, was a French Jew. Because the Jewish energy contrasted so eloquently with *pied noir* and Moslem listlessness, there was a bitter tradition of anti-Semitism in Algeria. Max Régis, Mayor of Algiers during the Dreyfus Affair, was one of the leading anti-Dreyfus deputies.

But, whatever the relationship between Jew and Christian, there was no question of where the Jews' loyalty would lie in a showdown with the Moslems. Measured in terms of economic strength, the Jews probably outranked the 9 million Algerian Moslems, and from the beginning of the Algerian war the Jews had been singled out as targets for the fellagha, who burned a synagogue in Orléansville, desecrated Jewish cemeteries in Algiers and Oran and formally boycotted Jewish merchants in Constantine, Batna, Sétif and Blida. On March 27, 1957, Jacob Chekroun, Rabbi of Médéa, was assassinated on the steps of his synagogue. "May God curse them because of their mischief," says the Koran (IV, 49) of the Jews, and the malediction intoned in mosques for centuries shows the deeper feelings of the Moslems against the Jews.

Aware that anti-Semitism could weaken the struggle for an independent Algeria and strengthen the French, the F.L.N. made an attempt to win the Jews over, but their words did not carry conviction, and one can see with what pain and reluctance they were even penned. According to one 1956 declaration:

> The disappearance of the colonial régime, which has used the Jewish minority as a buffer to absorb the anti-imperialist shocks, will not necessarily result in the pauperization of the Jews. It is an absurd hypothesis to imagine that, without France, Algeria would be nothing. Hereafter, national revenue will secure for all Algerians a more abundant life.

The presence, often a dominating presence, of the Jews in the O.A.S. was a constant embarrassment to *L'Humanité* and the left-wing press, which would have found matters so much simpler to analyze had they been able to equate the O.A.S. with the Nazis. Several of the O.A.S. Jews were Israeli secret agents, whose government had reason to view the independence of Algeria with concern. One of these agents was Jean Ghenassia, a veteran of the Irgun who had been wounded fighting the British in Palestine. Ghenassia later disappeared and was believed to have been captured and tortured to death by the F.L.N. One of General Salan's principal liaison officers was Captain Emile Lévy. Susini's principal assistant, secretary and confidant was a Jew, Dédé Saada. The Jews, caught between the *pieds noirs* and the Arabs, suffered more than any of the other groups. The Europeans of Bab-el-Oued did not love them any the more simply because they had become temporary allies, and the Moslems hated them far more bitterly than they hated the Christians.

And then there was the Moslem O.A.S., several hundred fighting men organized in their own commandos; their principal killer was a former sergeant in the Tirailleurs known to one and all as "Petite Soupe."

Finally, the O.A.S. sucked on the nipple of the Army. Officially the Army stayed aloof, and officers resisted their former comrades who lobbied among them. But the fact was that the Army, had it wished, could have crushed the O.A.S. in 24 hours. By doing nothing, it gave the Organization room to move in and air to breathe.

Because the fate of the O.A.S. was to become so inextricably linked with the Bab-el-Oued quarter in Algiers, one must understand what separated that community from the rest of the city and why it came to be written up on the front pages of the French newspapers as "the furnace of Algiers," and the "citadel of the ultras."

Bab-el-Oued means "mouth of the river," and there actually was a river once, later covered by the *pieds noirs* with cement, streets and bulldings. Bordered on one side by the sea and on the other by the Casbah, Bab-el-Oued was isolated enough to develop an extremely muscular and individual community personality. The majority of the citizens were of Spanish descent, followed by Jews, Corsicans, Maltese, Italians and Levantines, who together outnumbered the French about five to one. It was a melting-pot population, a fact that did not diminish its members' sense of being Frenchmen, any more than citizens of Brooklyn's melting pot feel less American. Bab-el-Oued was, indeed, the Brooklyn of Algeria. It even had a Brooklyn-esque name for itself; the inhabitants called it "Bablouette," and Bab-el-Oued jokes had a Brooklyn flavor. There was the one about the tourist who asked the citizen of Bab-el-Oued about the meaning of the initials "O.A.S.," which he saw on all the walls. "You must be ignorant not to know that," he was told. "It means 'Oz Armes Sitoyens.' "

Bab-el-Oued was partly a dingy, shadowed area of bars and cafés smelling of oil, tomatoes and garlic and partly a modern residential district with apartment buildings, shops, department stores, supermarkets and cinemas. The citizens were artisans, masons, shoemakers, waiters, plumbers. In the evening they made their promenade along the Avenue de Bouzarea between the tiny Place des Trois Horloges and the ramp of the Avenue Durando and sat for hours in the Café Alexandre consuming large quantities of anisette and making a great deal of noise.

The two best-known figures of Bab-el-Oued represented the extremes typical of the community. One was Dr. Jean-Claude Perez, "the Saint Vincent de Paul," of the area—urbane, well-read, rich. Perez considered himself a Frenchman, although his father had emigrated from Spain and had never even taken French citizenship, another Brooklynish trait. The other celebrity was an attractive, jolly little roughneck with legs like tweezers and shoulders like those of a boxer, "Jésus Giner, a former taxi driver with no particular means of support save a gang of local hoodlums he called "my commando," which accompanied him on all his jaunts through Bab-el-Oued. He liked to boast "I make the law around here," and he was popular, except with the Moslems, who fled at the sight of him. Perez and Giner were comrades in the O.A.S., although in later years Giner was to say, "If I ever get my hands on Perez I will kill him." It was a sentiment that others came to share, and with a certain amount of reason.

The inhabitants of Bab-el-Oued were referred to collectively and sympathetically as "the Hernandez family" after a popular vaudeville touring troupe. They did not resent the implied foreignness of their name; they saw themselves for what they were, second-class citizens, less than Frenchmen, more than Moselms. But nothing angered them more than to be considered other than French. They liked to point out that Réne Raphael Viviani, French Prime Minister and Foreign Secretary at the beginning of the First World War, had been a *pied noir* from Algeria with a foreign name but that nobody had considered him less French because of it.

When Jean Farran noted in *Paris-Match* that there were few French names like "Martin" in the Algiers telephone directory, readers pointed out with heat and with justice that there was as great a preponderance of Italian names in the Nice directory, of Spanish names in the Biarritz directory and of German names in the Strasbourg directory, yet no one questioned their Frenchness, least of all the bearers of the names themselves. Farran's article, "An Open Letter to the Hernandez Family," set off a correspondence that expressed the personality of Bab-el-Oued more vividly than had the article itself. A typical letter said:

> It it not true that there are only Jews, Spaniards, Maltese and Italians in Bab-el-Oued. There are people from Burgundy like myself, Arles, Brittanny, Auvergne, from all over France. I am a *pied noir* with honor and glory, and so are my children and my grandchildren. I make 30,000 old francs [$60] a month, and I will cry to my dying day: Long live France and French Algeria!

Another wrote:

> Always these cursed Europeans of Algeria who refuse meekly to having their throats cut! It does not stop the Moslems; we know them and love them better than you do. We are not "unspeakable colonialists," a lot of us have fought hard for our money. I am a third generation *pied noir*, and a "colonialist" who, with four children, does not have 10,000 old francs in his bank account.

And another:

> Algeria under the green and white flag of the F.L.N., is it conceivable? And our young men killed over the last few years? And what about all the Moslems loyal to France? Racism is to refuse integration.

Even in these brief extracts, a recurring theme is noticeable; the presumed existence of "loyal Moslems," "our Moslem brothers," "the Moslems we know and love better than you do," "all Moslems loyal to France." These Moslems were supposed by the *pieds noirs* to constitute the mass of the Moslem population silenced by the terror of the F.L.N. and to be waiting only for adequate guarantees of protection to throw aside their fears and join in the chanting of *Algérie française*. They were the millions of Ferhat Abbas' "Algerian Manifesto," which, alas for the *pieds noirs*, had been written twenty years earlier in a different world. The new idea of "integration," of one man with one vote, of replacing the unequal past with an equal future, of a marriage in which France would not lose a possession but would gain nine thousand new Frenchmen (which would give this Catholic land a population that was 20 percent Moslem), was an idea posing immediate and stupendous questions which the *pieds noirs* hoped would not be brought into the open.

The fact was that F.L.N. terror, far from cowing the peaceful Moslems, had given them the courage to envisage what had previously been unimaginable: independence and the end of European domination. F.L.N. terror against the Moslem population had been harsh and ruthless, as it is in every civil war, but it had been no less so than the terror of the Moslem harkis in the pay of France against areas with F.L.N. sympathies.

On the evening of August 5, the citizens of Algeria were at home listening to Radio-Algeria, when they were suddenly startled by a sound they had scarcely heard since May 13. Without any preamble, the program was cut off, and a military band played *Le Chant des Africains,* a rollicking Legion march that had become the theme song of the O.A.S. It was followed by the *Marseillaise*—how many times the *pieds noirs* had sung that song in recent months, sometimes hopefully, sometimes desperately, sometimes as a kind of prayer! Then the sound of a drum, boom-boom-boom *boom-boom,* and the electrifying words, "This is Radio Algérie française. The O.A.S. has decided today to interrupt the emission of the Gaullist radio. Delegated by General Salan, General Gardy, Inspector General of the Foreign Legion, will address you." A tremendous communal shiver ran through the city, a new kind of liberation. The telephone exchanges jammed as the word was spread. People shouted from window to window and then darted back so as not to miss a word. Car horns blared as motorists tuned in to their radios.

General Gardy's voice was a revelation. Somehow to the average *pied noir,* following his heroes of the Barricades, the Putsch and the O.A.S. insurrection, and to the foreign correspondents as well, General Gardy had always given the impression of relative senility. One had, of course, only to take such thought processes one step further and ask, what could be senile in an elderly retired general who could have been living comfortably in Biarritz or Nice, yet who chose instead to sacrifice his pension and the comforts of old age, not to mention his daughters and sons-in-law, for a French Algeria? He did it not because he had any particular interest in the country itself but to keep it for his regiment, for which Algeria was

"The cradle and the grave." When one came to think about it, and many people as they listened *did* think about it, Jean Gardy was one of the most resolute officers on the O.A.S. At every turning point in the O.A.S. story Gardy seemed to have been the toughest, to have been the last to admit defeat, to have acted most resolutely when there was a hiatus to be filled and to have then yielded immediately to men younger and more dynamic than he.

It was Gardy now who was to make the first pirate broadcast of the Secret Army, and his voice was not the voice of a foolish old man but that of an old soldier, full of anger, with slurred "s"s in the throat and a hint of suppressed tears. It was how the real King Lear must have sounded. The words were often inept and old-fashioned, gradually becoming pathetic and in the end deeply moving. No ghost-writer could have composed such a speech:

> Instead of the lying lickspittles of the régime, you are hearing the voice of truth, the word of those who fight to maintain the national community on both banks of the Mediterranean, and to reconstruct France on the ruins of the Gaullist dictatorship. In the O.A.S. are assembled civil and military forces, professional as well as working classes, all ferociously determined to resist being abandoned. My Army comrades and myself, shoulder to shoulder with civilians of all origins and professions have sacrificed everything—family, security, private interests—for the cause of French Algeria. We are apparently a joke as far as Monsieur de Gaulle is concerned. We are certainly outlaws, condemned to death. We do not care. The reverse we suffered in April has not beaten us or discouraged us. Our resolution and our faith remain intact. . . .
>
> I tell you, a day will come when you will have to choose between the personal service of Monsieur de Gaulle and that of the country. We have made our choice and we are sure that all soldiers worthy of the name will do the same.

He ended in emotional confusion, in answer to an F.L.N. gibe that the Europeans would have to quit Algeria "either carrying their bags or in a coffin." "Union!" he cried. "Discipline! Resolution! Frenchmen, European or Mussulman, who wish to live and die on French ground, I say arise. Neither suitcase nor coffin! The country and a rifle!"

Throughout Algeria goosebumps were raised. There was so much that was foolish in the speech—like the references to "Monsieur" de Gaulle, putting the upstart in his place—and so much that was courageous that many of the officers listening in the messes experienced emotions similar to those of the Pétainist officers when they first read of the Free French at Bir Hakeim.

The broadcast evoked memories of the Putsch, when old Gardy's determination had proved to be greater than that of General Challe. Admiral Querville, French naval commander at Mers-el-Kébir and one of the officers principally responsible for the failure of the Putsch, may have thought of Gardy's visit to him toward the end of the revolt, when its failure was already clear. Gardy had pleaded with him desperately to bring the Navy out in support, but Querville had refused; Gardy had slumped into a chair, beaten, exhausted and too old.

The Admiral poured him a large whiskey, which he took with a hand almost too weak to lift the glass. "Why, Gardy?" Querville asked in compassion. "Why did you do it?"

"The end of Algeria means the end of the Legion," said Gardy. "I love my Legionnaires. They counted on me. What else mattered?"

Now he had shown that he had not given up the struggle. The *pieds noirs* imagined the pirate broadcast to have been achieved in the most Rocambolesque manner, with heavily armed men in leopard camouflage taking over the radio station. In fact, the broadcast had merely been taped and inserted by the radio engineers of the Secret Army into the same broadcasting band as Radio-Alger. But it was a tremendous propaganda victory, and pirate broadcasts from Algiers and Oran became almost daily occurrences. Every day police helicopters circulated over the roofs to detect pirate radio transmitters, and the planes' presence was a confession of the authorities' impotence to stop the practice.

The broadcast coincided with an intensified campaign of terrorism on both sides. Commissioner Ouamri, a Moslem police officer, was machine-gunned to death in his car. An O.A.S. militant of Belcourt, a *pied noir* named di Rago, was wounded by an F.L.N. terrorist. Carried in an ambulance to the Mustapha Hospital, he was cared for by the medical staff for several days until a column of F.L.N. men came into the public ward where he lay and, ignoring the screams of the other patients, murdered him with machine guns.

Degueldre was told of the killing; he ordered a meeting of the ZA 1/A2/Q3 (Zone of Algiers/Subsector Center/Quartier Belcourt). The O.A.S. would reply in kind, he said. A leading F.L.N. terrorist, a man named Mirzak, had been wounded and also taken to hospital. On August 7, a squad of O.A.S. men led by Bobby Dovecar raided the hospital and shot Mirzak dead. The practice of shooting enemies in hospitals then stopped abruptly, at least for the time being.

A few days later there was a killing that seemed outside the pattern of the war established so far and, indeed, irrelevant to it. Previously, the adversaries had fitted very much into a civil-war pattern, brothers, cousins, Europeans, Moslems, Legion. Alfred Fox, an official in the British Consulate in Algiers, was driving home for lunch. He was 54 years old and dealt with shipping matters. As he got out of the car in the basement garage below the block of apartments in which he lived, a man stepped from the shadows, clubbed him to the ground with the butt of his tommy gun, then fired three shots into him, killing him. When Bobby Dovecar saw that the man was dead, he jumped into the passenger seat of his own car and was driven away. Britain and Britons figured little in the Algerian war, and the murder seemed meaningless.

Fox actually was an old Algiers hand who knew most of the prominent *pieds noirs* of the city. He was a regular patron of the bar of the Hotel Saint George and had from time to time acted as go-between for the French Army, the O.A.S. and the F.L.N. The O.A.S., however, had come to believe that Fox was telling the F.L.N. more than he should about the Organization, and Dovecar was delegated to dispatch him, which he did more efficiently than he had done with Gavoury.

After the pirate broadcast, the first O.A.S. publication appeared in the streets of the cities. The editor was Colonel Joseph Broizat, and its title was *The Centurions;* it was directed at a military readership in Algeria and France. Under the title, in each edition there was a quotation from General de Gaulle. In the first issue there was one taken from the speech of May 19, 1958: "In Algeria one sees a population which has been at war, with murders and ambushes for years. This population realizes that the system established in Paris cannot resolve its problems . . . How can one expect that in the long run this population will not rise up?"

The opening page was devoted to an editorial written by Broizat but signed "Scipio," after the Roman general who had defeated and destroyed Hannibal at the Battle of Zama in 202 B.C. The title of the article was "The Officer Faced With the Law and the Nation." The magazine contained eight pages and was well printed and edited; typographical students could recognize the printing styles and flourishes that characterized publications issued by the Foreign Legion print shop in Sidi-Bel-Abbès.

In the meantime, Broizat, former monk, former Catholic, former Protestant, former Communist and then Catholic again, was flirting with still a new faith; he was seeking to join, of all things, the Salvation Army.

✠✠✠

In Madrid, Lagaillarde's influence over Argoud remained powerful. Argoud, despite his threats to quit over the assassination of Commissioner Gavoury, stayed on in Madrid. He was there, living in a modern apartment block when Maurice Gingembre arrived in the city by car, on August 5, bringing with him Argoud's wife and daughters. Gingembre was keener than ever to put the O.A.S. into efficient working order. Despite the great propaganda victories in Algeria, the Organization was still badly divided among its three headquarters—Algiers, Madrid and Paris. Algiers had its *Comité Supérieure de l'O.A.S.* and Madrid its *Direction Centrale de l'O.A.S.* under Lagaillarde, who still claimed leadership of the entire Organization. To strengthen his claim, he hung on to Argoud, his trump card, rather the way Martel had hung on to Salan. The spirit of religious exaltation in Madrid made a spectacular contrast to the atmosphere in Algiers. Father Grasset was a regular visitor to Lagaillarde's flat, and he was treated with the deepest reverence by everyone.

With Gingembre's money, Lagaillarde came into the open and opened an office in Santiago Bernabeu; the sign on the door announced flatly: *Organisation de l'Armée Secrète; Plate-forme, Extérieure.* The office was filled with desks, typewriters, filing cabinets, pretty secretaries who typed, officers who composed tracts; it seemed almost an ostentatious gesture designed to mock the outlaws of

Algiers. The complications in such a situation were endless. One leader of the Right had written Susini that he did not intend to see Gaullism replaced by Salanism. Almost no one wanted Salan, who was there, and nearly everyone wanted Massu, who was not; many people wanted Argoud, who wanted Lagaillarde, who wanted Lagaillarde too, but few others wanted Lagaillarde at all.

Argoud and Lagaillarde asked Gingembre in effect to do a thorough market-research job and untangle the finances, the political decisions, the poles of interest and to arrange some coordination of policy without offending more egos than were offended already.

Gingembre accepted the commission with the alarcrity appropriate to his name, and on his return to Paris he called on Pierre Sergent. Sergent, de Blignières and Godot, with Adjutant Marc Robin were planning to direct, violent action and finding their job complicated by the fact that they kept butting into right-wing cells and conspiracies that wanted into the act in one way or another. Sergent, like the rest, was under sentence of death, a sentence that in French military law is automatically canceled as soon as the person concerned is apprehended. He was being sought by the Paris police as a matter of the highest priority, but he was an uncomplicated man who sought only to do his duty according to the orders imposed on him by Colonel Godard. His hero, in common with the rest of the disbanded 1st R.E.P., was Colonel Jeanpierre. Sergent was blessed with a mild face, rather like that of Stanley Laurel, and it fitted anonymously into any background.

Sergent had been born in 1927 and had spent his life since the age of seventeen in one resistance or another or in the regular Army. After the war, he had been graduated from Saint-Cyr and had fought in Indochina with the 1st R.E.P. At the beginning of 1961, he was serving in Metropolitan France, but, on hearing of the impending Putsch, he joined it with determination and became a vital courier among the various leaders. His virtues were loyalty, directness and an appetite for hard and uncomplaining work. Although several officers in, or sympathetic to, the O.A.S. outranked him and persisted in giving him the benefit of their advice and criticism, he remained the linch pin of the O.A.S. in Metropolitan France. Without him and his assistants, Godot and Robin, it would have quickly collapsed under the weight of right-wing screwballs.

Sergent introduced Gingembre to Barbier de Blignières, who was relieved to meet a gentleman for a change. Gingembre then returned to Madrid with letters from Sergent to Argoud and Lagaillarde. This time he met Colonel Lacheroy and Dr. Lefèvre; then he flew back to Paris for further conferences with Sergent, who asked him to go next to Algiers to see Godard and pass a letter to Salan. Sergent also gave him the accolade of a pseudonym, tantamount to acceptance into the club. From then on Gingembre was "Tacite."

Gingembre registered at the Hotel Saint George and was introduced to Godard, to whom he was conducted by a secret emissary. The meeting was held in a curious room, with travel and advertising posters on the ceiling, obviously the room of a young boy. Godard was quite impressed. Gingembre was then taken to see Susini, who wasn't. "Thank heavens it was night," Susini said later, "and thank heavens the name had been taken off the door of the apartment." Susini distrusted everything and everybody who came from Madrid. What appalled him as he listened to Gingembre was how much the man knew. He seemed to know the whole machinery of the Organization and wanted to show it. He delicately dropped names like "Laon," "Albatross," "Métro," "Soleil." The man, Susini decided, in addition to being a pretentious dandy, was also a buffoon but too dangerous to laugh at. As soon as Gingembre had gone, he telephoned Godard and Gardes and urged them to cover their tracks.

Once again Gingembre returned to Paris to report to Sergent and de Blignières. Gingembre had a girl friend, a vaudeville magician called "Barbra Gray." Her apartment became the poste restante center of the O.A.S. A letter arrived for Gingembre from Argoud, another from Argoud for Godard and the copy of a letter from Salan to Argoud.

Gingembre realized that the views of Algiers and Madrid were basically irreconcilable. Paris tended to support Madrid, but it had little influence, being the weakest of the three cities in the axis. Algiers, he reasoned, wanted to use any means at hand to create a power vacuum in France: Bombs, Putsch, terror, propaganda or whatever might succeed. Such at least were the views of Godard and Susini. Salan favored their point of view but issued an unexpected caveat against one project that had been widely discussed. There must, he said, be no attempt against the life of General de Gaulle. Salan had experienced one attempt against his own life and had found the experience decidedly unpleasant. Presumably, he hoped in time to step into General de Gaulle's shoes and was anxious to avoid disagreeable precedents.

At 7:00 P.M. on September 7, Gingembre drove to Orly in his car. He was frisked for firearms with the rest of the passengers bound for Algiers and boarded an Air France Caravelle. A few seats behind him Colonel Pierre Debrosse fastened his seat belt and watched him closely. The flight was uneventful, the cold cuts excellent, the service as courteous as usual. At Maison Blanche Airport, half a dozen plainclothes detectives closed in on Gingembre. Debrosse introduced himself politely, relieved Gingembre of his briefcase and arrested him.

12
AUTUMN LOSSES
September—November 1961

One of the basic hazards of clandestine warfare is that one does not always know who is for him, who is against him and, for that matter, who is who. This point was revealed significantly the day after Gingembre's arrest, when an attempt was made on the life of General de Gaulle at Pont-sur-Seine. O.A.S. propaganda in that case had been *too* good. "The O.A.S. strikes where it wants, when it wants, and against whom it wants" was one of its slogans, coined by Susini. Experience was showing that it frequently justified the claim. So French public opinion blamed—or praised—the O.A.S. for the deed.

But the O.A.S. was not responsible. That much was evident from the astonishment and confusion in the cadres of the Organization and the incoherent denials that followed it. Salan expressed his indignation at the accusations in a letter to *Le Monde* in words strongly resembling the style of his enemy, de Gaulle. "It has been ignominiously let known," he protested, "that I, Raoul Salan, twice Commander-in-Chief before the enemy, could be the instigator of an attempt to assassinate the Chief of State. I would not tarnish my past and my military honor by ordering an attack against a person whose past belongs to the history of the nation. . . ." But the embarrassment proved brief; the O.A.S. came to regret not that it was being blamed but that the ambush had failed.

Gingembre, held in the prison of Hussein-Dey, was defiant and unafraid. "You haven't a chance," he told Debrosse. "Why don't you join our side?"

Debrosse, in his shirtsleeves, his feet bare for comfort and showing his varicose veins, asked, "Who is your side?"

Gingembre, of course, told him at length and in detail. He told of meeting Susini and Godard. He did not know the address and would not tell Debrosse even if he could. He described the room in which he met Godard because it had posters pasted to the ceiling, obviously once a boy's bedroom; the apartment—it was on the seventh floor—clearly belonged to a well-to-do family. Gingembre was not confessing. He was boasting, tormenting Debrosse with knowledge that he had no intention of imparting.

Debrosse listened patiently, then issued orders to his men. Society in Algiers is small, and an apartment in an exclusive residential district, containing a room with posters on the ceiling, was not impossible to locate. The gendarmes in their lorries spread out through the night knocking on doors.

Within a few hours, the place had been traced. It belonged to a Madame Gasser, a middle-aged lady, member of an old *pied noir* family and well known for her militant support of French Algeria. But Madame Gasser was just back from a trip to Paris with her grandchildren. Her empty apartment had obviously been used as a neutral rendezvous, a common O.A.S. habit, and Debrosse knew who had given Godard access to it. It had to be Madame Gasser's daughter, Geneviève Salasc. Geneviève was the wife of a prosperous Algiers physician; she made a stimulating and volcanic contribution to Algiers society and was one of the most enthusiastic and tempestuous supporters of French Algeria. Although she was barely thirty, she was the mother of five, a pretty redhead with a *gamine* face and devastating reserves of energy. She drove fast cars at suicidal speeds, participated in every demonstration, looked after the poor, helped her husband in the hospital and shouted *Algérie française* on all the appropriate occasions. Her children kept signed photographs of Lagaillarde in their bedrooms.

At 2:00 in the morning, some six hours after Gingembre's arrest, police knocked on her door and told her to dress. Geneviève was not alarmed until one of the gendarmes whispered in her ear: "Try to hold out for 24 hours. The others will be warned." Men in civilian clothes were waiting in the car; they seized her, tied her up, blindfolded and gagged her. The car seemed to travel for hours, although Geneviève on the floor of the back seat suspected even in her confusion and horror, that they were going round in circles and were not traveling far.

She was taken from the car and down several flights of steps; her blindfold was removed, and she found herself in a dismal, dripping, ill-lit cellar facing five men, one of whom was an Arab. Before she knew what was happening, her arms were grabbed, and she was punched in the eye. It was not an ordinary punch. The closed fist is big enough to be stopped, however painfully, by the bone around the eye socket. In this case, the blow was delivered with the knuckles of bent fingers striking directly into the eyelid and the eye. It was followed by an identical blow to the other eye.

It is a well-known fact that clandestine organizations like the O.A.S., which make no pretensions to liberalism and democracy, are not permitted heroes or heroines, only villains. Nevertheless Geneviève Salasc was about to become the heroine of the O.A.S. Like Jean Moulin of the French Resistance, who was tortured to death by the Gestapo, Geneviève Salasc knew almost everything about the organization. She could direct the police to every leader of the movement. And the police were so desperate to know that they could not even wait. Even as Geneviève was being tortured, three police helicopters were landing at her mother's farm near Orléansville to see if Godard was hiding there.

Geneviève was so brutally gagged that she thought she would suffocate. She was stripped naked and beaten with fists. Water was turned on in a bathtub, but she could only hear it, for she had been blinded by blows. Heavy electrodes were applied to her breasts and other parts of her body, and the current was switched on. The fate of the O.A.S. literally rested on her endurance. If that endurance failed, the organization would be broken before dawn. A Christian woman, Geneviève prayed for death to come quickly. She heard someone saying, "When you are ready to talk, beat on the ground with your hand."

Geneviève beat violently. As the gag was removed, she shouted, "Take me to Colonel Debrosse."

The men appeared relieved. She was quickly dressed, tied again, blindfolded and taken upstairs, more gently this time, to a car. Once more it seemed to travel a great distance, and once again she thought it was traveling in circles, perhaps within the walls of Hussein-Dey Prison. When the blindfold was removed, she saw through her swollen eyes that she was in an office confronting Colonel Debrosse. She could also see the look of shock and horror on his face at her appearance. Playing for time, she threw herself upon him, grabbing his lapels, talking, saying anything that came into her head, knowing that the longer she stalled the more time she was giving the leaders to be warned. "Colonel Debrosse, you are a civilized man. You are not a brute. This is inhuman, appalling. You cannot do this to me. I am not someone dragged out of a gutter. My husband is a doctor, my grandfather a Senator."

"Who did this?" Debrosse asked her appalled.

"Your men did."

"They did not."

"Let me go at once."

"Give us the information we want, and you will be released immediately."

"And if I don't, I go back to where I was?"

"You will be kept here."

Geneviève kept talking, stalling, until she was near to fainting. Dawn came, and she was left sitting on a hard chair. Her mother was brought to her, and—though it was the spirit of the mother that the daughter had inherited—Madame Gasser screamed at the sight of her daughter. Gingembre was brought in and looked at her expressionlessly, not knowing who she was or what part he had played in her ordeal. Not until 5:00 that evening was she taken away and given a bed to sleep on.

But friendly gendarmes within Hussein-Dey had warned the O.A.S. of her capture, and during the night tracts were printed informing the citizens that Madame Salasc was being tortured. Godard, Susini, Degueldre and the rest had already changed addresses. Fortunately the family had political influence. Stories were published in the Algiers newspapers. In Paris deputies protested to the various ministries involved. Geneviève was released after a week and taken to hospital. She had been lucky insofar as she was a well-known figure. Other women with fewer social connections suffered worse.

As the story was touched on only lightly in the Paris press and even then in newspapers that Françoise Sagan and the others would have little reason to read, they can be forgiven for not hearing of the incident. If they had heard, it is unlikely that they would have protested or that Simone de Beauvoir would have written a book about Geneviève—or that Picasso would have drawn her picture. Geneviève, in her turn, had probably never heard of Djamila Boupacha. All that mattered to her was that she had said nothing and that, as soon as she was released from hospital, she was working for the O.A.S. as ardently as ever.

The reaction of the O.A.S. was to counterattack. On September 20, Dovecar, at the wheel of a scooter with a trigger man behind him, streaked through the tunnel of the university and shot dead another commissioner, Goldenberg. A "Night of the Casseroles" was ordered for September 23; the population of Algiers was called upon to bang pots and pans in an ear-splitting tattoo of *Al-gé-rie fran-çaise*. It was followed by a "Night of the Traffic Jams." Both were triumphant demonstrations of European support for the O.A.S. Delighted, the O.A.S. ordered a "Night of the Flags," calling on citizens to fly the yellow and black flag of the O.A.S. from their balconies. This demonstration was less successful, for it exposed private homes to possible police and F.L.N. reprisals. Degueldre and Nicole made a tour of the city by car to see how the demonstration was going and then, disgusted, went to Susini's apartment.

"French Algeria, fine!" Degueldre sneered. "As long as we don't get bothered by the police."

Susini rose quickly to the defense of the *pieds noirs*. "What do you expect? If one asked the people of Vichy during the war to fly the Free French flag, how many would have dared to obey?"

"Perhaps," said Degueldre, "but the people of Vichy had other cards to play and nobody was planning to kick them out of their home and country. The *pieds noirs* have no more cards to play. All I need is two hundred good men, and I'm damned if I can find them. There are plenty to stick up posters and xerox tracts, but for anything more. . . . And even the ones I do get . . . well, better avoid operations on Sundays because that's when they go out with their girls."

"Just wait," said Susini. "They will come. I know them. In a month you will be turning the crowds away."

They were curious days, so recent and yet so far away. The autumn of 1961 was a period when people lived simultaneously with unprecedented affluence and with the threat of global annihila-

tion. The Berlin Wall was erected on August 13. The Congo claimed
Dag Hammarskjöld among its victims. Miss Elizabeth Taylor was
at work on *Cleopatra* and still married to Mr. Eddie Fisher. Ernest
Hemingway shot himself. Gary Cooper and Marion Davies died, and
the *France* sailed on its maiden voyage. All these events were occurring in the same world as, yet a world apart from, the O.A.S.
war in Algeria.

A correspondent noted in his diary the atmosphere as he saw it
from his window in the Hotel Aletti looking up the ramp:

> By nine each evening the streets are deserted, except for
> patrols of battle-dressed soldiers. They hug doorways and
> move up one by one. The stillness is broken by the occa-
> sional passage of big gray vans filled with riot police. Two
> police commissioners are among the murdered. Two police
> chiefs in recent weeks were machine-gunned in their cars
> in the center of the city in broad daylight. A taxi driver,
> believed to be a police informer, was riddled at the steps
> of this hotel. There is no official score but in an average
> week two dozen honest citizens are shot down in public.
> It is all the work of the O.A.S. They place plastic bombs
> against the doors of known liberals, important Moslems,
> and any other opponents, real or imagined. On a recent
> night 38 exploded in the city. Never a night goes by without
> explosions. The shopping district is dotted with destruction,
> and newspapers no longer bother to report more than a
> paragraph, listing victims. How can this continue in the
> face of the massive array of the forces of order? The an-
> swer is complicity. Common policemen to colonels are
> secret supporters of the O.A.S. At every level of government
> from secretary to near the top there is sabotage of the
> official effort to combat the O.A.S. Records disappear,
> letters are lost, telephone calls go to the wrong office. Copy-
> ing the F.L.N. tactics the O.A.S. has begun to attack those
> who refuse to pay it taxes. Conspirators in banks and Gov-
> ernment bureaus supply precise information about in-
> comes. The Europeans nevertheless see the O.A.S. as their
> only hope for preserving French Algeria. . . .

There was another complicity, not yet mentioned perhaps but still
the most important of all—the complicity of the Moslems. Every
O.A.S. man was at the mercy of the Moslems, for every home,

even the most humble, had a Moslem servant. Moslems made Degueldre's bed, shined Salan's shoes, bought groceries for Susini, ran
errands for Godard, pimped for the Legionnaires. Admittedly the
Moslems were terrified of most of their masters, and domestic service
is not the breeding ground of heroes; nevertheless a brief, anonymous telephone call could have betrayed any one of the O.A.S. men,
and in the brief history of the O.A.S. not one important member
was betrayed by his servants.

✠✠✠

Previously the goals of the O.A.S. in Algeria had been simple.
It had sought to impose the will of the *pied noirs* on Paris and to
leave the Army free to finish its war with the F.L.N. At the end of
September, however, a new and disturbing note was introduced—not
in Algiers but in Madrid, where the irritating Lagaillarde group continued to insist on its own ultimate authority. In a manifesto entitled "A
Call to the French," the "Spaniards" proposed a corporate state for
France on the lines of Pétain's *etat français*. It had religious overtones
and reflected a yearning for ceremony, hierarchy and the old ritual
attitudes. It was almost as if the Spanish group were ashamed of their
colleagues in Algiers, with their schoolboy disguises and furtive, violent
ways. It was well known in Algiers that Argoud was under Lagaillarde's influence and that Lagaillarde was under the influence of
Father Grasset; still the presence of Argoud's signature on this
document was an unpleasant surprise for the most pragmatic colonels
of Algiers.

Broizat, who was sensitive to such things, spotted the religious
mysticism pervading the document and wrote a letter to Argoud
begging him to respect the freemasonry of the colonels. "That Lacheroy and Argoud appear to have joined the team of Laon (Lagaillarde),
and Grasset . . . No!" he wrote.

> You are above that scuffle, *cher ami!* The Army cannot lean
> on cliques. . . . You should in my opinion stay outside and
> above, and wait for another moment for action, or join the
> O.A.S. in Metropolitan France where your talents will enable
> you to work genuinely and usefully and closely with those

who work in the most difficult circumstances. . . . There are advantages in clandestinity; there is contact with immediate reality, facility of contact; meetings and reunions permit teamwork, even if one has different points of view as in my case. . . . Don't interfere. Leave the work of Algiers and Paris to those who are there.

But the damage was done. Various right-wing religious groups who had been watching the O.A.S. with sympathy now joined the cause with enthusiasm and, more important, with money. The consequences proved serious.

The O.A.S. man most vulnerable to the new turning was, of course, the most pragmatic, Jean-Jacques Susini. Susini was the new philosopher of the O.A.S. He had become the organization's Goebbels and had utterly obliterated the importance of Lagaillarde. It was a remarkable political victory against all odds, made all the more remarkable by the similarities, differences and contradictions of the two men. Both had been tempered in the turbulent political climate of Algiers University, but, whereas Lagaillarde, though born near Paris, had grown up the complete *pied noir*, sunny, noisy, a man of the day, Susini born a *pied noir,* was a man of the night, withdrawn, secretive, suspicious, with all the coldness of the north. In a straight fight, there would have been no question of the victor, but it had not been a straight fight, and Susini had won and Lagaillarde lost. In Algiers at least he had turned Lagaillarde's name into a joke.

Had Lagaillarde been in Susini's place, the O.A.S. would have been a very different organization, more flamboyant and less subtle, more mystical, but probably less lethal. But at that moment the O.A.S. as it stood belonged to Susini, and only by injecting a note of mysticism from Madrid did Lagaillarde wield any influence at all.

Although he did not often display it, Susini was not without a sense of humor. It appealed to his fancy to have a Jew as his bodyguard, for it balanced his references to fascism. "My brand of fascism is not racial," he liked to say. "Look at Dédé." André Saada, "Dédé" to his friends, was a former wrestler, but he was also courteous, witty and discreet. It was said that he had killed people. He doubled as Susini's secretary and chauffeur. It was often rumored that their relationship was homosexual, and although it was nothing of the sort the idea amused Susini, who said nothing to deny

it. All his cards were held close to his chest, even his virility with
the opposite sex.

Susini, like the colonels, had read Mao Tse-tung; he agreed with
Mao's delineation of three phases of warfare: first, political activity,
then guerilla warfare and finally mopping up the enemy in large-
scale fighting in military formations.

The first step had already begun. The second consisted of wearing
down morale in Paris through spectacular exploits demonstrating the
O.A.S.' omnipotence and power. The exploits included civilian demonstrations in the great Algerian cities, interspersed with "brutal
sporadic action," to use Salan's phrase. The pirate broadcasts and
interviews with Salan established a psychological climate of invin-
cibility. Mass action would then force the gendarmerie and the civil
administration back into their sandbagged compounds, leaving the
field to the O.A.S.; authority would rot away to such an extent that
the Army would no longer obey the régime's orders. The Army
would, in effect, merge with the O.A.S.

The task was being well performed, and so far the O.A.S. had
been sensationally successful, especially in the political field. But it
continued to feel the repercussions of the Gingembre fiasco. Shortly
after Gingembre's arrest, the police cornered Colonel de Blignières
in a Paris apartment. In trying to escape he was badly burned in the
face by a tear-gas grenade and was completely blind for several
months. That eliminated the designated O.A.S. chief in France. In
September the O.A.S. lost its friend and mascot, Noëlle Lucchetti.
The Gardes Mobiles received a tip that Colonel Gardes was at a
certain address in Algiers. They missed him by a matter of minutes,
but in his hurry to escape he had been unable to burn all his papers.
The Mobiles found information that led to the arrest of eighteen
members of the O.A.S. in Tiaret and three in Algiers, including
Noëlle. Salan and Madame Salan, well knowing Noëlle's loyalty and
enthusiasm had worried about her safety from the start, and Salan
had refused to allow her to join the O.A.S. proper. She shared a
refuge with Captain Ferrandi, hid any O.A.S. man who needed
sanctuary and provided a poste restante for any mail directed to
Salan.

The fear of torture is present in all rebels against established
authority, and upon hearing of her arrest Salan wrote an anguished
letter to police headquarters, assuring the police that she knew no
important secrets. Noëlle was nonetheless badly beaten though not

tortured as Geneviève Salasc had been; perhaps there was less satis-faction involved in torturing a plump lady of advancing years. The court at any rate was fairly chivalrous—Noëlle, in uniform, wore the Croix de Guerre among her many decorations; she was sentenced to one year in prison and expelled from Algeria. Afterward she retired to her home near Bordeaux but continued to serve the O.A.S.

The worst blow of the year to the O.A.S., however, occurred shortly afterward: Bobby Dovecar was caught. When the news came, Roger Degueldre, not a demonstrative man, rushed to the lavatory and was sick to his stomach. A deep friendship had grown among four men: Jean-Jacques Susini, André Danglade, Degueldre and Bobby. Objectively it is difficult to imagine a more disreputable and dangerous quartet: Degueldre, the architect of terrorism and death; Dovecar and Danglade, killers who did not hesitate to butcher unarmed men; Susini, a little Hitler who wallowed in the blood-thirstiness of it all. Yet each admired the other three enormously and simply. Danglade was the gentlest of people socially—unag-gressive, polite and cheerful company. Susini was a fascinating conversationalist, and Degueldre was as always overwhelming in his charm. Danglade later recalled Dovecar's talent as a pianist and considered him almost in the concert class. In the evenings the little group would gather with girl friends, sit on cushions on the floor and drink *pastis* and Scotch while Dovecar played Beethoven's *Pathétique Sonata*. Dovecar had become engaged to a *pied noir* girl. He, more than the others, had a strangely winning personality, which later, in prison, charmed even such intellectuals as Colonel de Blignières and Georges Bousquet, the right-wing journalist, who was one of the victims of the Gingembre incident.

What made Dovecar's arrest worse was that it was his own silly fault; no credit whatever was due to the police. It started with the drunken blabbing of a comrade. A Delta commander, Gaby Giorno, nicknamed "Fines Moustaches," was drinking with friends in a bar in the Rue Claude Debussy. He was one of Dovecar's principal subkillers, and he was boasting that he alone knew where Dovecar lived. Fines Moustaches was picked up, vehemently protesting his innocence, and taken to the Caserne des Tagarins. Twenty-four hours later, a large force of Gardes Mobiles surrounded the apart-ment house in the Avenue Marcel-Duclos where Dovecar, the second-most-wanted killer in the O.A.S. kept his *pied-à-terre*.

He saw them coming from the window and rushed to destroy

documents. Most of them were burning when they crashed in and overpowered him. Word of the arrest spread in a flash through the area, and the gendarmes leading Dovecar, handcuffed and with his face bruised, into the streets came face to face with a mob of raging *pieds noirs*. The police found their way barred. *Pieds noirs* had boarded a beer truck and pelted the police with bottles of beer. Reinforcements had to be summoned by walkie-talkie before Dovecar could be hustled through the crowds and the odor of hops to the waiting van.

"The question," said one of the Deltas to the vomiting Degueldre, "is what do we do to Fines Moustaches? He squealed."

Degueldre said: "You don't know if Fines Moustaches squealed or didn't squeal. If he went through twenty-four hours of treatment at the Tagarins nobody here can blame him for anything. I know *I* don't have the right. The only person to blame is Bobby. Damn! Damn! Why didn't Bobby *bouger sa viande?* Why didn't he clear out while he still had time?"

What he meant was that, when news spread that Fines Moustaches had been arrested, why had Bobby not moved to another address? The others had. It was an established Resistance lesson that only a fool presumes a captured colleague brave enough to resist torture. The correct presumption is the opposite. One presumes that *nobody* can resist tortures. Delay is the most that can be asked of a man or a woman. The moment word is received of a comrade's capture, the rest of the team vanishes immediately into thin air with arms, money and papers, leaving nothing behind. Bobby Dovecar knew about the capture of Fines Moustaches yet did nothing about it. But clandestinity is a rarefied condition. It is a great error to believe that a man hunted for his life lives constantly in terror; he may do so if he is a criminal but not if he considers himself a soldier. Far from being horrible, the sensation of being hunted is usually wonderful, exciting, heady. It is an infinite extension of the state of euphoria that a sports fan experiences after his team has won an important game. The team's apparent invulnerability spreads itself to the fan. And the quarry thinks no one can catch him.

In comparison with the loss of Dovecar, the next O.A.S. loss was almost comical and, as far as Algiers was concerned, not totally unwelcome. On October 8, the Madrid-Paris-Algiers axis was suddenly reduced to a Paris-Algiers axis. The Madrid group was eliminated. A squad of Madrid police presented itself at Number 10

Concha-Espina, a new apartment building near the Real Madrid soccer stadium, and asked for "Monsieur Leroy." The bearded young man who opened the door acknowledged the name—and Lagaillarde was arrested. He was taken to comfortable quarters in the police academy, where he found Argoud, Lacheroy and Ortiz also under arrest. Father Grasset had been spared because of his cloth; Spaniards do not like to arrest priests.

"Since when," Lagaillarde demanded, "does General Franco act under the orders of General de Gaulle?"

Argoud asked sardonically: "De Gaulle? Or General Salan?"

Salan was the intimate of Serrano Suñer, brother-in-law of Franco. The Madrid office of the O.A.S. was not bothering de Gaulle. It was bothering only Algiers. So Argoud assumed that the whole thing was a Salan plot. Actually neither Salan nor de Gaulle had put pressure on the Spanish authorities. The Spanish, more familiar with civil war than most, felt that they could no longer allow Madrid to serve as a privileged sanctuary in a war that was growing more and more bloody. The prison quarters were comfortable. The men, although they had little in common, dined together, served by a batman of the Spanish Army in a white jacket. After fifteen days they were flown to a luxury hotel in the Canary Islands, leaving one less problem for the Algiers O.A.S., at least for the time being.

❖❖❖

In the garden of an old presbytery in the village of Conflans-sur-Loiret (population 215, including, said the poster, 127 readers of *Paris-Match*) in north France, a middle-aged man was putting the finishing touches on his garden. He was as long and dry as a day without drink, and he could have played Cyrano de Bergerac without makeup. General Massu was no longer in General de Gaulle's bad graces; and he had accepted the command at Metz. Before that, for nineteen months he had tended his garden, with the help of his wife Suzanne, whom he had married in 1947. In the evenings he played with his three children, only one of whom was an issue of the marriage; the other two were Arab children whom the Massus had adopted in Algeria. The nineteen months had been quiet. Massu, suffering no qualms about the hereafter, felt no compulsion to auto-biography. From time to time he would summon his chauffeur Jean, one of his old paratroopers, and would drive in his Peugeot to the Montargis Tennis Club. There he would play a few vigorous sets, the scars of war livid on his hairy brown legs. Except before the military tribunal, he had never spoken for the record since his ill-starred interview with the German journalist, Kempski. At the tribunal he had told his judges, "I had the mentality of a *grognard*, the *grognard* of the Empire who loved dearly his Emperor, but could still grumble."

"I have no intention of embarrassing my chief," he said, "no matter what I think of his politics." So, after a year and a half in which he was left to repent his sins, he had been forgiven. There would be no more colonels, majors and captains coming to him from the O.A.S., as there had been for nineteen months. He would leave the fighting to others. He disappeared into the ivy-covered mansion in Metz, which served as his headquarters. He had fought with his conscience and had made his decision: The inspiration and almost the incarnation of the O.A.S. disappeared from its history without having written so much as a page of it.

13

PROBLEMS

Autumn 1961

✤✤✤

On a sunny Sunday in October, an O.A.S. militant was seized in the street by a patrol of the Gardes Mobiles. After a short but violent struggle, he managed to free himself and sprinted through the streets, pursued by the police, until he saw a youth starting up a motor scooter. He leaped on to the back seat and pleaded in the boy's ear: "Dash! I'm O.A.S., and I'm escaping from the Mobiles."

The boy did not turn. He switched off the ignition, looked straight in front of him and said, "Monsieur, I do not know you, and I refuse to carry you."

It was no time for dialectic. The O.A.S. man jumped off the scooter, kept running and managed to shake off his pursuers; he reached safety exhausted.

Roger Degueldre and Nicole were in the habit of visiting Susini at midday on Sundays, Degueldre usually wearing rather sharp, light-gray suits and pointed Italian suede shoes.

Susini showed him a report of the incident, which Degueldre read impassively. "We can't kill the kid just for that," he said.

"No," said Susini. "This is a job for my Z commandos."

He issued telephone orders to trace the youth. By evening he had been identified as Barnabé, the son of a local shopkeeper. That night the contents of the shop were blasted over the pavement with plastic bombs, and Susini drafted a report that was distributed in pamphlet form throughout Algiers next day:

> An O.A.S. fighter who fell into the arms of the Gaullist forces escaped. Closely followed he begged the help of the

son of the Barnabé Company. Although the youth had a
vehicle he refused to help the patriot. That same evening,
on the orders of the Commandant of Algiers-Sahel, special
sections of the O.A.S. destroyed the premises of the Barnabé Company. Signed Jean-Jacques Susini.

In September a seventeen-man commando attacked the television
station at Cap Matifou and destroyed the technical installations. A
pirate broadcast replaced the regular program; it called for four
days of demonstrations, plastic explosions, nocturnal *casserolades*
and complete stoppages of traffic in Algiers, Oran, Bône and Constantine. The O.A.S. ordered all vacations canceled: "While we are
struggling to keep Algeria French it is unthinkable that citizens
should laze on beaches or enjoy the sights of Paris," it declared. Duti-
fully the *pieds noirs* remained at their posts.

It seemed so easy. In the hothouse atmosphere of Algiers, the Fifth
Republic seemed to be on the point of total disintegration. From
Algeria an eerie atmosphere was seeping into France, a sense of
dread, as if fear traveled by osmosis. It was incredible that, in the
1960s the police commissariats in Paris had to be sandbagged
against plastic-bomb attacks ordered from some secret cold-water
flat in Algiers—or that an antiaircraft gun had to be posted on
the roof of the Élsyée Palace in case O.A.S. "paras" were to land. It
was indicative of the jittery state prevailing in Paris that, when on
October 9 General Salan announced in a pirate broadcast that by
the end of the year he would command an Army of one hundred-
thousand men, few disbelieved him. General de Gaulle's Free French
Army had not achieved that number until after the invasion of
North Africa in 1942, more than two years after the fall of France.
But Salan made his announcement only six months after the rebels
had been decimated by the collapse of the general's revolt and the
disbanding of the 1st R.E.P.

The truth was more modest, though no less spectacular. A great
deal of noise, propaganda and violence was being generated by
comparatively few people. The basic militant force of professional
O.A.S. killers consisted of fewer than one thousand men. They
included perhaps a hundred from the 1st R.E.P. and other paratroop
units, under the command of Degueldre; the rest were demobilized
soldiers and militant civilians under Susini in Algiers and of General
Gardy in Oran. General Salan commanded, and Colonel Godard did

the paper work. These five men constituted the summit of the pyramid.

They were supported by some three thousand district leaders, who were sympathizers but not usually fighters; they were mostly men and women who worked in police and government bureaus, spied, distributed propaganda leaflets and raised money. There were further cadres of military and civilian specialists: to forge papers, to make bombs, to crack safes. There were also trained cadres to print magazines, repair motors and organize pirate broadcasts. Not least important were the construction workers and masons, with their Moslem handymen, who had honeycombed Algiers and Oran with false walls, underground passages and secret rooms. Even in the modern apartment blocks, areas large enough to conceal fleets of cars and even tanks were sealed off. Unless searchers had an architect's plan of a building, they could never hope to find the hidden rooms, which were often comfortably furnished and equipped with telephones; the O.A.S. leaders could hide there when security forces were making a sweep.

O.A.S. money was entrusted to varous leaders. Each fighting man received between $150 and $200 a month. The leaders themselves drew from a special fund, the source of which was private subscriptions augmented by bank robbing. They lived in reasonable comfort in new apartments lent to them by sympathizers, but the Legionnaires often lived in squalor. It was not unusual for seven or eight Legionnaires to share a small flat in Bab-el-Oued or Belfort, together with arms, grenades, lubricating oil, wine, anisette and girls; they often slept on mattresses or in sleeping bags on the floor.

The real power of the O.A.S., its grip on its enemies both in Algeria and in France, lay in the brilliance of its intelligence network. There was not a single profession or trade that had not been infiltrated, and it was this network more than anything else that gave the O.A.S. its jaunty self-confidence and contributed to the low morale of the administration.

One example: After the failure of the Putsch, the wives of officers who had remained loyal set up clubs to help the wives of officers who had been arrested or gone underground. These unfortunate women were often penniless, with children to bring up. They could no longer look forward to Army pensions. But many of them were *pieds noirs,* ardent supporters of French Algeria and skillful persuaders. The sympathy and charity of the "loyal" wives gradually changed to discontent with their own situations and then to violent partisanship. The O.A.S. officers were more romantic and swashbuckling than were their own barracks-bound husbands, and the charity clubs gradually grew into active O.A.S. intelligence agencies. Many loyal officers found themselves in the intolerable position of having to protect wives whom they knew were helping the O.A.S. They dared not bring home confidential documents or tell their wives about their activities. As a result, family life became impossible. Officers fretted when their wives went to play golf or bridge with their women friends.

Not infrequently, an O.A.S. man would approach a foreign correspondent and say, "Tomorrow, at midday we blow up such-and-such a prefecture." The following day the prefecture, despite rings of barbed wire and sandbags would go up with a bang. The defenses were useless. The person who had placed the bomb worked inside the building, and the bomb itself had been put in place days before.

And clandestinity all but ceased to be clandestine at all. General Salan gave interviews to the press and, on one occasion, to American television. On several occasions, he was actually seen in the back seat of an Army staff car, lent by friendly brass, and escorted by Army outriders. Degueldre, Susini, and Dr. Perez moved openly in the streets of the city Because of their disguises, they were not easy to recognize. Degueldre, for example, had dyed his hair a kind of ginger and had used a chemical to darken his complexion. A gendarme who did recognize an O.A.S. man would turn his back to preserve his own life, for it was prudent to presume that any O.A.S. leader abroad in the streets was followed discreetly by armed bodyguards who would not hesitate to kill. A sweep by the police could be frustrated by the ability of O.A.S. quarry to disappear into the first automobile or apartment house and be reasonably sure of sanctuary. So the activists were therefore able to lounge openly in the sidewalk cafés, especially the Café Otomatic, their favorite meeting place, reading *Rivarol* and *Les Centurions*.

But there were indications that the O.A.S. fortress had shaky foundations. Too much was being done too quickly, and it was already beginning to shed bricks and tiles like a modern Moscow skyscraper. In the Second World War it had taken the French Resistance four years to reach maximum efficiency. The F.L.N. reached its peak in 1957 after the Algerian war had been going on for nearly four years. The *pieds noirs* and the Army, had they had eyes to see, could have foreseen de Gaulle's intentions as early as 1959 and made preparations, instead of wasting their time on the sterile braggadocio of the Barricades. Because of the momentum of events in Paris and the negotiations going on between the French and the Algerian Provisional Government, at Évian, the O.A.S. was being forced to do in months a job that required years.

And the police were becoming better organized. Colonel Debrosse had all but eliminated the *pieds noirs* from his force and was relying on less corruptible reinforcements from France. Debrosse was detested by the O.A.S. but no more so than another strange figure, Major Bernard Allaire, who had been a parachutist in Indochina and later an officer in the 1st R.E.P. His son, a second lieutenant, had been killed by the fellagha. This tragedy had a curious effect on Allaire. He decided that the only hope for the future of Algeria was cooperation between Europeans and Moslems. He became an open supporter of an Algerian Algeria, a friend of many of the leaders of the F.L.N. and a counter intelligence officer in the Army—one of the most ruthless enemies of the O.A.S.

As Lagaillarde had tried to convey to Algiers before his arrest, the very basis of resistance is a privileged sanctuary from which control can be administered. The precedents were known to everyone. The French Resistance from 1940 to 1944 had depended on control from London; the average life of a Resistance leader in France was three to four months, for an active fighter often no more than a week. Only in Britain could enough cadres of saboteurs receive the training and professional experience to make up the losses. The Irish in their war with the English, the Vietminh in Indochina and the F.L.N. in Algeria were all directed from outside. Even Fidel Castro was only able to win in Cuba because of the enormous backing he enjoyed from outside, principally from the United States.

The regular Army was still depressingly inert. Although more than a thousand officers had resigned their commissions in protest against de Gaulle's Algerian policy, nearly all had preferred to go home and take jobs as champagne salesmen or automobile dealers rather than to enlist in the O.A.S. Officers released from prison, men whom the O.A.S. liked to represent in its propaganda as martyrs, showed little desire to risk second terms. (One important exception was Colonel Roland Vaudrey, former aide-de-camp to Godard in the Algiers Sûreté, who had been arrested after the Putsch and condemned to ten years in prison; he escaped from the Fresnes after four months and turned up in Algiers shortly afterward.)

Gaullist officers tended to speak less loudly than did anti-Gaullist officers, but they were more numerous than the O.A.S. liked to believe, and they kept a quiet brake on the Army hotheads. Often it seemed that companies and even battalions were on the point of making a break for the O.A.S., but somehow never quite enough officers were ready to agree, and no one moved at all. Of them all, officers sympathetic to the O.A.S. suffered the worst crises of conscience. Secretly they hated themselves for lacking the courage to join, and they envied the O.A.S. cadres. But a conscience needs rationalization, and truth is bound to become what one needs the truth to be. The contempt in which they were held by the O.A.S., the *pieds noirs* and in some cases their own wives wounded their feelings and gave them the necessary excuse for increasing the psychological barrier between themselves and the O.A.S. It could almost be stated as a rule of thumb that, in that period in the messes of Algeria and France, the louder an officer argued against the O.A.S. the more he secretly wished to join it.

The Legion still refused to budge. It was like mountain snow, creaking and groaning, but it failed to start an avalanche. The Legion had no supreme commander. Each regiment was largely autonomous, and all had witnessed the fate of the 1st R.E.P. If one commander moved, it is likely that others would have followed. The officer they principally looked to was Colonel Vaillant, commander of the 2nd R.E.P., who hesitated and hesitated and . . . hesitated.

An able and devoted officer, a deserter from the 1st R.E.P., Captain Philippe le Pivain, had been assigned to liaison and proseletyzing work with sympathetic Legion officers and N.C.O.s; he sent an ominous report to Colonel Gardes. Of the 5th Regiment he wrote:

> . . . in spite of the transfers there is still a small core of officers absolutely sure and decided, ready from now onward to accept missions for us. Some will only be acquired 100 per cent when a satisfactory doctrine has been presented to them. The last defeat has made them fear action for the sake of action.

Le Pivain continued with a warning that had special significance, for it concerned the very basis of Legion existence, the status of the N.C.O.s who effectively ran the Legion:

> The Legion problem is not an officer problem but a problem of the senior N.C.O.s. Most of the adjutants and chief adjutants have only one thought, their retirement. The treason of Pfirrman and Brothier [two commanding officers who had personally stopped their Legionnaires from joining the Putsch] reinforces their position. A few might be recovered, and we have one strong card to play; the survival of the Legion depends on our success.

Le Pivain's findings at Sidi-bel-Abbès were more depressing still: "Contact was possible only with two or three officers of the 1st Regiment."

But in Oran and Algiers there were few who would listen to gloomy prognostications while the whole country was enjoying its passionate love affair, its orgiastic long lost weekend with the O.A.S.

14

THE FLIGHT OF COLONEL ARGOUD
September 1961–February 1962

✠✠✠

From the Canary Islands the plastic-bomb warfare of Algiers and Oran, the narrow escapes, the tortures and atrocities and the screaming of police sirens all sounded the faintest of echoes, and the word "activist" evoked only ironic laughter. The leaders of O.A.S.-Madrid lived in a Sartresque hell of wholly unwanted comfort—together. They ate at a large dining table in the Hotel Mayantigo, Santa Cruz de Tenerife. About a score of people shared the table; they had nothing in common, not even the O.A.S. Even Argoud and Lagaillarde had fallen out at last, over a question of money; Argoud complained that Lagaillarde helped himself too liberally to the O.A.S. funds.

With Argoud, Lagaillarde, Lacheroy and Ortiz sat Michel Fechoz, Lagaillarde's court jester, as outrageous as ever and as happy to be a "prisoner" as he had been in Madrid; loafing in the Canaries as he had loafed there. Several assistants of both Ortiz and Lagaillarde had been arrested at the same time, and the social segregation of the Barricades repeated itself in a smaller way; Lagaillarde's men were former students, whereas Ortiz' were artisans. Lagaillarde once more had the opportunity to pull rank and demonstrate his intellectual superiority.

Ortiz had brought with him a newcomer, a Monsieur Dantès, a former secretary to Pierre Laval in the Vichy Government. Until the O.A.S. had come to life in Spain, Dantès had been living in near penury with a wife and child; Ortiz took pity on him and gave him a job as secretary on his own O.A.S. budget, so that Dantès was one of the few who could claim to have enlisted in the Secret Army solely for the money. Unfortunately he had the bad judgment to admit it and to acknowledge his indebtedness to Ortiz, which enabled Lagaillarde to cut him as not *pure race* O.A.S." Four women shared this uneasy company: Fourry Argoud, Babette Lagaillarde, Andrée Ortiz and Madame Dantès. It is to the credit of their sex that they avoided the backbiting of their men and got along quite well.

All the men at the table, however, made it a point to be glacially polite to one another; even Lagaillarde. Although he had not forgotten that Andrèe Ortiz had once tried to spit in his face, he occasionally passed up tempting opportunities to needle and humiliate her husband.

Occasionally there were explosions. Fourry Argoud, who was neither French nor Algerian, could not help seeing the funny side of this ill-mated and bizarre company and occasionally had to stifle a giggle.

This attitude annoyed her table companions, one of whom turned on her and said acidly, "It is obvious you do not understand the O.A.S."

"I never did," Madame Argoud replied and was immediately contrite, sensing that in her very lack of understanding was the element of genuine tragedy. "Admitting that they are right in their convictions," she confided to her notes, "it is all the more reason to be understanding and patient with them."

The Hotel Mayantigo is one of the pleasanter hotels in the Canaries, and the dining room was divided into three sections for the involuntary guests. There was a table for the prisoners, an adjoining table for the guards and other tables for tourists. Although the O.A.S. prisoners became, in time, something of a tourist attraction in themselves, the other guests quickly found themselves little better off than the prisoners. Their cameras were confiscated, and, although a certain amount of fraternization was permitted, they were carefully watched to make sure they were not newspaper reporters or planning to help the prisoners escape.

If one is compelled to be in prison, it would be difficult to imagine a prison more comfortable than this one. The detainees were allowed to come and go as they pleased, but each was followed by two guards on walks, to the beaches and nightclubs and even skin diving on the ocean floor.

But, despite the informal and even friendly relationship between the O.A.S. and the guards, the Franco Government was taking no chances; the guards were always alert for attempts at escape or coup. Helicopters flew overhead. The dock and the small airfield were guarded day and night, and precautions were taken even against the possibility of an attempt to penetrate the harbor by submarine. The O.A.S. in Algeria was at the height of its power, and nothing seemed beyond its capabilities or inventiveness.

In this enforced and languorous companionship, there was little room for pretense, and everyone was obliged to fall back on his own intellectual resources. Lagaillarde spent most of the day attending to his suntan on the beach. For a man so violent and dynamic, his inertia since the Putsch had puzzled many. He seemed drained of ambition, with no desire to go back to Algeria. The truth was not quite that. Lagaillarde, as he admitted to some of his close friends, was frankly frightened. "If I try to go back," he said simply, "Susini will kill me." Jean-Jacques Susini, his former disciple, ran the Z commandos. That Susini looked indifferently upon the deaths of others was a well-known fact. That he was capable of actually killing became apparent later. Lagaillarde was no coward. He was facing facts. If he had gone back, Susini *would* have killed him.

Fechoz patrolled the dock to study the new arrivals. As usual, he sought girls. "English girls," he emphasized. Their nationality was very important. He could not tell the difference, he said, between English and American accents, but he recognized the quality of performance as soon as he put it to the test.

Argoud fumed at the inactivity and wrote angry letters to General Franco ("whom I have always considered, Sir, a lover of freedom"); he was aggrieved at receiving no answer. Broizat wrote to him from Algiers and sent him copies of *Les Centurions*. Broizat was little comfort, however. For Argoud, in intolerable confinement, Broizat's preoccupation with joining the Salvation Army had a certain irrelevance. Joseph and Andrée Ortiz pined for Algeria; they read every newspaper, snatching at bits of hope as chickens peck for grain. "It was as if Algeria were their own daughter, dying of an incurable disease," said Madame Argoud, "and they hoped against hope for a miracle to cure her."

Colonel Lacheroy was a broken man. He had had his fill of the O.A.S. and bitterly regretted his decision to have anything to do with it. All day long he sought in his mind for some way of detaching himself from it and resuming his military career and family life, but no formula had yet been devised for resigning a commission in the O.A.S. Like Colonel Gardes, he had been a specialist in psychological warfare and a press-relations officer; unlike Gardes, he had not made himself popular. He was xenophobic; he lumped American and British correspondents together and disliked both. In later years, correspondents informally polled usually recalled Lacheroy as a "bastard."

Lacheroy walked in an aura of personal ruin and decay. It seemed to him that his life had been one of consistent waste—a brilliant education come to nothing, a frustrated and mediocre military career. Now he was shattered by news that he had dreaded from the start: his son, a cadet at the naval academy, had been arrested because his father was supposed to be one of the leaders of the O.A.S.

Fourry Argoud, on walks with him, tried to console him. "Everything will sort itself out, Colonel," she said as they strolled through the narrow streets of Santa Cruz, followed idly by two guards.

Lacheroy smiled wanly. "When?"

"Tomorrow . . . or the next day." She could think of nothing more positive than that. The beautiful Oriental wife of the most brilliant colonel in the French Army had once been promised the Élysée Palace. She could have used some comfort herself.

Boredom played tricks on them all. One of the party was found cheating at cards. He was one of Lagaillarde's men and narrowly escaped a bad beating at the hands of his furious chief. The prisoners next refused to pay their hotel bills and were politely informed by the manager that they were the guests of General Franco. "Only the drinks are supplementary, Señores."

They went on a hunger strike for more freedom. Lagaillarde gave up after 24 hours, declaring the effort childish and absurd. After four days, Lacheroy begged permission to give up because of his greater age. Argoud, Ortiz and Dantès lasted eight days.

Finally, Argoud could stand no more of this tomfoolery. His quicksilver brain was atrophying in the life he was leading, and he could sense it almost physically, as one feels the slackening of muscles. One day in late December, he told his wife that he intended to escape; the very idea worked as instant intellectual therapy. As soon as the idea took hold, it transformed him, and he could think of nothing else.

On his walks he studied the guards at the dock and the structure of the houses in the area. Fourry bought him dark glasses, a dark raincoat and a hat that could be pulled low over his eyes. He studied the hours of moonrise and fixed his date of escape for February 26. A friend bought him a Tenerife-Madrid air ticket, and another bought a ticket on the night boat from Santa Cruz to Tenerife.

He had noticed near the dock a crack in an old wall, which was big enough for a man his size to squeeze through; it led into a stretch of waste ground that was not overlooked by any windows. It would be his hiding place, and his wife would carry his escape clothes and glasses in a parcel while bringing their two daughters from school.

The night of February 25 was spent in clearing up O.A.S. business. Argoud, in his room, counted out money, sealed it in envelopes and wrote the recipients' names on the cover. These envelopes held the wages of the men covered by his budget, and he instructed Fourry to distribute them 48 hours after he had gone.

Only two of the prisoners, Lacheroy and Ortiz, were taken into his confidence, and on the day of the escape they busied themselves bothering the guards and distracting their attention. Lacheroy demanded an escort on a long walk to see the island volcano. Ortiz asked for volunteers among the guards to go skin diving.

The night ferry to Tenerife was to sail at 11:00 in the evening, but Argoud would have to slip his guards by 7:00 and hide for the intervening four hours. After 7:00 the guards and the prisoners would be in the dining room or lobby, and he would attract attention if he tried to leave. Shortly before 7:00 Madame Argoud told the guards that she was going to pick up her daughters from school, and Argoud said he would accompany her. It was the promenade hour in Santa Cruz, and the Argouds trusted that the wholly unsuspicious guards would find things to distract their attention if only for a few seconds. Fourry carried with her a small briefcase containing her husband's papers, false passport, tickets, diary and some money.

The gap in the wall was near a corner, and, as they turned, Fourry looked back and saw to her immense relief that the guards had stopped to chat with a couple of girls. She quickly gave the briefcase to her husband, who disappeared into the darkness without a kiss or a farewell.

Fourry walked as casually as she could back to the officers, who were still talking but saluted as she approached. "My husband has already gone back to the hotel," she said. "Didn't you see him?"

"Thank you, Madame," they said and resumed talking. Fourry collected her daughters, telling them nothing. Behind her in the shadows, her husband was donning his coat, hat and dark glasses and settling down for the long and dangerous wait, which might, at any moment, be punctured by the wail of alarm sirens.

At the hotel Fourry Argoud pressed her face to the window of her room. She had telephoned down to the dining room that she and her husband would have only some broth in their room, which they did frequently. The dock itself was hidden from her sight by some intervening buildings, but she would see the boat when it put to sea. Eight o'clock, then 9:00 passed. She put her children to bed, making some excuse for their father's not coming to kiss them goodnight. She knew that, at three minutes to eleven precisely, a small man with a hat pulled low over his dark glasses would present a ticket at the gangplank. At 11:00 the boat's foghorn signaled its departure, and she saw it move slowly out to sea. She did not feel nervous, only terribly weary. Yet she could not sleep. She walked down to the waterfront to listen to the waves beating against the rocks. She was consumed with lassitude, and before she was aware of the passing hours it was dawn.

The police had not noticed the disappearance, but the word had spread among the prisoners, and a delegation knocked on the door of the Argouds' room at 10:00 A.M. The spokesman said, "Madame Argoud, we consider it essential to divorce ourselves from any responsibility for your husband's escape, and to make it known that we were never informed of his intentions."

Nobody intended to give the game away, but the meaning was clear. Fourry Argoud was being kicked off the team. She was to face the music alone, and she could not count on her husband's colleagues for moral support. She remembered him as he had been two nights earlier, the night before his escape, facing an agonizing future in which he might be recaptured, beaten, punished and perhaps even shot if he tried to resist arrest. Knowing him, she knew very well that he would resist; yet he had sat at his desk occupying himself with matters of detail like the O.A.S. payroll. With tears in her eyes, she ran to the drawer. Although her husband had told her not to distribute the money until 48 hours after his departure, she handed them the envelopes. "As long as you have your money you will be happy, Messieurs," she declared. "Now leave the room, keep your distance and leave me alone with my children."

Alarm bells convulsed the island at 3:00 that afternoon, awakening Fourry Argoud from an uneasy nap. She was arrested, and by early evening Santa Cruz was full of angry police chiefs from Madrid. The guards were summarily dismissed and replaced. The prisoners were ordered to remain on the hotel grounds. Every airport in Spain was alerted. Fourry was not ill treated, but she was questioned closely for the rest of the day and into the night and then the next day and the day after, for a month. After that she was released and permitted to take her children back to Paris. Argoud's getaway had been complete.

✥✥✥

The ferryboat had docked at Tenerife at 8:00 the following morning, in time for Argoud to catch the Madrid plane; he landed in the capital shortly after midday. He was immediately dismayed to realize that the plane schedules he had studied in Santa Cruz were out of date and that the flight times had been changed. He scanned the departure board for the first outgoing plane to Brussels, Rome, Geneva, anywhere except France or Algiers, where he would be immediately arrested. The first was a Lufthansa flight to Stuttgart, leaving at 3:00. He had two and a half hours to wait. He bought a single ticket and examined the layout of the airport. He was disturbed to see that there was no barber shop; he had planned, if he heard the alarm or saw policemen, to order a shave. The soap would have made a crude disguise. He retired to the lavatory and locked the door. There he stayed until he heard the flight called. The Spanish immigration officer stamped his passport incuriously, and he boarded the plane and fastened his seat belt. He had friends in Germany in the French NATO Army. He could not have a better destination, once the plane took off. Only when the wheels of the airplane left the tarmac of Spain did he permit himself a sigh of relief.

15
PARIS BY NIGHT (BLUE)
October 1961–February 1962

✢✢✢

Three months before Argoud's escape, at the end of October, an appalling Moslem riot took place in Paris. The police, to counter the plastic-bomb attacks of Moslems, as well as of the O.A.S., imposed an 8:30 curfew on Algerians working in the capital. But the Algerians lived in corrugated-iron *bidonvilles* on the outskirts of the city, black holes without electricity, sanitation or water. The roofs were bare of television masts, the opiate of even the poorest. Such homes were places to escape from, not to be caged inside. Thirty thousand Moslems took the *métro* to the heart of the city to demonstrate in protest.

But the police, sorely tried in every direction, had a score to settle. Fourteen of their number, innocent men, had been murdered by the F.L.N. in Paris in the course of 1961. The gendarmes charged into the demonstrators with clubs and loaded capes; tourists who admire the cut of the Paris policeman's jib are often unaware that the hem of the cape is weighted with lead; in the hands of a professional it is a stunning antiriot weapon. Reporters, television photographers and bold tourists were knocked aside and given bloody heads. The Algerians were severely beaten. Pictures showed them running and stumbling through gauntlets of gendarmes, with hands on their heads to protect themselves against the drumming of the clubs. The following morning corpses were found floating in the Seine. Victims were strangled in the woods. The Palais des Sports was opened and turned into a concentration camp, even as the Gestapo had used it for the Jews during the war. Broken limbs were left unattended for days. All this brutality was reported not only by the communists but also in the conservative press.

The Algerian riot gave fresh ammunition to newspapers like *France-Observateur, L'Humanité* and *Le Monde,* all of which had been bombed. They renewed their attacks on the Government, which seemed to them timorous in its attitude toward the O.A.S. and ineffectual in keeping the peace. The *Journal Officiel* finally printed a Government decree pronouncing the O.A.S. dissolved, an announcement both belated and premature. It called forth an impudent riposte: Even as the city councilmen were meeting in the City Hall, the flag of the O.A.S. was raised on the roof of the building, not once but three times.

The apogee of O.A.S. fortunes in Metropolitan France occurred a few weeks later, on November 8, in the Assembly. Eighty deputies voted for a private motion before the Chamber to reduce military service to eighteen months. This proposal would have eliminated a large proportion of the conscripts, who as a bloc were opposed to anything that would prolong their service in Algeria. It was a motion for which Jean-Jacques Susini, speaking through General Salan, had been calling. The motion thenceforth became known as the "Salan Amendment." The O.A.S. had achieved parliamentary representation!

On November 23, General de Gaulle went to Strasbourg to address 2,000 officers and to demand their loyalty. Two bombs were exploded in the city before he arrived. His reception was cool, and when at the end he burst into his arm-flailing, tuneless bellowing of the *Marseillaise,* scores of officers pointedly remained silent. At the same time the negotiations between the French and the Algerial Provisional Government at Évian were broken off over the question of who would control the Sahara and its oil deposits. The event was greeted in Algeria as a tremendous victory for the *pieds noirs.*

A week later the "Committee of Vincennes" to keep Algeria French held a public meeting in Paris. The leaders were Georges Bidault; Jacques Soustelle; André Morice, former Minister of Defense; Max Lejeune, former Minister of the Sahara, and Robert Lacoste, former Minister-Resident of Algeria (equivalent of Governor; in wartime Algeria titles seemed to change with each change of policy). The meeting attracted almost every notable in France associated with the Right, both moderate and extreme. Every time the name of Salan was uttered it received an ovation. Léon Delbecque said, "It is the O.A.S. which is saving Algeria." Bidault, hero of the Resistance in the Second World War, said, "A new Resistance is declaring itself day after day. The Army of the new Resistance is organizing itself. Its ranks never cease to increase."

This material was highly inflammable and the alarmed Government ordered the Committee to disband on the grounds that "it was defending the liberty to assassinate."

Both Jacques Soustelle and Georges Bidault stood on the threshold of conspiracy. As a young man Soustelle had gone to Mexico and Guatemala to study the Mayans, and he became sensitive to the idea of catastrophe so enormous that entire civilizations could be destroyed. When he returned he found himself completely out of tune with the subtleties and compromises of French politics, and took an active dislike to politics in themselves. It was for this more than any other reason that he became and remained de Gaulle's most faithful supporter. Soustelle was made Governor-General of Algeria in 1955 at a time when de Gaulle was still living in retirement at Colombey-les-Deux-Eglises, and before he left Soustelle called on his former mentor for guidance. De Gaulle told him, "It is you, Soustelle, who will be responsible before history if Algeria is abandoned." Although distrusted at first by the *pieds noirs*, Soustelle became their idol, and he in turn became bewitched by Algeria, and by the Sahara. "It is in this desert region" he said "that the future of the French Republic will be decided." Both Soustelle and de Gaulle believed that Algeria was the ultimate test of French virility, but after de Gaulle came to power that same belief led to their taking opposite directions.

Georges Bidault was a more complex man. Under the Fourth Republic he had been almost continually in office, twice Prime Minister and frequently Foreign Minister. But bitterness and an increasing irrationality, certainly accentuated by a serious drinking problem, marked his activities. There was an element of hysteria in his appeal to President Eisenhower to send in the U.S. Air Force to save the French garrison at Dien Bien Phu. In 1958 he, like so many others, had hailed de Gaulle's accession to power: "The grandeur and the hope for the safety of fundamental rights and the future are no longer impossible thanks to the return of General de Gaulle." He soon regretted his words. Intellectual brilliance and lack of common sense make a dangerous combination. With the Algerian war almost over, he was having hallucinations, as is obvious from his own memoirs. He imagined Gaullist spies following him everywhere and dark plots against his life. His was the biggest name to adhere to the O.A.S., but he had long ago lost his capacity for coherent leadership.

The O.A.S., however, had every reason to be delighted at these massive manifestations of dissatisfaction with the Government. The Algerian plague had infected Metropolitan France. The O.A.S. policy of violence and terrorism was achieving exactly what it had been intended to achieve: creation of such nervous tension among Frenchmen and such friction between the Moslems and the forces of order that an independent Algeria would seem impossible. The French of France and the French of Algeria would be left shoulder to shoulder willy-nilly—wrong, perhaps, but wrong together.

Paris, like Algiers though not to the same extent, was rocking from plastic-bomb explosions. Attacks were made on journalists and public figures who opposed the O.A.S. A plastic bomb was detonated in the Saint-Cloud home of Pierre Lazareff, editor of *France-Soir*. Later *France-Soir* itself was bombed under the most disturbing circumstances. The bomb was placed on a narrow staircase and detonated at a moment when the editors of the paper were usually holding their editorial conference. On that occasion the conference had broken up early, and the bomb did nothing more than start a fire and slightly wound an elderly woman clerk, but it proved that the O.A.S. had agents within the editorial department.

The bombers could not refrain from injecting a note of symbolic anti-Americanism by bombing le Drugstore at the top of the Champs Élysés; it was one of the favorite rendezvous of young Parisians, and the scent of perfume from its smashed stocks and shattered windows pervaded the avenue for several days.

The apartment of Jean-Paul Sartre was blown to rubble. A plastic charge was left on the windowsill in the home of André Malraux, Minister of Cultural Affairs. Malraux was not at home—the terrorists were usually cautious enough to make sure that their victims were out —but the explosion disfigured a small girl who lived in the building.

On the level of the ridiculous the terrorists sent a threatening note to Brigitte Bardot demanding money. B.B. rejected it and became a heroine. That such a note actually came from the O.A.S.-Métro is doubtful. The maiming of a small girl, threats to a cinema actress and destruction of a drugstore were enough to show that the O.A.S.

in France was, to put it charitably, a mess, the work of hooligans, justifying the demands of Argoud, Lagaillarde and the other "Spaniards" that O.A.S.-Métro restrict itself to propaganda. A wiser leader than Salan might have gone further and told the O.A.S. to stay out of France altogether. It took no political genius to see that once the O.A.S. tried to organize on the mainland, every crazy political movement in the country would seek to jump on the bandwagon. There were innumerable right-wing conspirators who sought the glamor of the O.A.S. imprimatur and called themselves "activists." Among them were crackpot mystic organizations inspired by Martel. There was the fascist Jeune Nation, Father Grasset's Cité Catholique and many others. There were also bands of delinquents with "O.A.S." emblazoned on the backs of their black leather jackets; many of them knew the art of plasticating but lacked a sense of where and when, not to mention why.

For these and other reasons, it is clear that Captain Pierre Sergent, head of O.A.S.-Métro, in many ways had the most thankless job of all. It was hard for him to see the wood for the trees. Salan did not help. He seemed available for interviews and help to whoever visited Algiers, and people coming back to Paris with letters of introduction from the Mandarin plagued Sergent's life. The most important of these people was André Canal, known as "the Monocle" or "the Colonel"; he had been put in charge of "Mission III," which took care of exploding plastic bombs and liaison among Paris, Algiers and Spain. Canal was a Frenchman married to a *pied noir,* and he had lived in Algiers since before the Second World War. He made his base in France and actually suggested to Sergent that he (Canal) was the superior officer. He changed his mind only when Sergent told him that he and Godot were thinking of killing him. Canal, like Lefèvre, Lagaillarde, Bidault, Soustelle, Grasset and others, had a personal ax to grind; dealing with him diverted Sergent from his own tasks, the principal one of which he considered to be recruitment of officers and spreading of propaganda.

Ridiculous as it may seem for the leader of a clandestine organization dedicated to action and sometimes even murder, Sergent's greatest problem was, of all things, rank. He constantly found himself at a disadvantage in talking with senior officers, even though he had the most famous O.A.S. name in France. The absurdity was typified by "the Verdun Affair." The Algiers police, when they arrested Gingembre, became excited about a certain "General Verdun," supposedly the mastermind of the O.A.S. in France. The police combed the lists of all the sympathetic generals for those whose names began with "V," having already noted O.A.S. tendencies in the field of pseudonyms. The list was not large, and General Vanuxem was given the compliment of an arrest and accusation of being "General Verdun."

As is usually the case, the truth was less melodramatic but funnier. The officer appointed to command the O.A.S. in France had been a colonel, de Blignières, but he was in prison exchanging letters with Father Grasset. Salan was upset when he heard that O.A.S.-Métro was left in the command of a captain. He talked to Godard and insisted that the command be given to a senior officer, however honorary; but those approached—Crèvecoeur, Mirambeau and Massu— had all reluctantly declined. Finally Vanuxem had agreed, but before arrangements could be agreed upon Gingembre was arrested.

In the meantime, however, orders had been issued under the name "Verdun"; as far as the police were concerned "Verdun" was therefore an important leader, and the arrest of Vanuxem was considered a big victory for the forces of order. Sergent was a philosophical fellow and would have been happy to serve under Vanuxem, Faure or de Blignières, but he could see that, after all the good men had either declined or been eliminated, there were few left in the barrel. Salan had a lot of cronies with general's rank who lived abroad on the retired list. Sergent, fearing that one of them might be foisted on him, wrote Godard a letter that showed that even a Legionnaire, accustomed to unquestioning obedience, can tell a man from a myth. *He* was running O.A.S.-Métro, said Sergent, and his sole criterion was *efficiency*. "We don't need some inspector general [a rank formerly held by both Salan and Gardy], and we have confidence only in generals who have already taken the plunge or are in prison for their pains. The generals have had their chance and they only needed to take it. They are now a length behind."

The arrest of Gingembre, however, settled the hash of "Verdun," and neither he nor his like was ever again found in the ranks of O.A.S.-Métro.

Altogether, Sergent was a remarkable man and, in his quiet way, a fine leader of men. It was impossible to guess how many telephone calls had identified Sergent in how many places—and how many thousands of policemen had broken into how many homes to look for

him. He could have lain low and issued tracts. There were many
O.A.S. leaders in both France and Algeria who considered their continuing liberty a triumph but who actually achieved it by never leaving their hiding places. They were not caught, but they achieved little.
Resistance, or clandestinity, demands constant movement. For purposes of liaison it was necessary for Sergent to keep in contact with
people who had no known political background that would arouse
police suspicion, He also had to expose himself to danger, to call
meetings even with subordinates whom he suspected were being followed, to visit men with whom he had no real business. For clandestinity is a lonely way of life, and comrades need contact with one
another just to be reassured that company exists. The best Resistance
group is the one least spoken about; whatever captured O.A.S. men
were compelled to reveal, if they could cloak themselves in convincing ignorance, their friends could escape. Only Pierre Sergent knew
everything.

One of Sergent's assets was his appearance. Even in uniform he
had never had much military bearing. He walked with an unsoldierly
slouch, and his face was pasty and unhealthy looking. Perhaps because of his own lack of presence and stiff back, he was not as instinctively distrusting of civilians and politicians as most soldiers are.
As he had written to Godard, he was interested only in efficiency. Jean
Reimbold, a civilian leader of the O.A.S. who was ultimately condemned to fifteen years in prison, said of him:

> With Sergent there were no problems. Our friendship was
> total. He had the qualities I loved in a man, courage, mental
> balance, consistency and constancy. As a captain in the
> Legion he maintained its spirit, but his intelligence per-
> mitted him to orient himself into a world new for him, the
> world of politics. He lacked presumption, and never con-
> sidered himself a great genius. Between Sergent and myself
> there was never the slightest difference. The military man
> he no longer was, and the civilian-at-war that I had be-
> come, we complemented each other completely.

The difficulties of O.A.S.-Métro were endless. In Algeria, the
O.A.S. played a role largely similar to that of the Resistance toward
the end of the German occupation, that is to say, a force fighting an
oppressive enemy in the heart of a sympathetic population. In France
the situation was different. The need to remain underground was total.

One did not use the telephone except to exchange noncommital words with people whose names one never mentioned. One could not afford the luxury of useless phrases like "How are you?" or "Do you understand?"

Almost never could one write directly. Everything had to be done through intermediaries. One never stated specifically where and when he would make a rendezvous. And the greatest source of danger was not the possibility of police recognition in the streets but simply of paper. All operations require papers, documents, files. In France the O.A.S. leaders destroyed every scrap of paper not immediately needed, and the rest was hidden in half a dozen places. Because the documents had to be consulted by the various leaders, their notes and address books were coded in such a way that, if they fell into the hands of the police, not even O.A.S. prisoners could help to decode them. For example, 37 Rue Saint Roch might be referred to in one man's book as "Pierre Gabrielle" and in another's as "Marseilles Caen." In the former "37" might be the age of a friend called "Pierre," and "Gabrielle" might be a girl to whom he recalled making love in a hotel on the Rue St. Roch; in the other man's book "37" might be the year in which Marseilles won the football cup, and "Caen" might refer to a butcher in the Rue Saint Roch who made his favorite tripe.

A car was indispensable, but it involved all kinds of risks. Roadblocks sprang up like magic, and false papers were scrutinized. A minor traffic accident could lead directly to the Santé. To rent a car required filling out forms, and car-hire firms were required by law to report rentals to the police within 24 hours. Ideally the O.A.S. man traveled with a driver whose papers were in order and who was under no police suspicion, but it was a rare friend who could put himself at someone's disposal on a moment's notice and then be available all day or for a week or a month.

To an extent, Sergent's task was simplified by the fact that he recognized only Godard and, through Godard, Salan as his commanders. But Godard himself was not fully in control of his own actions. Active leadership had passed, whether Godard liked it or not, into the hands of Degueldre. Salan made no decisions. Argoud was not there. Godard was overwhelmed, or perhaps he deliberately overwhelmed himself, with paper work, "organigrammes" and such, in order to seem busy. He had a meticulous, filing-cabinet mind, and to

Sergent he addressed endless demands for more men, experienced officers to reinforce the cadres in Algeria.

Sergent could not supply enough, but he did enjoy some spectacular propaganda triumphs. He was able to announce the defection of Lieutenant André Curutchet of the 9th R.C.P., one of France's more colorful and extroverted officers, on the very day that Curutchet's promotion to captain was announced in the *Journal Officiel*. At the end of September he and Godot, a deceptively mild-looking young man with dreamy eyes behind steel spectacles, sprang two important officers from prison: Colonel Roland Vaudrey and Captain de Saint Rémy. Both were serving terms of imprisonment in Fresnes for their parts in the Putsch. They were permitted to go to the Val de Grâce military hospital to be examined for imaginary maladies. On the way, they were met by Godot with false papers and civilian clothes, and by that evening they were both in Algiers.

On December 14, Sergent's lobbying in the Army messes led to a bizarre propaganda success for the O.A.S., one that it hailed as a great victory. In the middle of the night, in the forests of northern France, a section of the 2nd Company of the 43rd Regiment of Infantry was taken out on exercise by Lieutenant Roger Bernard. Bernard was another small fellow, 5 feet 4 inches tall, and his former job had been as a combat officer in the 2nd R.E.P., in which regiment he had taken part in the Putsch. His new duty was the crash training of aspiring officers. At 2:00 in the morning, in bitterly cold weather, under a black and starless sky, he summoned his troops. "We are going to practice a night march in the direction of Fort Englos where we will make a surprise maneuver," he told them. On arrival at a bivouac near the fort, the cadets formed their rifles in pyramids and were told to get some sleep.

Alone with the sentinel, Lieutenant Bernard proposed an exercise. "Now we begin a test of initiative," he said. "We are going to plot a theft of arms. I shall tie you up and in half an hour, not less, free yourself and sound the alarm."

It was better than standing guard in the cold. Bernard tied the cadet's hands and feet, threw a cover over his head and wrapped him warmly so that he would not die of exposure. He then walked to the main road and flashed a light. Two cars, with only their sidelights glowing, approached from the cover of trees. One was a large station wagon, the other a Volkswagen. One of the two men who alighted was Adjutant Marc Robin, one of Captain Sergent's principal assistants. The arms were loaded, quietly and professionally, by men who had fought the F.L.N. in the black silence of the Kabylia. The car crossed the Belgian border, and the arms arrived with Bernard by private plane in Algiers. The ordnance department of the O.A.S. gained one bazooka, ten MAT 48 machine guns and twelve MAS 36/51 rifles, as well as ammunition and hand grenades.

It was an extraordinary exploit and one that made Roger Bernard a hero of the O.A.S., but the reaction within the O.A.S. was interesting. The senior officers were *furious.* In prison Generals Challe, Vanuxem and Faure raged against the act in terms that included blasphemy. "It isn't military," was their basic attitude. "We have wounded the pride of potential officers by making fools of them," they said. "One does not humiliate boys."

Their anger took the junior officers and civilians by surprise. "Nonsense," they protested. "This is revolutionary warfare, and Bernard made a revolutionary gesture. The F.L.N. slits the throats of Moslem boys who were loyal to the French. We simply take the guns of boys who are serving de Gaulle."

"You don't deceive and trick and lie," said the generals. "That was the reason given by Major Saint Marc for taking part in the Putsch. The Gaullists dart hither and thither. We don't."

"Are we serving a cause, or are we not? Which Army are we fighting for, de Gaulle's Army or the O.A.S.?"

So, as in 1940, the French Army was split over what was correct and what was incorrect, what was honor and what was dishonor, what lay in front of one's nose and what on the other side of the rainbow. What was not in dispute was that Roger Bernard was one of the heroes of the O.A.S., the new pinup of *pied noir* children. Coindidentally, both Degueldre and Bernard were from the North—Degueldre from Nord and Bernard from Alsace. Sergent was from Britanny, Godard from Savoy, Dovecar from Vienna, Argoud from Lorraine. The southern representation was smaller and subtly different. General Jouhaud was from Algeria and General Salan from Provence.

✠✠✠✠

Yet, despite the bombings, the schoolboy gestures and the general futility of the O.A.S. campaign in France, a large number of people were drawn to the Organization. It was a strangely paradoxical situation. Colonies had become the most useless bric-a-brac of world power, and the French, after Indochina, had shed them with even greater alacrity than had the British, except for Algeria. An important section of the French press consistently defended the O.A.S., notably the powerful *Le Parisien Libére*, with its circulation of 850,000, and *L'Aurore*. The weekly *Rivarol* was the boldest and most ribald in its anti-Gaullism. "De Gaulle can puff himself up all over France," it claimed, "but it is only the ignorant or the imbecilic who believe he is qualified to preach about *obedience*."

Even among the most distinguished politicians there was open sympathy for the O.A.S. One sympathizer was former President Coty, who continued to defend the statement he had made in 1957, a year before de Gaulle replaced him in office, in which he said:

> To states that dare accuse France of colonialism is there not a Frenchman proud to answer, in which country is there less imperialism, less racism, less enslavement than in ours? It is not to the French but to civilized public opinion that I pose this simple question: If a number of your compatriots were established anywhere for a long time, would you be so cowardly as to abandon them? Do not count on us to sacrifice the other side of the Mediterranean as if it were a new Alsace-Lorraine.

Another was Antoine Pinay, the former Prime Minister and economic genius, whom France could largely thank for the recovery of the franc and the whole national economy. He was asked, and refused, to denounce the O.A.S.

Camus denounced both the F.L.N. and the O.A.S.; his views had been expressed in 1958 in the course of his running fight with Sartre:

> If some Frenchmen consider that, as a result of its colonizing, France (and France alone among so many pure and holy nations) is in a state of sin historically, they do not have to point to the French in Algeria as scapegoats ("Go ahead and die; that's what we deserve!"); they must offer themselves up in expiation. As far as I am concerned, it

seems to me revolting to beat one's *mea culpa* as our
judge-penitents do, on someone else's breast . . ."*

And he added later, "When violence answers violence in a growing
frenzy that makes the simple language of reason impossible, the role
of the intellectuals cannot be, as we read every day, to excuse from a
distance one of the violences and condemn the other."

In the social order of the Metropolitan O.A.S., the most significant
element of all was the network of Jean-Marie Vincent. Vincent was
the explosives expert of André Canal's Mission III, and he was just
nineteen years old, the son of a well-to-do family from Niort. Patric
Edel, head of another plastic-bomb group, was seventeen, and he had
under his command boys who were scarcely older. All came from
good families and were on the way to successful careers. They were
not in the O.A.S. for "kicks." Their involvement could be explained
away on the grounds of youth and adventure. But then, when the
Brittany network was blown open by the police, it was found to include career officers, landowners, well-known local aristocrats; it was
headed by Count Horace Savelli, President of the National Union of
Ex-Servicemen. The Toulouse network counted in its ranks the Deputy Mayor of the city and Dr. Jean Castaigneau, the leading heart
specialist in southwest France. All these men were representatives of
the French Establishment, men whom one would have imagined to
be models of conformity, eager to protect the prosperity of the present
against the chronic insecurity of the nation's past, certainly the last to
rebel and go underground. Some were old Pétainists. Although that
background would account for their extreme anti-Gaullism, the Pétainist tradition took precedent and the authority of the law as
absolute.

The campaign in Paris was climaxed by the famous "Blue Night"
of January 17–18, when eighteen plastic-bomb explosions were recorded in the capital. Between January 15 and 21 there were forty
plastic-bomb explosions in Metropolitan France. Thirty-four more
were reported between February 5 and 11, including 27 in the sub-
urbs.

The police recovered a certain measure of ground on February 26,
when they captured young Jean-Marie Vincent in his headquarters,
an apartment in the Avenue Émile Zola. Vincent had been suffering

* Preface to Algerian Reports," quoted in *Resistance, Rebellion and Death*.

painfully from conscience because he accepted that it was his plastic bomb, placed near the apartment of André Malraux, that had disfigured the child. The capture of Vincent led quickly to the capture of André Canal and the crippling of Mission III, but even that setback was not really bad news for Pierre Sergent, Daniel Godot and Marc Robin.

Nothing seemed to work for the police. They had arrested Gingembre with all his documents, but all they had gained was Geneviève Salasc, who would not talk, de Blignières and a few minor figures. They had caught Dovecar, but Dovecar would not talk either. Vincent yielded up Mission III, but Sergent remained as elusive as ever. The morale of the anti-O.A.S. forces in France had reached rock bottom. The police had been infiltrated. The civil administration was full of sympathizers with the O.A.S. Within the Government the sympathizers were said to reach up to Cabinet level. That a majority of the Army wished the O.A.S. well was reflected in the tactics of General de Gaulle himself. De Gaulle, as everyone knew, could have crushed the O.A.S. in a matter of hours had he sent the Army to do the job. He did not issue the orders, and there was only one reason why. He believed that the Army would not obey or at least that it would obey no more rapidly than it had done at the Barricades. On no occasion, however, did he give any indication of losing his aplomb. He strode through a city that humbler men considered on the verge of civil war as if no enemy existed, and occasionally the situation seemed to appeal to his special sense of humor. Roger Frey, Minister of the Interior, warned him that if France held elections the O.A.S. would probably succeed in killing at least fifty Deputies.

"What does it matter, Frey," said de Gaulle, "providing they are well selected?"

16

THE BARBOUZES

November 1961–March 1962

✣✣✣

The war to which Antoine Argoud returned after his months of captivity was very different from the one he had known before, and he remained in Germany for a while to catch his breath and take stock of the new situation. New forces had entered the struggle, new officers had risen to lead the O.A.S. and other officers had faded. Above all, even from Germany, Argoud sniffed the scent of victory.

Few modern wars have been uglier and dirtier than the Algerian war. It had about it a sordid unnaturalness, like abortion. It pitted comrade against comrade, forced one to hate opponents one would have preferred to admire and compelled soldiers to assume attitudes repugnant to them. It resembled the mythical succubus, the female demon supposed to haunt the sleep of mortal men and sap their virility, the feminine counterpart of the incubus, which ravished mortal women while they slept and was responsible for the birth of demons, witches and deformed children.

Soldiers in Algeria who took pride in their métier found all pride drained from them; indeed that was why the O.A.S. had been born in the first place. The last thing necessary was a new element to make the war even worse. But ever since November 1961 Paris had been providing just such an element. Agents who were neither detectives nor soldiers were arriving in Algiers and Oran. They were not officially part of the Secret Service. They were not answerable to anyone in Algeria. Their status and even their existence were unrecorded in any Government budget. The nearest they came even to definition was that they seemed to be a shadowy offshoot of the S.D.E.C.E., the *Serv-*

ice de Documentation Extérieure et de Contre-Espionnage. Yet they existed, they were there and while they lasted they were extremely disagreeable. They left arrests to the police. Their mission was to eliminate.

They were, in fact, a special force loyal to the person of Charles de Gaulle. Their origins dated back to 1940, to the curiously exciting and idealistic days of the Free French in London. The Free French Army of 1940 was not a very impressive lot; indeed among the armies of the world it held a position resembling that of Charlie Brown's baseball team. Some of the members were dispossessed Englishmen who had grown up in France. Many were French Jews in transit to New York. Yet a small hard core, under the inspiration of de Gaulle, held it together until it throve and became the French Army. That hard core was at de Gaulle's side on the day of his entry into liberated Paris in 1944. When he retired, the hard core retired too; most of its members returned to their families and businesses. A few remained in the Army and fought in Indochina. But they lived for only one man, Charles de Gaulle, and awaited his return as others awaited the second coming of Christ. So far there is nothing dishonorable in the story. This band of men, of whom perhaps 50 percent were Jewish, could be credited with loyalty and idealism. But the men who came to Algeria to help stamp out the O.A.S. were reinforced by others, French Black and Tans attracted by the pay, which sometimes amounted to $300 a day. Nor were these men the worst. There was also a large number of Vietnamese, among them killers from the former Bande Noire, specialists in torturing Vietminh prisoners.

Because the public was aware of this group's existence and because the members had no official name, they were given one—*barbouzes,* which means "the bearded ones," clowns with false beards, stock figures in French vaudeville. The chief of operations in Algiers was Yves le Tac, a Gaullist who had been captured by the Germans in 1942 and had spent three years in a prison camp. One of the heads in Paris was a sinister individual named Georges Figon, who some years later died mysteriously after being implicated in the abduction and murder of Ben Barka.

The Vietnamese were particularly detested and detestable in the view of the O.A.S., although it is doubtful that the philosophy of the Vietnamese was sufficiently advanced for them to understand why they should be so hated. Eight years earlier the French Army had watched the Vietnamese fleeing the North by the hundreds of thousands after Dien Bien Phu. It was partly compassion, partly guilt-complex for these refugees that had caused the intellectual and moral crisis among the officers that was the earliest germ of the O.A.S. The same refugees were now employed to destroy and torture the force that their plight had helped to create.

As soon as the *barbouzes* arrived, their losses began. The O.A.S. was too well entrenched and the population too small for strangers not to be recognized. O.A.S. intelligence men were always on the look-out. As the *barbouzes* disembarked at Maison Blanche Airport, hidden cameras took their pictures and airline agents copied their names from their passports. Later the same day posters would be pasted on the walls of Algiers with photographs and names and the words *"Barbouzes,* dead or alive." It was warning enough to chill the bravest of men.

As psychological warfare it was tremendously effective. The *barbouzes* changed their addresses every night, but four times in succession Degueldre's Deltas caught up with them and blew their headquarters to bits. The O.A.S. coined a name for these anti*barbouze* operations. They were called "punctualities."

On December 30, a real-estate agent called on Degueldre, and they took a taxi to Hydra. "I want to show you something," he said. They stopped the taxi and got out. "You see the villa down there," he said. "I've just rented it. Guess who to?"

"Everybody's looking for a villa," said Degueldre. "I'm looking for one myself."

"I've rented it to the *barbouzes.* They are moving in tomorrow night, New Year's Eve. Together. They are scared of being alone, and they need each other to give each other courage."

"It's not possible," Degueldre exclaimed. "All of them together at the same time!"

At his apartment on the Boulevard Telelmy he summoned twelve men from Delta 1, and, while Nicole listened, he outlined his plan. Two bazookas would be placed on the terrace of a nearby building. If the first did not score a hit, the other would adjust its range instantly. As the *barbouzes* sought to escape, they would run into an ambush. The operation was timed for ten minutes before midnight. Curfew was at midnight, and there would be little traffic in the streets.

At 11:30 the commandos took up their positions. They could hear singing and laughing from inside the villa. A single sentry sat on the step at the entrance, but he went into the house at 11:45 and was not replaced. The first rocket went through a window and exploded, stopping the singing. The second miraculously landed in the *barbouzes'* armory, and the villa went up as if it had been bombed. The *barbouzes* ran out and into a stream of submachine-gun fire. Within seconds it was all over. The police were at the villa in two minutes, but the commandos had faded away into the night. O.A.S. observers among the ambulance men counted seventeen bodies taken from the villa.

The next day three lorries came to take the surviving *barbouzes,* their weapons and their documents to a new secret address near El Biar. To shake off any O.A.S. groups that might be seeking to tail them, the police set up a series of roadblocks, which closed behind the trucks as they passed. The driver of one truck, however, was an O.A.S. man and identified the new headquarters and the Villa Rejana, a three-story building that a hundred or more *barbouzes* were using. This time security precautions were stronger, and it took Degueldre nearly a month to formulate his plans. The result was the greatest O.A.S. victory of the war. At 5:00 in the evening of January 29 the villa crumbled to its foundations. When the cranes removed the rubble, 36 dead *barbouzes* were counted. The O.A.S. had booby-trapped a crate of duplicating machines, which had imprudently been left standing on a dock for several days before removal to the villa; forty kilos of plastic, an enormous charge, had been packed inside. The bodies of the *barbouzes* were flown to France and buried in the Santenay cemetery in Seine-et-Oise. Only one person, a Vietnamese woman, attended the burial ceremony.

At the beginning of February, the O.A.S. wounded Yves le Tac. They had almost gotten him once before with a bomb in his car. This time he was shot as he drove his "deux chevaux" through the tunnel under the University. He managed to drive to the Maillot Hospital and collapsed at the door. The hospital was not considered safe enough, and he was flown to the Val-de-Grâce military hospital in Paris, where he was put under police guard. The O.A.S. tried again. Pierre Sergent ordered a military commando of eight men under the personal direction of Godot and Robin to go in and finish him off, but they found the room guarded by police. There was a flurry of shots, one policeman was killed and the O.A.S. made off.

Nobody loved the *barbouzes*. The police, used to the norms of criminal detection, resented their immunity and clandestinity. The military commanders were angry when *barbouzes* appeared in their areas and often declined to cooperate. The Vietnamese, although easily identifiable, had an advantage in their language; their radio communications, though tapped, proved difficult to decode. They knew the subtler and more painful arts of persuasion, so much so that, on more than one occasion when the O.A.S. heard that one of its number was in Vietnamese hands, they informed the police in hopes that the latter might "rescue" him.

Once an O.A.S. commando opened fire on a car that was taking four wounded and bandaged *barbouzes* to hospital. The car swerved and crashed into a lamppost. Without waiting to see whether the occupants were dead or alive, the O.A.S. men threw gasoline over the car and set it on fire. As they fled through the streets, the crowds cheered, and the police made no effort to stop them.

Altogether the intervention of the *barbouzes* was a bad psychological error. It achieved little except to intensify the venom in the Algerian atmosphere, which was poisonous enough to begin with; but as no one in authority even so much as admitted their existence, who could be blamed?

✠✠✠

It was with the greatest optimism that General Salan issued his New Year message. It was addressed to "all regional commanders in Algeria, General Challe (Toul), General Faure (Santé), Captain Lucchetti (la Petite Roquette), and all regional commanders in Metropolitan France." In it he proclaimed that "1962 is the year of hope, the year of triumph. As we have shown in combat we shall find ourselves again united for the victory which we shall all have earned equally." The message was counter signed by Captain Sergent.

Two weeks later the Captain was able to report still another propaganda triumph, the acquisition of a new colonel, one of the most formidable of them all, Colonel Pierre Château-Jobert. Château-Jobert was one of France's most legendary soldiers. When the 1939 war began he had been 27 years old. He was wounded in the Battle of France but escaped to England a month later and joined the Free French under the name of "Captain Conan," a name that stayed with him throughout his career. He fought in the unpleasant, fratricidal campaign in Syria. Later, in Libya, he was one of the heroes of Bir Hakeim. He fought through the Indochinese campaign as a colonial parachute officer and was made commander of the 2nd R.C.P. in 1955. He parachuted into Port Saïd in November 1956 and was considered France's first hero of that brief campaign. Afterward he returned to resume fighting in Algeria.

He was another small colonel, no bigger than Argoud, tempestuous, almost impossible to control. In 1959 he was judged politically suspect and sent to simmer down in Bayonne, where he commanded a brigade of parachutists. He was one of the "Committee of Colonels" that planned the Putsch, but he was far away in Niamey, Niger, when it took place. Château-Jobert was no man to temporize. He immediately announced his support of the revolt, and, as it collapsed almost before the words were out of his mouth, he was brusquely recalled to France, where because of his exceptional combat record he was given only 45 days house arrest. He was next appointed to the 3rd Military Region at Rennes and so carefully watched by security officers that it was not until January 16 that he was able to escape to Algiers.

Château-Jobert was a frightening little man, with a prim, cruelly pursed mouth and a disdainful nose; he looked as if he were used to dealing with people beneath his dignity. A small but thick black beard contrasted startlingly with a head shaved bald, making him seem a kind of latter-day Landru. But what struck one most forcefully were his eyes, fixed and glowing with the light one associates with Savonarola or the early saints. Château-Jobert was ideally cast. He was a religious mystic and reminded one observer of the Carlist Pretender who named the Vírgen del Pilar as general of his armies. Châeau-Jobert lived on a precarious mental platform that threatened to tilt at any time into serious madness.

He frightened even Roger Degueldre, although not for any conventional reason. A rendezvous had been arranged at a certain café in Algiers, where it was planned that Degueldre would brief the new prize recruit and at the same time weigh him in his own mind. As it happened he was able to do the latter but decided against the former. Degueldre had lived in hiding and disguise for nine months, and it came naturally to him, even to the dark glasses equipped with small rearview mirrors. It scarcely occurred to him that disguise was an art that had to be learned. As he was about the enter the café, he was stopped by a startling apparition. Château-Jobert was sitting at a table with a glass of beer in front of him. He still wore what was probably the best-known beard in Algeria. He also wore a green Tyrolean hat complete with feather and puffed a huge Tyrolean pipe, the bowl of which he cradled fondly at chest level. The other customers in the café were staring at him and whispering "Château-Jobert" and "Conan" to one another. A man sitting with a girl at a neighboring table leaned over and said excitedly, "Colonel, have you joined us?"

Château-Jobert smiled conspiratorially and put a finger to his lips. Degueldre in the doorway, went white and fled.

Although the O.A.S. announced Château-Jobert's arrival as a major propaganda victory, his actual reception was cooler than one might have logically expected. Susini especially distrusted the sudden appearance of a man capable of dominating the whole O.A.S. apparatus. General Salan had suggested to Susini that Château-Jobert should go to Oran to help Jouhaud, but Susini had other ideas and persuaded Salan to send him instead to Constantine, which was a backwater of the O.A.S. war and where the Colonel stood an excellent chance of being killed. The F.L.N. almost from the beginning of the war in 1954 had remained entrenched in the Constantine countryside, defying all French attempts to eject it. The French retained control of the cities of Bône and Constantine, but even there their position was uncomfortable. Constantine had the smallest European population of any major city in the country—fifteen thousand, of whom only eight thousand were Frenchmen, living among 220,000 Moslems.

Susini did a good sales job on Château-Jobert: "You will be really impressed when you get there, Colonel," he argued. "It is the most enthusiastic area in favor of French Algeria. What it needs is a real leader capable of uniting the military and civilian elements. Also the police there are with us to a man. Quite honestly you would be wasting your time in Oran. Jouhaud and Camelin have done a fabulous job and there really isn't anything to do. Constantine is the place for you."

"The bastard literally kidnapped me," Château-Jobert recalled later. "I had no reason to be suspicious. Nor did the others try to explain the situation to me because if I had really been put in the picture, and saw who was running what, I'd have packed my bags and gone back to France."

As it was, he went to Constantine. Some of the more thoughtful members of the O.A.S.—men like Captain Ferrandi, who had plenty of time for reflection—were disturbed by the mystical quality that Château-Jobert contributed to the band. The original designers of the O.A.S. after the Putsch were, in their own way, pragmatists, practical men who understood what they were trying to do. They were Godard, Gardes, Gardy, Susini, Perez, Degueldre and, from a distance, Salan. Since then, the organization had been progressively splitting between the realists and the mystics. Nearly all the latter were graduates of the monastery of Father Grasset. Beside Château-Jobert they included André Canal, Philippe le Pivain, Delhomme, Broizat (despite his warnings to Argoud and his flirtation with the Salvation Army), Lacheroy and even Lagaillarde. Hovering uneasily between the two were Argoud and de Blignières. The realists had simple aims: to keep Algeria French, to force the Army into violent action against the F.L.N. and, if possible, to bring down de Gaulle. The mystics were introducing all sorts of mumbo jumbo into the movement and talked about monarchism, antirepublicanism, corporate statism, Pétainism, the supremacy of the Church. Their enemy was not so much the F.L.N. or de Gaulle as the freemasons, the Jews, the Rosicrucians. If the influx of mystics continued, it could be safely predicted that the O.A.S. would ultimately change into a completely different kind of force.

✤✤✤

They were dangerous and exciting days in Algeria, and escapes were narrow and frequent. Colonel Godard was arrested for carrying false papers. At the commissariat he told the police chief: "You know who I am and I know you. I am 'Claude,' Colonel Godard. I appeal to you as a Frenchman and a patriot to let me go." The police chief turned away and looked out the window. He did not turn back until Godard had gone.

Degueldre, driving an old Citroën, crossed a busy main street on an amber light and was stopped by a traffic policeman well known in Algiers for his severity. He peered into Degueldre's car, examined his papers and handed them back. "If children had been crossing at that moment, you would have been in serious trouble," he said. "I could

bring a criminal charge against you. Fortunately for you we have
other things to worry about these days. Now get going and don't let
me or any other flic see your ugly face again, Lieutenant Degueldre."

Philippe le Pivain, hearing noises that sounded like policemen in
the street, sprang from the bed he was sharing with a friend, dressed
hastily and left by the back door even as the front doorbell rang. He
was promptly seized by a second group of gendarmes who, being
French, could recognize a fleeing paramour when they saw one. "We
understand your problem," they said. "But don't be caught out in the
curfew." They released him, and the girl he had left called to him:
"Philippe come back. The police have brought my dog back. It was
lost."

But le Pivain did not survive much longer. Since the beginning of
the O.A.S., he had been working hard trying to persuade the Legionnaires at Sidi-bel-Abbès to join the revolt, and he had become one of
the Organization's most respected leaders. Driving through Algiers one
evening on a certain specific mission, he was stopped by a sudden
roadblock of Gardes Mobiles, who flashed a spotlight on him. Desperately le Pivain braked and threw the gears into a crash reverse, but
before he could turn a whole battery of tommy guns opened up and
killed him. Le Pivain's loss was a bad blow, but it was the manner of
his death that was disturbing. The police had known that he was
coming and were waiting for him. The only people who knew of le
Pivain's mission were the senior officers of the Organization. For the
first time, the suspicion arose that one of the inner circle was playing
a double game.

✛✛✛

Nevertheless, Salan was well content with the achievements of his
men. In a proclamation dated February 23, he noted that he was
"particularly satisfied to note that the past week has been marked by
actions of high value at all levels" and addressed his congratulations
to all those responsible.

> Whether it be the lifting of arms at Oran, Bône and Boghari,
> with the magnificent intervention at El Biar on the villa
> of the *barbouzes,* or of the explosion of the radio station

on the Igamie of Algiers, or the sabotage of a ship at Bône, or the spectacular holdups at Algiers and Oran, they are the witnesses of initiative and uncontestable physical courage. . . .

In the form of war which we are now waging everything is to be commended that demoralizes and neutralizes the adversary, consolidates our positions and ameliorates our means. Once again we must take the arms that are in the depots of our adversary, we must take the money that is in his banks.

Salan then became slightly defensive:

I do not deny that certain actions can lend themselves to criticism and entail certain regrettable errors. . . . We are not making war or coming down into the streets with choir boys and lounge lizards but with men of stout heart, and that must be understood. . . . I am taking this occasion to renew the green light for all profitable and spectacular actions, such as those that have just been executed. Signed, Salan.

Two weeks later, a Delta commando in Oran obliged the Mandarin by robbing the Bank of Algeria of $4,250,000.

❖❖❖

All these events occurred during the period of Argoud's incarceration in the Canaries, creating new situations, new problems of leadership and decision, with which he had to come to terms. His escape, coinciding with the bank theft and the triumphant pronunciamentos of Salan, was jubilantly hailed in Algiers as a new victory for the O.A.S. At last it was possible for the O.A.S. to have a real leader. Previously there had been little overall control. Salan was little more than a figurehead. Degueldre was the master technician but overworked and hampered by his low rank. Lagaillarde was distrusted by everyone. Susine concentrated on politics and intrigue. Gardy was too old, Château-Jobert too unstable. The worst disappointment was Godard. Godard, more than any other of the officers, fretted at his clandestine existence. As head of the Sûreté in Algiers he had been a person of great power, commanding many men and much respect. The colonel of a regiment is in many ways like a ruling monarch. A colonel without a regiment is nothing more than a *Monsieur*. Another bitter problem for Godard was his love for the city of Algiers. Almost every man has in his heart a city in which everything seems to go right for him, usually one quite different from his place of origin. For Godard Algiers was the personal battlefield on which he had won his dramatic victory over Yacef Saadi in the Battle of Algiers in 1957. Godard loved the smells of Algiers and the intrigues. He loved the Moslem markets and the sounds of Arabs at prayer. He had selected Tipasa, a bay about forty miles from Algiers, as the place where he would build a house on retirement.

Retirement, there was the rub. There was no retirement in the O.A.S. Godard missed his uniform. He missed the salutes. He was a shadow of the man who had done most to start the O.A.S. the previous May. Ultimately it was Degueldre who lost patience with him. There was little love lost between the two men, and in February Degueldre told him what he thought of him after Godard had spoken in dreamy fashion about "honor."

"You don't do what I have been doing as a matter of honor," said Degueldre. "Your *armour propre* has no interest for me. Forget the big words and the scruples, and all your pangs of conscience. Our business is French Algeria. I've done my part. Everyone in Algeria knows that I am the head of the Deltas. If I get caught I am under no illusions about what they will do to me. But I've accepted my responsibilities. Now you accept yours or move over for someone else. The Deltas are winning all their battles but you bosses are losing the war."

Godard thereupon and without protest removed himself from active command; his job was given to Colonel Roland Vaudrey, who had seen the inside of prison and did not like it and was thus less nostalgic for his decorations and lace bars. As a result of the gradual shifts of emphasis in the Organization, the inner council now consisted of Susini, Gardes, Vaudrey and Degueldre. Dr. Perez, like Godard, had been gradually edged to the sidelines, and Jacques Achard, a *pied noir,* had become, more than Perez, the spokesman for the Bab-el-Oued lobby. A new leader was urgently required. Argoud should have been the man. Only Susini was against him. Not only would he have been welcomed in Algeria as an effective commander of the O.A.S., but also several Army units that had no time for Salan would have rallied to him; at least that was the considered opinion of Colonel de Blignières. The preoccupation of the O.A.S. with Antoine

Argoud was curious. So far he had been worse than useless. He had been responsible for drawing in Maurice Gingembre. He had loafed around Madrid mixing with the wrong crowd, and he had allowed himself to be shut up in the Canaries for nearly five months. Even so, most of the O.A.S. preferred to study his potential than his record.

Alas, Argoud was still not prepared to accept the Organization as it was. Once more impulsive action had been followed with indecision. The Hamlet of the O.A.S. had gone broody again. He made a tour of French Army messes in Germany, talking to officers and urging them to back the Organization, but he made no move in the direction of Algiers.

As usual, the one who understood Argoud best was Broizat. In a note to Argoud he gave his impressions of the O.A.S. as it stood at that moment, that is to say, at the crest of the wave. Broizat could understand the policy of violence even while deploring it:

> Violence could oblige the Army to come to the aid of the Resistance in spite of itself. Violence worked for the F.L.N., indeed without it de Gaulle would never have abandoned Algeria to the Algerian Provisional Government. I have said that personally I was always opposed to blind terrorism. I opposed it as a Christian and I opposed it as a man of the west. We have absolutely no right, even on the question of efficiency, to use methods which are the negation of the values we are defending. It is for this reason that we condemned the F.L.N. and that we condemn the Gaullist régime which uses the same processes with the *barbouzes*. [Our condemnation] is one of the essential reasons that justifies our resistance.

He added wearily, "The O.A.S. point of view is different." It is not irrelevant that the Bay of Pigs disaster had taken place only six months before. Although Broizat never mentioned it and may not even have thought of it, the nightmare of some parallel disaster haunted his mind. "Under no circumstances," he continued "must the O.A.S. conduct a pitched battle or hole itself up in a building or even a defined area. The consequence would be the rapid end of our fighting teams, which in spite of appearances and propaganda, are not very numerous."

But a pitched battle was precisely the subject on the agenda of the inner council of the O.A.S., and neither Argoud nor Broizat was there to oppose it.

PART THREE:
THE FRENZY

17
BATTLEGROUND
March 1962

❖❖❖

Negotiations between the French and the Algerians were resumed on February 21 under conditions flattering to the O.A.S. They were begun, not at Évian as before, but in the obscure ski resort of Les Russes in the Jura. The negotiators wore ski clothes and dark glasses and arrived by helicopter with strong police escorts. The O.A.S., whether absent or present, haunted them all. Otherwise, the Algerian leaders held all the trumps. They were well aware that General de Gaulle urgently needed an agreement to restore calm to the country and free himself to pursue his own wider policies. But the O.A.S. was *there,* a malevolent ghost that set the negotiators' nerves on edge and made them lose their tempers. One of the Algerian delegates complained about the French police in Algeria, "who should be 'Algerianized' immediately because the Commissioners are too passive, and the administration is hand in glove with the O.A.S."

Louis Joxe, the chief French representative, replied angrily: "Let's be serious. If there is a difficult and painful job to be done, as there is, you know quite well, it's not a question of whether the police is more Algerian or less Algerian. The only force that can keep the peace is the French Army."

But the negotiations continued, and little by little agreement was reached on all matters: on the Sahara, on the conditions for a cease-fire, on the great naval base at Mers-el-Kébir, on the cooperation between the police forces.

But consciousness tends to lag behind reality, and in Algeria the O.A.S., concerned with its own tasks and problems, worked from

day to day with little idea of the changing mood of France or of
how quickly the Organization was becoming an anachronism. In
France even the anti-de Gaulle press had become less critical and
derisive. *Le Monde* in a major front-page editorial said:

> For the first time perhaps in seven years . . . we are close
> to our goal and, before that, an end to the fighting. There
> is something moving, tragic, in seeing, in hearing, this
> lone man, intrepid, immovable, sure of himself, seeking to
> communicate here and elsewhere the certainties at which
> he has arrived across the eddies that for three years carried
> him so far in the opposite direction from what he had
> hoped, planned, declared and which events cruelly gave
> the lie at a time when he believed himself powerful enough
> to command them. These certainties, which he gained at
> the cost of his own disavowals, are that there is a deter-
> minism to history, that Continental France retains its po-
> tential as a great power, with an eminent role to play . . .
> and that no alternative exists to the phenomenon, soon to
> be universal of decolonization.

Such views, like the developments at Évian, were received in
Algeria with almost total incomprehension, and life continued as
though Algeria were quite alone in the world. At the beginning of
March, General Salan, chafing at his disguises, sought dignity by
writing a series of open letters. Some were challenging, some queru-
lous, but all seemed designed, as publicity people would say, to
improve the Mandarin's public image. He wrote to Michel Debré,
the Prime Minister, to *Le Monde*, to Antoine Pinay, to Guy Mollet,
to all the prefects of France. Typical was the letter he wrote to Roger
Frey, who as Minister of the Interior was responsible for the forces
of law and order:

> You know that in spite of all the luxury of your means
> you have not succeeded in neutralizing our Organization.
> In answer to your tortures, your exactions, your brutalities,
> our combatants are replying with exemplary faith and de-
> termination. You have created, and this is one of the
> principal disgraces of your régime, the "barbouzes" (be-
> cause that is what we call them). To do it you have been
> obliged to appeal to the Communist Party and to unprinci-
> pled mercenaries. Not only have their actions failed to

reach the heart of our movement, but we have handed them such severe blows that in spite of the fabulous sums you have paid them they have been filled with terror, and you can see them leaving for yourself.

Of the tactical victory of the O.A.S. there could be no doubt. In Algiers the *barbouzes* were penned in secret hideaways and had all but given up. In Oran, where a stranger is quickly recognized, they were eliminated almost as soon as they alighted from train or airplane. But even as the power of the O.A.S. in the Algerian cities reached its peak, it began to atrophy and die. It was like a play that had attracted a fortune from backers and an all-star cast but was unable to find a stage. What happens in the theater is that the backing withers away.

What was eating at the foundations of the O.A.S. was, as always, time—or the absence of it. Realizing that the negotiations at Évian were almost at the point of agreement, the O.A.S. ordered demonstrations and strikes that were almost 100 percent effective. It also ordered "Operation Rock and Roll," a series of 120 plastic-bomb explosions in Algiers. The *pieds noirs* desperately hoped to goad the Moslems into a riot that would have to be put down by the Army, but the Moslems could sense the approach of independence and maintained an almost inhuman calm and discipline in the face of murderous provocation.

A sense of futility was growing within the fighting cadres of the O.A.S. It had already been summed up by Degueldre in his attack on Yves Godard when he said, "My Deltas are winning their batles but you bosses are losing the war." This feeling that victory was slipping away led to a meeting in El Biar at the end of February to discuss some form of spectacular mass action. Susini represented Salan, and Major Camelin came from Oran to represent Jouhaud. Jacques Achard represented Bab-el-Oued and Colonel Vaudrey, Colonel Gardes and Lieutenant Degueldre represented themselves.

Gardes reported that he had been recruiting young men wanted by the police and had turned them into an efficient military force in the bled. "For six months," he said, "I have been touring the officers' messes, both European and Moslem, and I believe that an uprising, properly planned would stimulate them to come out on our side."

"Where would you arrange the uprising?" Vaudrey asked.

"The Ouarsenis," said Gardes. "It is wild. It is a natural fortress.

It is not far from Sidi-bel-Abbès. It has good lines of communication to Algiers and Oran, and the Moslems are pro-French."

Susini disagreed rudely. "Any mass action that we take," he said, "must be taken here in Algiers. Algiers is the heart and the soul and the symbol of French Algeria. We almost run the city as it is. The Mobiles hide behind sandbags. Now would be a good time to take it over formally."

Achard was doubtful. "We might be the masters of Algiers but even so about ten Europeans are killed every day by the F.L.N. First of all we have got to put the fear of God into the Mussulmans and put them down. The *pieds noirs* will have to feel they are at home and safe in Algiers, not simply living in a town honeycombed with fellagha."

Gardes, who was as always intensely pro-Moslem, was pained by this sentiment. "I have been working and living with the Moslems for months," he said. "Without Moslem cooperation you can throw your French Algeria into the sea."

Susini sneered. "Your so-called friendly Moslems will turn into F.L.N. ultras the moment they think the F.L.N. will win."

Degueldre said nothing. He was watching Susini curiously. He had heard rumors that Susini was secretly planning to negotiate with the F.L.N. It had also been reported to him that Susini had informed the police against le Pivain for reasons of his own. It was strange how the emphasis of the O.A.S. was changing. Godard was more or less in retirement. Broizat was gone. Château-Jobert had been hastily rusticated—by Susini. Lagaillarde was afraid to come to Algeria—because he thought Susini would kill him. The inner councils of the O.A.S. were thinning. But there was always Susini.

"You can do nothing without Army help," Gardes was saying. "With the Army . . ."

"Oh, damn the Army!" Susini shouted. "I'm fed up to the gills with the Army. The Army had its chance on May 13, 1958, and on January 24, 1960, and on April 22, 1961, and it messed it up every time. We are on our own, and this time we have to rely on what we have got."

Gardes replied angrily: "Without the Army you are nothing. It is thanks to the Army and its sympathetic passivity that we are all sitting here now."

"Here in Algiers," Susini said, "we have the men and the means for a rising. It is not going to be pretty, but it's either that or we have to pack our bags. We have to do *something*."

'I don't like it," said Degueldre, speaking for the first time. "But I agree with you that some form of mass action is necessary or we will simply wither on the vine, and in two months we won't have anybody left. My boys are getting restive. They need action. If they don't get it they will start looking for trouble."

"I'm not saying my plan is easy," said Susini. "I don't say it is perfect, but it is the only way we can act as a catalyst for all the forces in favor of French Algeria. I repeat we can only count on ourselves, and there are just so many solutions."

"All right," said Gardes. "I am not going to stop you. But I am not going to help either. I'm going to keep my forces intact, because I have an idea you are going to need them some day."

The Évian agreement was signed March 18; it included an automatic cease-fire between the French Army and the F.L.N. Officially the war was over. At 5:30 in the evening, General de Gaulle, his voice breaking with emotion, appeared on television to proclaim the end of hostilities and an agreement that "would henceforth enable Moslems and Frenchmen to walk along the road of civilization together as brothers." His only reference to the O.A.S. was an oblique mention of "certain former Army elements" whom he called "misguided chiefs and criminal adventurers."

Half an hour after de Gaulle spoke, Ben Khedda, who had replaced Ferhat Abbas as head of the Algerian Provisional Government, spoke from Tunis and announced to Algerians the end of the war. He called it a great victory for Algeria and ordered a cease-fire. He also warned:

> The period of transition will demand the greatest vigilance. A cease-fire is not a peace. The dangers are enormous. The Fascist hordes and racist-minded O.A.S., despairing of maintaining their French Algeria, will try once more to drown the land with blood. Up to now, the French civil and military authorities have been more or less the accomplices of the O.A.S. In the prior interests of peace and cooperation between the two countries, this complicity must come to an end.

The irreverent Paris weekly, *Le Canard Enchaîné* made its own Buchwald-esque comment on the end of the war:

When a gentleman says one day to his nation, "Algeria is a
French land today and forever" (de Gaulle, June 6th,
1958) and another day proclaims "Algeria will be a sov-
ereign independent state" (October 2nd, 1961) that is
rather crazy. Well, let's skip that. To the man who would
bring us on a silver platter the end of the Algerian war,
whoever that man was, we were ready to take off our hat.
You could say we have been waiting for that man. It could
have been Guy Mollet but it wasn't. It could have been
de Gaulle in 1958, de Gaulle in 1959, de Gaulle in 1960,
de Gaulle in 1961. But it was not any of those de Gaulles.
It could have been Salan in 1964 if he had managed a
successful revolt in 1961. However, at the end of it all,
it was de Gaulle just the same. So, long live de Gaulle. . . .

France sighed with relief. So far as the Métropole was concerned,
the agreement marked the end of the Algerian affair. Whatever
sympathy the majority of Frenchmen might once have had for the
pieds noirs, the cause of French Algeria and the O.A.S., it drained
away before the cold inevitability of the cease-fire. The French had
been sufficiently devoted to Algeria to spend eight years fighting to
keep it. But that was all over. Algeria was like a star actor stranded
in the middle of the stage halfway through his speech with the lights
of the auditorium on and the audience making for the doors. The
French saw quite clearly that Algeria was not French at all and
never had been. Almost all the Europeans who lived there were
clustered in the seaport cities, a foreign and unassimilated body in
a vast country. The problem was not French Algeria or Algerian
Algeria. It was the simpler one of what to do with a million stranded
Europeans with Spanish names and French citizenship.

But the Algerian soil is fertile in illusions, and the *pieds noirs*
could still not really believe the extent to which their cause had
been abandoned. There was still a referendum to come in Metropolitan France in April, and that, they assured themselves, would undoubtedly result in an unqualified rejection of the Évian agreement.
France had invested too much money and too many lives in Algeria,
they said. In the meantime, there was no waving of flags or pealing
of bells. The agreement was signed. The ball was in the court of the
O.A.S. It had to crown its victories or admit defeat.

As the altercation between Gardes and Susini had shown, the

O.A.S. was still divided into two uneasily matched sections: one military and stratified, and the other *pied noir*, civilian, committed, still conditioned by the bittersweet nostalgia of May 13, 1958. The military plan drawn up by Gardes was ingenious and well thought out; if successful, it would have permitted the O.A.S. to leave its cellars, abandon its pseudonyms and emerge as an established force with which the authorities would have had to deal, whether they liked it or not. Susini's plan, in the hands of *pieds noirs*, led to the kind of party to which one goes with the precise intention of getting drunk, and to hell with the hangover.

It happened first in Bab-el-Oued. But who now spoke for Bab-el-Oued? Perez, the good doctor, was in political eclipse. After the Putsch he had made the mistake of agreeing to share the direction of O.R.O. with Roger Degueldre, but the force of Degueldre's personality had so overshadowed him that Perez was left with almost nothing to do except write "subversive" letters to Lagaillarde and the other "Spaniards," fulminating against Degueldre and Susini, words that were extremely well received by the Canaries community.

Achard was a comparatively minor figure. The only other possible leader was little Jésus Giner, the tomtit taxi driver, and his band of goons. One invariably spoke of him as "little Jésus," usually with the kind of smile one keeps for the rapscallion who is always getting into trouble but at whom one cannot really get angry because of his disarming smile. He was good-looking in the feral, Mediterranean manner, scarcely 5 feet 6 inches tall, heavily sunburned, with thick black hair, bushy eyebrows and eyes that twinkled with the pleasure of a dirty joke, for example, or a punch on somebody else's nose. He was a compulsive bottom pincher, and it was said that after he had made his tour of the Algiers bordellos the girls were given a day or two of rest to recover their strength.

Giner was a complete man of the earth. By speaking of food he could make one hungry. Rarely can a human personality have been less aptly christened than he. He was more a combination of Bill Sykes and Dennis the Menace than the Savior.

Giner as a boy had had a brief spell in 1st R.E.C. at the end of the war, and he liked to speak of himself as a Legionnaire. He had also been a boxer, a jockey, a construction worker, as well as a taxi driver and drifter. In the capital of the ultras he was king, a good king in that he showed a certain prudence. With the others, he plasticated the premises of *pieds noirs* who had fled to France, but in his own way he was a family man and had sent his wife and children to the safety of Europe.

The events of March had played into Giner's hands. The military operation planned by Colonel Gardes had resulted in a thinning of the O.A.S. forces in Algiers. Delhomme, operational commander of the Z commandos under Susini, had disappeared with other members of the elite cadres. As the bulk of the Z commandos in Algiers was based in Bab-el-Oued, Delhomme's absence left a hiatus into which Giner moved quite naturally.

In the days following the cease-fire, the walls of Algiers were adorned with posters showing a European child embracing a Moslem child. On the morning of March 22, these posters were ripped down in Bab-el-Oued, and Giner's men substituted their own posters, which challenged the Army: "If you do not evacuate by midnight you will be considered troops of an alien Government." The Lycée Bugeaud, which formed a kind of frontier post between Bab-el-Oued and Climat-de-France, was reinforced. The formation of the Bab-el-Oued district, bordered by the sea, Climat-de-France and the Casbah, was such that no one could enter it without being seen from the Lycée, and for several months a system of telecommunications had been in operation between the school and the various command posts (for "command posts" read "bars"). At the same time drums of oil were placed at every crossroad, and five hundred kilos of rusty nails were distributed in bags for throwing onto the greasy streets.

The Bab-el-Oued poster would have been a bellicose statement at any time, but it was especially foolhardy when most of the O.A.S. professionals were away and Roger Degueldre had promised no more than diversionary incidents in other parts of the city in case of an uprising. But the Army might have shown greater discretion at such a hypersensitive hour of Algerian history. The posters demonstrated nothing more than traditional Bab-el-Oued bravado. The citizens always talked that way, and they could be a nasty lot. What it amounted to was that Jésus Giner was saying, "I can lick any man in this bar." Colonial paratroop or Legion officers would probably have understood and stayed away from the area until the shock of the Évian agreement had lessened a little. The citizens of

The Bachaga Boualem. "If I said I approved of the O.A.S. I would be lying. If I said I disapproved I would be lying. I believe in only one thing, French Algeria." A.F.P. *from* PICTORIAL

Pierre Lagaillarde. "A man of charm, good looks and charisma . . . but removed to the sidelines he could only watch the machine he had created destroy itself." *Paris Match*

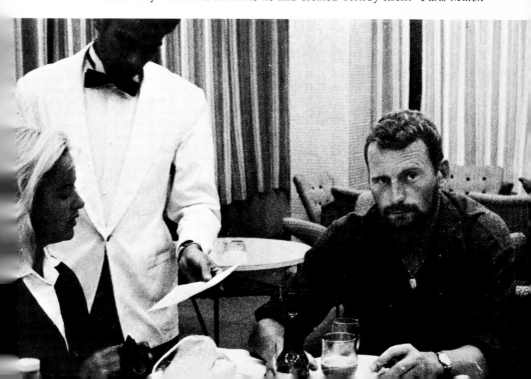

Joseph Ortiz. The cafe proprietor who became a kind of symbol of French Algeria. His supporters called him "Uncle Joe." *Wide World*

Sergeant Dovecar. The paradox. "Gentle, much-loved. He could play Beethoven beautifully and killed unarmed, defenseless men without compunction." *Property of Chantal de Blignières*

Colonel Chateau-Jobert. "A brilliant officer. He lived on a precarious mental platform that threatened to tilt at any time into a serious madness." *Paris Match*

Colonel Argoud. "The Hamlet of the O.A.S. . . . whose instinct for violent action was interspersed with periods of agonizing reappraisal." *Paris Match*

Lt. Degueldre. With cigarette. He liked to say, "No photos, no letters, no souvenirs." This is a rare snapshot. *Property of Jacqueline Coatalem*

Captain Sergent. O.A.S. head in Paris. "Uncatchable, almost invisible . . . How does one find a master-terrorist when he looks like Stanley Laurel?" A.F.P. *from* PICTORIAL

General Gardy. "The old warrior was angry . . . 'Violence certainly' he said 'We are not a party of academic opposition.' " A.F.P. *from* PICTORIAL

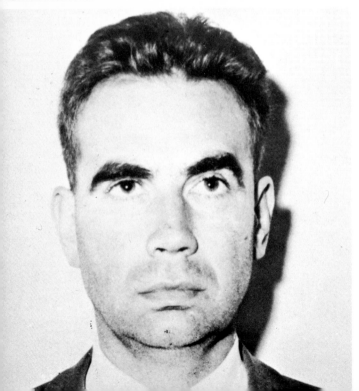

Bastien-Thiry. A prison photo. "A devout Catholic, he believed that in attempting to assassinate the President he had the blessing of the Church." *Paris Match*

General Katz. "When the O.A.S. became his enemy, he allowed no feelings of former comradeship to deter him from his duty as he saw it." *Paris Match*

Tixier-Vignancourt. "He was to the French Bar what Jean Gabin was to the cinema. One feels that neither would have had any difficulty in playing the other's role." *Wide World*

Cap Madrague, near Algiers. The O.A.S. still keeps guard on sunbathers. But the end was near. Photograph taken two months be-

Massacre on the Rue d'Isly. The main post office, April 7, 1962. "The worst atrocity of the war . . . it had to share headlines with the capture of a general." *Paris Match*

The Exodus. Maison Blanche Airport, Algiers, May 1965. In order to leave one needed an exit visa issued by the O.A.S. Otherwise no ticket. A.F.P. *from* PICTORIAL

Bab-el-Oued were entitled to their human grief. But the troops stationed in the area were conscripts who scarcely knew what was happening and knew only that they might be going home.

Reports were sent to Giner in his command post in the Bar Alexandre. One hundred and twenty men, mostly wearing camouflage uniforms and O.A.S. armbands, were at their posts ready to report any Army movement.

At 7:00 in the morning of March 23, a patrol of troops was surrounded by a band of heavily armed *pieds noirs* and, after a brief argument, submitted to the inevitable, giving up their arms and withdrawing. Two hours later an Army truck was ordered to stop. The French officer in charge told the driver to accelerate, and the truck rammed into the line of cocked tommy guns. The attackers, scared by the noise of war and the screams of the dying soldiers, fled. The truck was taken in tow and brought back to the military roadblock at Climat-de-France, where the appalled troops came to the assistance of their comrades. A truck full of dead and dying men is an obscene sight. Five men, all Army conscripts with an average of three months' service, were dead, and twelve more were wounded. The officer in charge died on the way to the hospital. The story spread and was magnified through the military ranks of the city. The soldiers had already had their fill of the arrogance of Bab-el-Oued, and they were enraged at this senseless killing of innocent boys. A military cordon was set up around the district. It was not the kind of friendly cordon that the soldiers had set up before, the kind through which the *pieds noirs* and O.A.S. moved freely. Instead it sealed the district tightly, and the Army, supported by Gardes Mobiles, filed through the streets. Ever since the Barricades, the Mobiles had been waiting to come to terms with the *pieds noirs,* who had killed fourteen of their number on the steps of the Forum. The *pieds noirs* knew that the Mobiles detested them, but they could never really understand why; it was one of the character failings of the Europeans of Algiers that they failed to understand why the victims of their hysteria did not appreciate the high principles that motivated it.

At sight of the invaders, the *pieds noirs* tossed Molotov cocktails from the windows of their apartments; they fired mortars from the roofs and bazookas from behind sandbagged barriers. They strewed oil and nails in the streets, and trucks skidded and spun like

tops but somehow continued their slithering advance. The trick had
worked at the Barricades, but it failed to stop angry soldiers. Resistance was determined, progress slow and casualties heavy on both
sides.

At midday, the angry fighting stopped. By a logic that was
inarguable in *pied noir* philosophy, there was a truce for lunch. At
first the Army commanders could scarcely believe it, and requests
for orders were sent as high as General Ailleret, Commander in
Chief of the Army in Algeria, who was directing the operations
personally. Ailleret was a man who jumped out of airplanes for
the fun of it, and he knew his *pieds noirs* from experience. Delighted, he told the Army and the police to accept the truce and to
prepare for more fighting afterward.

While the guards faced each other at the barbed-wire barricades,
fantastic scenes were occurring in Bab-el-Oued. The whole community flocked into the streets, the girls in their spring dresses, to
fill the sidewalk cafés, drink anisette and contemplate the devasta-
tion in the streets. Outside one café in the Place des Trois Horloges,
a military vehicle blazed. Meanwhile the police had invested the
heights of the Frais Vallon, from which they could direct fire down
into the streets. At 2:30, after coffee and cognac, the settlement of
bills and the arrangement of tips, the *pieds noirs* withdrew, and
the fighting started up again.

By now General Ailleret was deploying forty infantry battalions,
24,000 men in all, and four armored units. Colonel Broizat's nightmare had turned into brutal reality. The O.A.S. was fighting a
pitched battle in which it could not hope to escape annihilation. But
Bab-el-Oued fought back. Armored cars, nosing their way into the
Avenue Bouzarea, were hit with grenades and mortars. They withdrew but came back with reinforcements, accompanied by tanks,
which advanced up the avenue twenty yards apart and firing into
the shops. Helicopters drove the snipers from the roofs with tear-gas
grenades. Four American T-6 fighter planes flown by French Air
Force pilots made strafing runs at low altitudes over the roofs, firing
their machine guns at random.

The more disciplined O.A.S. commandos withdrew in reasonably
good order, barricading themselves in street block by street block,
but little by little they were driven first into the houses and then out
again by cannon fire. The end was only a matter of time. At one

roadblock a line of escaping cars was halted. The officer in command looked into the window of the first car and said, "No one leaves."

There were five men in the car, two in front and three behind. In the front passenger's seat, Jésus Giner smiled and pointed his tommy gun at the officer's face. "Do you stop us?" he asked. "Or do we kill you?"

"Keep going, Giner," said the officer. "I am not for you, or against you."

"Not just me," said Giner. "My men too. I haven't lost a man all day, and I want to keep my record clean."

"All of you," said the officer, and the line of cars passed through into the larger anonymity of Algiers.

Other Deltas, too, showed enterprise in penetrating the roadblocks. Ambulances took out O.A.S. men disguised as doctors and priests, and at least one left clad in top hat and morning coat at the wheel of an undertaker van, with his colleagues hidden in the two coffins.

The Battle of Bab-el-Oued was the first pitched battle of our affluent era. For the first time in history institutions like supermarkets stood in the firing line. Smashed television sets and transister radios were part of the rubble in the streets. Dishwashers and spindryers were victims of machine-gun fire. Some of the smashed and gutted shops announced in blue, silver and white that they honored the credit cards of the Diner's Club and American Express; in the bars, littered with broken bottles and reeking with the smell of cordite and aniseed, calendars askew on the wall advertised Air Algérie and "Pan American World Airways, the world's most experienced airline." Parked cars took a terrific pounding. Their petrol tanks exploded, and on streets like the Rue Cardinal Verdier between the Place des Trois Horloges and the Rue des Moulins every car was riddled with bullet holes.

The battle was over by nightfall, and silence, if not peace, came to Bab-el-Oued. While a chill rain fell, a house-to-house search for O.A.S. leaders began. In the old days, when sympathy for the O.A.S. had pervaded the Army, such searches had tended to be perfunctory, excuses for a rest, a chat and a glass with the locals. This time the Army, excited by the battle and by the bloodshed, was in the mood for outrage. The O.A.S. men who had not succeeded in escaping the roadblocks had hidden their uniforms and emblems, but pretense did not save them. Any man who looked as if he might have carried a gun was beaten and thrown downstairs to the Black Marias that lined the streets. The Army had recently received a report on anti-O.A.S. combat by General Joseph Katz, Army commander in Oran, who had made a detailed study of the subject. "The O.A.S. commandos are ingenious," General Katz had said. "They hide their arms and even themselves behind false walls and in false bottoms of cupboards and closets. A vase of flowers might conceal one or more grenades. . . ."

Soldiers wielded axes to smash down doors and walls. Goldfish bowls were upended to see what might be hidden among the pebbles at the bottom. People in their own homes, among them girls and children, were stripped naked and searched for arms.

General Katz had said, "A special source of danger is the upstairs window, from which bombs may be thrown on to patrol cars. . . ."

When the search was finished, a rigid curfew was ordered, and any open window or jalousie received a volley of 20-millimeter machine-gun fire. Many homes were wrecked in this fashion, and several people died.

The following morning, from the heights above the city, the troublesome suburb of Bab-el-Oued seemed drowned in black smoke, broken by an occasional belch of orange flame. While the rest of the city went about its business, shopped or attended the cinema, Bab-el-Oued remained sealed off. The casualties were grave. The French Army reported 16 men dead and 91 wounded. The *pieds noirs* admitted to losing 21 killed and 80 wounded, among them women and children, including Ghislaine Grès, aged 10, whose memorial notice recorded that she was "killed by a bullet in the head in Bab-el-Oued in the apartment of her parents." The actual casualty figure of the *pieds noirs* was probably double the official figure, for many wounded men were hidden and treated secretly by the local doctors. It was a tragedy, but it could be said at least that the O.A.S. had given Bab-el-Oued its martyrs, its Budapest, its Commune.

The loot, when it was counted, did not amount to much. The Army listed 579 hunting guns, 43 army rifles, 9 tommy guns, 263 grenades, 5 army radio sets, a ton of radio equipment, several hundred rounds of ammunition and two and a half tons of assorted military equipment.

For three days, Bab-el-Oued remained as cloistered as Tibet, occupied by soldiers, its citizens forbidden to leave and strangers, including journalists, forbidden to enter. All blinds were ordered closed, and civilians were not allowed on the streets even to buy bread or milk. Refuse piled up in the streets, which swarmed with rats. The *pieds noirs*, in their shadowed rooms, gathered their breath and their courage and tried to restore order to their ransacked homes, to sooth their children and to replenish their reserves of hatred. It was not only the Army and the Mobiles they hated. Nor was it only General de Gaulle or Metropolitan France or the brutal manual of General Katz. They were all too easy to hate. They also hated the leaders of the O.A.S.—Salan, Susini and the rest—who for a year had expended the energy, money and blood of the *pieds noirs* in a hopeless cause. The *pieds noirs* had given everything they had, at least as they saw it. When the O.A.S. said "Strike!" they had struck. When the O.A.S. said "Demonstrate!" they had flocked to the Forum by the thousands. For a year they had lived at the very limits of their nerves. And the net result was that scarcely a single soldier had been won over to their cause. Bridges had been burned between the Europeans and the Moslems that could never be rebuilt. If, a year earlier, they had been told that an Algerian Republic was inevitable, they could have tried to make some accommodation with the new régime as the French had done in Morocco and Tunisia. But the killings had gone on too long, and it was too late.

18
CRACK-UP (ROGER; OUT)
April–May 1962

❖❖❖

When a nation re-awakens, its finest sons are prepared to give their lives for its liberation. When Empires are threatened with collapse, they are prepared to sacrifice their non-commissioned officers.—Menachin Begin of the Irgun

The disaster of Bab-el-Oued effectively cut the lifeline of the O.A.S., by depriving it of the sympathy, or at least the detachment, of the Army. The sympathy could perhaps be regained by a new victory or by the right tactics, but any dangerous undertaking, any game played for high stakes, requires, in addition to courage and enterprise, a certain *esprit,* what is called in the Arab-French argot of the Army, *baraka,* something like luck with flair added. The O.A.S. seemed to have spent its precious capital of *baraka.* A perfect example of *baraka*—and its absence—occurred on March 25, the day after the Battle of Bab-el-Oued, when General Jouhaud was arrested in a routine checkup in Oran without anyone's suspecting who he was. Jouhaud had been incredibly imprudent, spending hours chatting with friends in the cafés. A note delivered to police headquarters suggested that the apartment building at 15 Boulevard du Front-de-Mer seemed to attract a suspicious number of O.A.S. men. The gendarmes knocked on the door of an apartment that had been indicated to them on the fourteenth floor and asked that Monsieur Jerbert, the tenant, come to police headquarters with the friend who was with him, Dr. Sabatier. Although the drive was short, it took the police nearly an hour to reach the police station because O.A.S. patrols, more heavily armed than they, seemed to be everywhere. The O.A.S. knew, even though the police did not, that "Monsieur Jerbert" was, in fact Jouhaud, and "Dr. Sabatie" was his aide, Major Julien Camelin. In the end the police reached headquarters without being intercepted.

All the documents seemed to be in order. One of the detectives was dubious, especially of Jouhaud's claimed profession—"Inspector of Schools." He telephoned his wife, who was a schoolteacher and asked her to give him some questions that a school inspector should be able to answer. Jouhaud fluffed, but even so the police let the men go with apologies ("These are unusual times, Messieurs"). Jouhaud and Camelin, were free to leave, which is what happens to men who enjoy *baraka,* as Godard had enjoyed *baraka* that time in Algiers when the police officer had let him go, as Degueldre had enjoyed it in his encounter with a friendly traffic policeman.

But as the two rose to leave, General Katz came into the room and recognized Jouhaud. At least, he thought he recognized him and asked him to sit down again. Jouhaud's hair was dyed, and he wore a thick moustache. Katz sent for an album of photographs of O.A.S. leaders and flicked them under Jouhaud's nose one by one. It seemed to him that the man's jowls tightened when he came to the photograph of Jouhaud in his Air Force days, but Katz gave no indication that he had noticed anything unusual. He finished the album and sent for police doctors. To Jouhaud he said simply, "Stand up."

Jouhaud scowled but stood. Katz could have sent to Air Force headquarters to ask for someone to come and identify Jouhaud personally, but Katz had been fighting the O.A.S. for a year in Oran, and he played the game differently. He had an interesting personality, one that will be explored in greater detail later. He ordered Jouhaud to strip, ignoring his indignant protests. The doctors looked up his nostrils, and fingered and touched him, although without hurting him. Jouhaud was ordered to touch his toes, and the doctors examined his anus; finally, humiliated beyond endurance, he burst out, "I am Edmond Jouhaud, and you cannot treat an Air Force general like that."

That was all Katz wanted to hear. Jouhaud and Camelin were placed under arrest and flown to Paris. And that is what happens

when one's *baraka* has run out. F. Scott Fitzgerald described it in
The Crack-up: "All life is a process of breaking down," he said.

> The blows that do the dramatic side of the work—the big
> sudden blows that come, or seem to come, from outside—
> the ones you remember and blame things on and in mo-
> ments of weakness tell your friends about, don't show
> their effect at once. There is another sort of blow that
> comes from within—that you don't feel until you realize
> with finality that in some regard you will never be as good
> a man again. The first sort of breakage seems to happen
> quickly—the second happens almost without your knowing
> it but is realized suddenly indeed."

Only three days before, the O.A.S. had been riding the crest, the
masters of Algeria. And now . . .

The Battle of Bab-el-Oued, while it lasted, was unique in many
ways. In the center of Algiers, life had gone on as if the fighting
were being waged hundreds of miles away. The cinemas remained
open. Citizens sat at bars and watched the smoke rising in the distance. Bab-el-Oued, said the people in the cafés, is not Algiers.
Bab-el-Oued is an entity in itself. Bab-el-Oued is getting only what is
coming to it, they said. But 24 hours later, even as Jouhaud was
being arrested, the virus of Bab-el-Oued came roaring into the center
of the city, to the Rue d'Isly itself, as jittery Tirailleurs of the French
Army fired into a massed crowd of *pieds noirs* who were protesting
the Army's behavior. Within a few minutes nearly fifty people lay
dead in the street, and 120 were injured. The police and Red Cross
arrived to restore some control to the panic-stricken soldiers. As an
incident of the atrocities committed by those in power it ranked
with Sharpeville or the massacre of the citizens of Petrograd by the
Tsarist Guards after the Potemkin mutiny. But it was a tragedy lost
in the confusion of the headlines. The individual story is always
more moving than the mass story, and the massacre on the Rue
d'Isly had to share space on the front pages with the arrest of
General Jouhaud.

For these momentous shocks, comfort came only in crumbs.
Colonel Henri Dufour, former commander of the 1st R.E.P., chose
this moment to desert the garrison at Offenburg, Germany, where
he had been stationed for more than a year, ever since he had stolen
the colors of his regiment before the Putsch. His achievement was good

propaganda, but it belonged to the cloud-cuckoo-land in which the O.A.S. increasingly lived. Dufour answered an appeal from General Gardy, who told him that three regiments in the Legion were ready to join the O.A.S., providing they were led by the former commander of the 1st R.E.P. "You are our last hope," said Gardy. Dufour flew to Oran next day, made a rapid tour of the officers' messes and realized that Gardy had been dreaming. The regiments had no intention whatever of coming out. As a consolation, General Salan gave him operational command of Oran.

On March 30 Salan, still seeking respectability, announced the creation of the *Conseil Nationale de Résistance* under the leadership of Georges Bidault and Jacques Soustelle, with Antoine Argoud as military representative. The name was designed to evoke heroic memories; it was the same as that of the organization Georges Bidault had so courageously led during the German occupation of France. It held some meetings in Rome but had little impact in Paris or, for that matter, in Algeria.

Reaction to disaster, real disaster, is always delayed. Like the pain of a wound, it is never felt at once. The shocked mind seals itself off until it is ready to cope. The Battle of Bab-el-Oued had little emotional effect on Colonel Gardes's plan to create an area of Algeria that the O.A.S. could occupy openly, where it could abandon its clandestine existence and draw in, quickly or gradually, the Army and the rest of the citizens.

The plan could be feasible only if the premises on which it was based was accurate. The O.A.S. persisted in the belief that the majority of Moslems preferred French rule but had been terrorized into silence by the F.L.N. Convinced that the O.A.S. had men and arms to protect them, these loyal Moslems would throw aside their fears and rise to support French Algeria. It was a comforting idea, and O.A.S. sentiment tended to embroider it. In rosier moments the leaders of the O.A.S. pictured a vast, spontaneous rising, as Soviet painters and filmmakers picture the October revolution. Certainly, if it were true anywhere, it would be true in the Massif Ouarsenis, the arid, mountainous area south of Orléansville that was the personal fief of the Bachaga Boualem, Algeria's most uncompromisingly Francophile chieftain. The Bachaga was Vice-President of the National Assembly in Paris and the traditional chief of the tribe of Beni Boudouane. During the Second World War, his men had formed the celebrated and dreaded Goums, who fought through the Italian campaign and were feared equally by enemy German males and otherwise-friendly Italian females. Their advance up the peninsula had left a strain of Berber blood among the unfortunate Italian masses. Stories of the Goums in the Second World War are endless. It is said that they were taught to recognize Germans by their helmets and that the last memory of many Germans was the touch of light fingers fluttering over the visors before the knife sank in. Once, it is said, probably apocryphally, the Brazilians, the only Latin-American people to fight actively with the Allies in the European campaign, moved into the front line; as they wore helmets similar to those of the Germans, they were supposedly raped then knifed or vice versa by the Goums—the lucky ones were taken prisoner, but only the really lucky ones preserved their virginity.

The Bachaga himself was a man of magnificent appearance, 6 feet tall and a creature of the desert. Everything about him was lean and spare, from the tip of his long, pointed nose to his thin toothbrush moustache. He uttered sharp, clipped phrases in perfect French through which the guttural harmonics of Arabic echoed. His fingers were slim and long enough to span an octave on the piano— and his nails were very dirty, despite which it would be difficult to find in any society a more complete aristocrat. He also knew how to hedge a bet.

The Bachaga's fifteen thousand harkis had fought alongside the French against the F.L.N. for seven years. They, even more than the *pieds noirs,* had a vital stake in French Algeria. Their cause, even more than that of the *pieds noirs,* was represented by the O.A.S. Rulers of an Algerian Republic, knowing how much they would have to rely on Paris for financial aid, would hesitate to take mass reprisals against Europeans, but they could make a fiesta out of the Arabs who had been loyal to France.

The Bachaga had expressed his views frankly both to correspondents and to Colonel Gardes, who had visited him several times. "If I told you I approved of the O.A.S. I would be a liar," he said. "If I said I disapproved of the O.A.S. I would be a liar. Only one thing matters to me and that is French Algeria. But not by the shedding of blood. I am more of a soldier than a politician, but I don't believe that French Algeria can be preserved by murders and bomb explosions."

The O.A.S., however, had received news calculated to change the Bachaga's mind and had worked out its plans accordingly. The plan was based on exciting news from General Gardy that a regiment of the Legion, some 2,500 men, was ready to come out in support of the O.A.S. Furthermore, according to Gardy, a regiment of Cavalry had agreed to come out if the Legion did. The news was passed on to Gardes by Captain Branca, formerly of the 1st R.E.P., who had been arrested after the Putsch, had served a year in prison and had rejoined the O.A.S. immediately after his release.

Contact was then made with the Bachaga's son, Mohammed, a big-boned, good-looking, uncomplicated young man, who had been educated in France. He was immediately enthusiastic and believed, no less than the O.A.S., that the Ouarsenis could be occupied. The Bachaga himself was sympathetic but aloof. He wanted to see what happened first, but he did convey to Gardes that his chieftains would match man for man, that, if the O.A.S. could produce five thousand soldiers, they would produce five thousand harkis.

It is interesting to note the increasingly dominant role of Roger Gardes at that period. After a year of existence, the O.A.S.—this "job for the colonels," as Argoud had forecast it—was obliged to turn to its least considered member for genuine leadership. The "colonels" had become singular. Gardes's flair and resourcefulness throughout the previous year contrasted vividly with the qualities of the others. Château-Jobert in Constantine seemed to be going out of his mind; his communications were full of accusations and angry replies to imaginary insults. Godard in Algiers had all but given up any claim to leadership. Broizat, though continuing to publish *Les Centurions,* seemed to have been squeezed dry intellectually and physically. There was no more energy in him. It was hard to remember that he had been one of the toughest paratroops in the French Army, that only nine months earlier he had been talking of going to the Congo as a mercenary. Argoud continued to grind loudly in neutral gear in Germany and Italy, accomplishing nothing.

But Gardes, with his need to participate fully in anything he undertook, had been liberated both spiritually and physically by the O.A.S. His inhibitions were gone, and although he remained as taut and nervous as ever, he also seemed rather like a child at play with mud pies. Whereas most of the O.A.S. men, particularly the senior officers, tried to maintain a martial appearance and wore

khaki bush shirts or paramilitary clothes, Gardes, who had always looked so trim in uniform, began to look quite awful. He had
grown a Groucho Marx moustache. His shirt was dirty, and his
creased, unpressed trousers flopped over carpet slippers or open
sandals. He played endlessly with his pipe, smoking it, filling it,
emptying it, pointing with it, spilling tobacco over his clothes and
even getting bits in his hair. Although he remained punctilious about
calling his fellow colonels *mon colonel*, he had little use for protocol
himself. His slovenliness bothered Europeans more than it bothered
Moslems, who are not the cleanest of people in their personal habits;
Gardes had a flair for handling Moslems and a love and trust for
them that, after having lived hidden among them for a year, he had
no reason to regret.

Gardes had originally asked Roger Degueldre to take actual charge
of the Ouarsenis operation, but Degueldre replied that he was too
busy in Algiers, and Gardes had turned to Captain Pierre Montagnon. Montagnon, yet another small man, was a veteran of the 1st
R.E.P. who had been condemned with Captain Branca to a year in
prison. On his release, he had accompanied Branca back to Algeria. He
was known to be an able but conservative soldier, with little taste
for life in the Maquis.

A hundred and fifty of the O.A.S. key men, including Lieutenant
Roger Bernard and Second Lieutenant Bernard Delhomme, head of
the Z Commandos, took the train from Algiers to Zaccar. All but
two or three held officers' or senior N.C.O. rank, as a matter of
deliberate policy. They would command the five thousand eager
recruits who were about to join them. From Zaccar, they made
their way to the Marguerite Farm, owned by the parents of Geneviève
Salasc. There they were divided by Montagnon into three groups,
each of which was assigned to a large truck. Montagnon himself,
with a small group, boarded a 403 Peugot station wagon and Gardes
an armored and heavily armed Citroën DS. All wore paratroop uniform with insignia of rank and green berets; at 2:00 in the morning
on March 30 they set out.

The convoy traveled through the night to cover the fifty kilometers
to the Ouarsenis. Some of the men in the station wagon sensed
that one of their companions was unusually light and soft-bodied
but they could not see in the dark and presumed that it was a boy.
Youths of fifteen and even younger often joined O.A.S. operations.

When, however, the station wagon stopped for the usual reasons of nature, the "youth" seemed unusually reticent and disappeared behind a rock.

One of the men said to Montagnon, "Captain, I believe that boy's a girl."

Montagnon admitted it. "It's my fiancée," he said. "She is coming along for the ride." On the girl's return, he introduced Miss Bernadette Pujol, uniformed like the rest, to her fellow travelers. Stimulated and in merry humor, the party continued on its way.

The immediate object was to capture three forts, Moulay Abderrahman, Dra-Messaoud and one called simply "Post 505," which was held by conscripts of the French Army at the entrance to the Ouarsenis mountains. Gardes had given orders that under no circumstances must the O.A.S. fire on them. If the O.A.S. bluff was called, the order was to retreat.

Trucks presented themselves at the gates of all three forts, simultaneously. Sleepy sentinels, surprised, found the Legionnaires taking over. They surrendered their arms. Young soldiers in their pajamas were awakened and told to go to the mess and treat themselves to coffee and brandy; in half an hour it was all over. The three posts had been taken without a shot.

Gardes toured the forts at daybreak and was delighted. He was introduced to Bernadette and congratulated Montagnon on both his excellent job and his good taste. He left the rest of the operation in Montagnon's hands and drove back toward Algiers. On his way, he ran into a police roadblock and rammed through it, his guns firing. The Citroën, although reinforced, was badly damaged. It continued for a few kilometers to a village, where Gardes changed cars and went home.

All day long the men waited in their three captured forts, in radio contact with one another. Mohammed Boualem tried to call his father, but the wily Bachaga had locked himself in the fastness of his home. He, like the others, was waiting. If the Legionnaires appeared on the scene, so would the harkis. Montagnon waited for the harkis, whose arrival would encourage the Legionnaires to move out. There was no sign of either of the phantom armies. The sense of loneliness was oppressive, intensified by the cheerfulness of the conscripts, who, relieved of their military duties, were drinking beer in the mess. The captive officers fraternized with their captors and at

first seemed inclined to join the enterprise if it looked like suc-
ceeding, but they grew increasingly aloof as the hot day wore on.
The night passed even more uneasily than had the day; shortly
after dawn Mohammed made contact with his father and reported
to Montagnon that the Bachaga was unbudging. It was not actually
so. The Bachaga had, in fact, made contact with General Katz in
Oran, who was making his dispositions to recapture the forts. Montagnon did not know of this betrayal but realized that his operation,
brilliant success though it had seemed so far, had failed and lost his
nerve. He told Mohammed at length what he thought of his father
and actually, in a moment of sheer lunacy, ordered the Bachaga's
arrest. Who was going to penetrate into the Bachaga's territory,
through thousands of armed guards, was an interesting question to
which Montagnon gave no answer.

He did not, in any case, have time to go into details because at
that moment a reconnaissance plane flew over the command post,
followed by a fighter with its guns blazing. The pilots were aiming
to warn and frighten, not to injure, because of the presence of the
conscripts, and they succeeded completely in their mission. Montagnon realized that the Army had been called in to retake the forts and
ordered the retreat; the O.A.S. reboarded the lorries in disorder.

It was a hellish flight. Pursued by troops and police and tracked
by the Air Force, the O.A.S. men found out what life had been like
for the fellagha over the past seven years. To make it worse the
fellagha themselves heard from the Moslem Prefect of Orléansville
about the retreat and joined in the hunt. Major Bazin and two others
were killed. Other O.A.S. men struggled on foot through the in-
hospitable wilderness of the Ouarsenis and, crazy with thirst, gave
themselves up for a drink of water. Lieutenant Roger Bernard was
captured at Rouiba, near Orléansville, with Captain Madaoui, a
Moslem. Mohammed Boualem faded into the geography and escaped. Montagnon was captured with Bernadette. Delhomme was
captured by police but leaped out of the police car. He escaped into
an Arab village and begged for asylum. The inhabitants thought it
was more amusing to stone him to death, but he was rescued, unconscious, by French soldiers.

Of the 150 crack officers who began the operation, 40 were taken
prisoner and another dozen killed. As for Roger Gardes, he as usual
blamed himself, not the Foreign Legion whimsies of General Gardy,

the double-dealing of the Bachaga or the indecisive leadership of Montagnon, whose girl friend was given a year's suspended sentence and kicked out of Algeria. Even while the campaign was taking place, Broizat, detached as always, was noting in his diary:

> I have just had a long talk with some young O.A.S. leaders, among them two Moslems. One of these gave me a pretty severe picture of the Bachaga Boualem who is no man to take risks and would prefer to be set up tranquilly in France. There are other sections of Algeria, he suggested, more favorable, and the Sheikh Ben Tekouk would be helpful. . . .

Such opinions might have been useful earlier.

Whatever the general opinion of the Bachaga, he, no less than Gardes, was racked by the failure of the Ouarsenis operation. He had known from the start about the plans and had prayed for their success, but he was also frightened of antagonizing the Army. He was afflicted by pangs of conscience, which he sought to rationalize. "I gave them my son, didn't I?" he said to a correspondent. "Gardes is a fine man, a gentleman. But I could not afford to trust the O.A.S. I cannot afford *not* to trust General de Gaulle. Besides," he added wearily. "I am 56 years old, and you don't join a lost cause at my age."

So, in addition to losing elite officers it could not spare, the O.A.S. lost, in effect, its best fighting colonel and one of its most important Moslem allies. After the fiasco of Bab-el-Oued and the massacre of the Rue d'Isly, the Organization seemed to have taken all the punishment it could absorb. But even worse was to come—and quickly.

✠✠✠

The police in Algiers received a secret tip that Roger Degueldre could be found alone in an apartment near the Boulevard Telelmy, which runs roughly parallel to the Rue Michelet. Extra roadblocks were set up, and, because the police were infiltrated with O.A.S. sympathizers, the plans to capture him were made in the greatest secrecy. The policemen themselves did not know the object of the operation until they were packed in their trucks and on their way. They stopped near the apartment building, and rubber-shoed gendarmes climbed on to the roofs to prevent a skylight getaway. Detectives carrying tommy guns pressed themselves against the wall on either side of the door of Degueldre's apartment while a locksmith silently opened the door.

Degueldre stood in the living room alone, with what was described by one officer as "a smile of stupefaction" on his face. His hair was now dyed blond, and he seemed to be preparing to leave, for he had a felt hat in his hand.

"There must be some mistake," he said and reached for his papers, the signal for a row of tommy guns to point at his chest. His papers were taken from his pocket, and he was identified as a schoolteacher named Gauthier, a name he had sometimes used in his early days in the Legion.

But the police knew they had their man, and he was conducted back to the police station with an escort of outriders, horns blaring in excitement. At the police station there were scenes one usually associates with weddings or New Year's Eve. Debrosse ordered champagne for all, and the corks exploded. Policemen cheered, sang, slapped each other on the back. Degueldre himself was offered a glass and sipped it morosely in his cell. Within two hours the star prisoner was on his way to Paris.

✤✤✤

The appalled leaders of the O.A.S. were faced with a completely new and disastrous situation. They ordered an immediate inquiry into how Degueldre came to be captured at all. Certainly he was the most wanted man in the Organization, much more important than Salan, but for that very reason his security was the tightest. To the average O.A.S. man he was as misty and mysterious a figure as he was to the police. He had long since ceased to see the ordinary troops and communicated only with the Delta chiefs. He slept in a different bed every night. He traveled everywhere with bodyguards, and his car was always preceded by a radio car, which warned in advance of roadblocks.

But in life events do not happen in logical order. The fact was that Degueldre was at the end of his tether. He was ripe to fall, and he fell. For a year he had lived under almost inhuman pressure, carrying the O.A.S. almost on his own. The arrest of Dovecar had shaken him more than he realized himself. He had endured a fearful quarrel with General Gardy when the General learned that his daughter was pregnant. Gardy had taken a train from Oran, confronted Degueldre and Nicole and ordered her to have an abortion. Nicole refused. Degueldre's sense of doom was never far below the surface. To be shouted at and insulted by a senior officer whom he revered was deeply mortifying to him. Since the arrest of Dovecar and even more so since the quarrel he had began to drink heavily. He was half drunk when he was captured. Usually he went out with his men, but on this occasion they had left him alone while they went to bring the two cars to the door, and the police had taken advantage of their absence.

But how did the police know that Degueldre would be caught alone and without his bodyguards? That was the nagging problem, and the agonizing conclusion that none wished to face was that Debrosse's men had finally infiltrated the highest echelons of the Organization. Who was the traitor in their midst? The night after the arrest there was a meeting of Delta chiefs in an apartment near the port. The meeting was open only to the men who had known where Degueldre was to be when he was arrested; they numbered about eight. A trial of elimination was held, as each in turn proved the guilty one could not possibly be he. Finally only one man was left without conclusive proof of innocence. His name was François Lecca, and his O.A.S. credentials could not have been better. He had been a paratroop sergeant and had served under Colonel Bigeard in Indochina and Algeria. He had been in the O.A.S. almost from the beginning and was one of its most ruthless and efficient leaders. Degueldre trusted him completely. But, for reasons that will never be known, he had moved over to the side, not of Debrosse but of General Allaire. After a long interrogation marked by much brutality and pain Lecca confessed that he was indeed the spy. With a gun pointed at his head, he wrote and signed a confession. As soon as it was done the gun blew his brains out. Lecca was then stripped and his body bound tightly in chicken wire. He was taken out to sea and dropped overboard. As the body decomposed and became bloated by sea water, the flesh was progressively shredded by the unyielding chicken wire and attracted swarms of fish, which devoured it until there remained only an unidentifiable cadaver.

19
SUSINI SEES
REASON (OF A SORT)
April–May 1962

✤✤✤

News of Degueldre's arrest caused consternation in Algeria. Bab-el-Oued and the Ouarsenis were simply lost battles, but Degueldre was the heart, spirit and embodiment of the O.A.S. It was realized that morale must be restored at all costs. Degueldre had been arrested at 6:10 P.M. on April 7. Twenty-four hours later, the Caserne des Tagarins, the prison most feared by the O.A.S., was blasted by mortar fire, and three days afterwards the control tower of Maison Blanche Airport, although heavily guarded, was blown up. The O.A.S. had to prove that it had not lost its teeth when it lost Degueldre.

But its efforts were futile, and on April 20 Salan himself was caught, betrayed by an adjutant captured in the Ouarsenis. He had arranged to meet his wife and the children to celebrate Easter in a ground-floor apartment at 25 Rue Desfontaines in Algiers. It was a year almost to the day since the generals had started their Putsch. Captain Ferrandi was captured at the same time. Fortunately for the Organization, the arrest was witnessed by a sympathizer, who took a taxi to the Ferrandi apartment. All his documents were removed and passed on to Susini just before the police arrived.

Salan's security arrangements had always been too lax for comfort, and he knew it, but he had never lacked courage; he realized that a leader must be seen to be believed. He was available to foreign correspondents, television people, photographers, politicians, lobbyists. Only a month before his arrest he had written to André Canal that thenceforth he would receive only people he knew personally or in whom he could feel confidence. But it was too late. The head of the O.A.S. was taken by helicopter with Madame Salan and Captain Ferrandi, to the French military base at Reghaïra. There was a brief confrontation between Salan and his former subordinate, General Charles Ailleret. "You know who I am," Ailleret said curtly. "You are responsible for all the crimes committed by the O.A.S. in your name, and you are going to pay for them. I shall see to that myself," Salan turned his back.

"It had to happen sooner or later," Salan told the police. "I saw too many people, for too many ridiculous reasons. People I did not even know, who could not help the O.A.S. in any way. What difference does it make? Everything is collapsing around us."

In the Santé Salan found himself in company with hundreds of other captured O.A.S. men—though not Roger Degueldre, who was kept in reinforced seclusion. None of the men in the Santé had been treated particularly well, but some of the older members of the club could remember having been there before when they were in the Resistance, and they agreed that conditions were better than under the Gestapo.

Salan had never been an effective commander of the O.A.S. The task was wholly foreign to his temperament. But then Salan had never been an effective commander of anything. Throughout his career, he had been merely adequate. What he did give to the O.A.S., however, was presence and a certain style. His comment that "the Mediterranean divides France the way the Seine divides Paris" put into one sentence the whole mythos of French Algeria. His presence at the head of the Secret Army lent respectability even to its atrocities. But, despite the desperate propaganda of Susini, who tried to make him appear a fearless, swashbuckling commander who could swallow General de Gaulle in a gulp, Salan persisted in presenting the image of a rather benign but humorless father figure. From the point of view of the O.A.S. as a fighting force, the unfortunate thing was that it had not been led by Massu. The larger tragedy was that it had never found a de Gaulle.

Now that Salan was gone, it could be argued that the O.A.S. would be more rather than less effective, for it was left wholly in the hands of the professionals. In practice it did not work out that way at all.

Gardy, Gardes, Vaudrey, Dufour, Susini, Broizat, and Château-

Jobert continued their propaganda, their efforts at recruitment, their attacks on their enemies. In Rome, Bidault, Soustelle and Argoud issued pronunciamentos on behalf of the O.A.S. and the C.N.R. But their task was daily becoming harder, for more and more effort was required to remain in place without losing ground. Every day four or five or six good O.A.S. men fell into the hands of the police. Even Dédé, Susini's faithful Jewish friend, found it prudent to vanish. Unfortunately, he made the tactical error of trying to vanish with Susini's treasury; he made it only as far as the Algiers railway station, where his body was found full of bullets. The money was restored to Susini by the Z commandos. Susini himself had ordered the execution. He was not a sentimental man.

The man most embarrassed by Salan's arrest was General Gardy. He was the last surviving officer of general's rank, and he wrote to the Colonels asking that they agree to his declaring himself Commander in Chief. Still bound by the seniority system in which they had spent all their careers, they agreed and left him to his dreams of conjuring the Foreign Legion out of thin air.

General Jouhaud was sentenced to death. At his trial he said, "There is a wall of total incomprehension separating France and Algeria." Bobby Dovecar, Petri and Tenne, three of the four men who had killed Commissioner Gavoury, were sentenced to death, and so was the *pied noir* Piegts for complicity in supplying the key to Gavoury's apartment. When the sentence was announced, the three Legionnaires tore off their decorations and flung them at the judges.

Weeks of political chaos ensued. On May 4 André Canal was arrested in Paris. On his person was found a note in Salan's handwriting, dated April 1, that named Georges Bidault as head of the O.A.S. A second note ordered General Gorel, the treasurer of the O.A.S., to put at Bidault's disposal the sum of $200,000. Bidault never received the money.

Meanwhile, on May 8, General Gardy tried a new political approach. He sent a circular to all ambassadors in France whose nations were members of the North Atlantic Treaty Organization. He stated that the O.A.S.-C.N.R. was staunchly faithful to NATO and formally substituted itself "for the illegal authorities installed by the personal power of de Gaulle." It was a plaintive declaration, part of the simplistic philosophy of the O.A.S. that, if one kept on assuring the United States of one's anticommunism, the United States would give support and money. But the circular also contained a warning, subsequently vindicated, that de Gaulle was not to be trusted at the heart of NATO. The ambassadors unanimously refused to receive the communication.

An O.A.S. man, Axel Nicol found Susini in a pensive mood. Susini had lost faith in everybody. He jeered at the name of Argoud, despised Perez and Lagaillarde and was bitterly anti-Army. He had, however, lost none of his lucidity. "The situation has greatly changed in the last three months," he said. "Our men had good reason then to think that a large part of the Army would join us. We now know for certain that they will never expose themselves. We also know now that they never intended to. On the sentimental level—and saber-carriers, my friend, are always sentimental—the Army favored our fight, but it never went beyond kind words. I have no time for kind words. It is not with these you can win a war, any more than with whimsies." For a moment Nicol thought that his friend was going to cry, but Susini was too tough for that. He was merely facing facts as he saw them.

"You surprise me," Nicol said. "I thought Charlie was in Bel-Abbés getting the Legion out."

Susini sneered. "Charlie, Château-Jobert, Dufour are all good fellows in their own way, but they are plunged to the heart with ancient history, and don't see what is going on all round them. I repeat and I assure you there is not a single unit ready to take the decisive step. And, of course, the Government is making a big thing out of it, and talking about loyalty. Loyalty! It's enough to make you puke. It is not a question of loyalty at all. It's a question of money at the end of the month, it's a question of ranks, promotions and decorations. The French Army, no matter how much sympathy it might still have for us, will entrench itself behind the holy principle of obedience. The kids who have been drafted don't give a damn. They want to get back to their villages as soon as possible, and Algeria can go to hell."

It was all news to Nicol. In war the serving soldier rarely understands the implications of either defeat or victory until much later. "Surely there are still officers on our side?" he said.

Susini laughed cynically. "One in ten. And that one is lost among the civil servants in uniform, watched over by Security and by all those little pals with nice officers' commissions who don't want to get themselves involved. . . ."

Nicol was depressed. "I didn't think things were so bad. What do the others think?"

"It's possible that some of the colonels still nurse their illusions. But as for me, no. Have you realized the blows we have taken lately?"

"I know."

"You don't. It is worse than you think. We have lost Delta above all, Bobby Dovecar, Piegts, de Blignières, Bernard, Delhomme and how many others? Our men are physically and nervously exhausted. The Gardes Mobiles are exhausted too, I'll admit that. But they can go on leave, be replaced, have a rest. We are stuck."

"So what do we do now?"

"Continue as we have done before, make as much noise as possible to make the Fels consider us as legitimate interlocutors. As long as Paris continues to think that the Algerian French don't matter, and as they don't ask our opinion about what they intend to do with us, we will have to make a little Évian of our own."

Nicol was appalled. He, like the others, had heard rumors that Susini wanted to negotiate. "All this means defeat?"

"Yes."

"Have you started negotiations?"

"Not yet. But we will have to start soon."

"How do you think the *pieds noirs* are going to take it? With gaiety in their hearts?"

"With gaiety or not, they must see reason. It is up to us to prepare them as gently as possible."

"What do Gardy and the colonels think of your point of view?"

Susini shrugged. "I haven't spoke even to them. To tell you the truth I have had very little contact with them since the arrest of the General. Salan was the only man able to put a little cement into the Organization."

"They won't love you for this."

"I know."

The two men shook hands and parted. They did not see each other again. Poor Susini, Nicol thought. Susini, the master ventriloquist had lost Salan, his four-star mouthpiece. He had lost Dédé. He had lost Degueldre. As always he needed someone stronger to manipulate. There weren't any such men left in the O.A.S.; he was therefore going to try to find what he needed in the camp of the enemies. But for the moment the best brain in the O.A.S. was cut off from the rest, a man alone.

That at least was Nicol's reading of Susini's mood, but it was dead wrong. Susini, far from being downcast, was in a state of exultation. He had *become* the O.A.S. In the negotiations he was planning, he would be the sole leader and spokesman. He had climbed to the crumbling summit. What Lagaillarde had created he had inherited. Lagaillarde had been in at the birth, but he, Susini, would be in it at the death. His victory over Lagaillarde was complete. In truth, Jean-Jacques Susini was beginning to go a little out of his mind.

20

DOUCETTE

April–July 1962

✦✦✦

On April 8 the referendum was held. Even then the *pieds noirs* allowed themselves the luxury of hope. The Mediterranean Sea is a marvelous filter through which realities penetrate as baby food comes through a straw. France could never abandon her compatriots across the water. When it came to approving once and for all the Évian agreements, the citizens would reply with a thundering and decisive *non*. They would never give up a land they had been civilizing for 130 years, especially not when oil had been discovered in the Sahara. But France could—and did—vote *oui*, at the rate of 90 percent.

Georges Bidault denounced the result in the name of the C.N.R. Violence, as Susini had foreseen, was all that remained to the O.A.S. as a bargaining point, and new waves of explosions rocked Algiers, Oran and Constantine.

And the violence began to provide its own satisfaction. It seemed that the *pieds noirs* had, in a way, been psychologically freed by the referendum. They were able, after all the years, to hate with good conscience, to shed the cant about "Moslem brothers." They had wound themselves tight to accept integration, but the elastic had snapped, releasing a spinning top of rage and violence. Any Moslem was fair game. The *ratonade*, the rat hunt, became the vogue. The fashionable new attitude was "there are nine million Moslems in Algeria and one million Europeans; if we each kill nine the problem is solved," after which there was the inevitable comparison, once uttered in derision but now in admiration, of the American precedent with the Red Indians.

A new word reigned in those spite-filled days: *doucette*. It is a pretty word, the result of saying "twelve-seven" quickly in French. It could be a girl's nickname, but it had come to mean the 12.7 Hotchkiss heavy machine gun, which the O.A.S. would mount at street corners to give other O.A.S. men covering fire while they massacred Moslems.

Death was everywhere, a commonplace, a hysterical joke; all over Algiers there was blood, fresh, bright and uncongealed. Blood splashed the ramp in front of the Hotel Aletti, and some days it was difficult to walk five hundred yards without stepping over a corpse. Men and women walked crabwise, looking over their shoulders for assassins. Life was ruled by fear, the fear of everyday things: of meeting a person of different race in the street, of a slowly moving car, of a parked car with people inside it. The O.A.S. had forbidden the *pieds noirs* on pain of death to quit Algeria, and a man who decided to escape feared his own people as much as he feared "the others." He had come to fear a knock on the door by day or night, even a note left on his table by a waiter. Even the traditional *billet doux* had become a death warrant.

A few scenes taken at random suggest the daily pattern of life in Algiers: People pass without stopping to look at the remains of a policeman spattered against a wall like a vast insect against a windshield, the victim of a direct hit by an O.A.S. two-pound shell. Children in school pinafores and carrying briefcases pause to see if the body lying in a gutter of the Rue Michelet is European or Moslem; they cheer when they see that it is the latter.

A young Moslem is lying in the street, apparently shot dead by an O.A.S. squad. He stirs. A European girl says to her escort, "Finish him off with your gun." The Moslem climbs dizzily to his feet and stares blindly at the hostile ring of Europeans; because no one wants the blood and dust to rub off on his own clothes, they make way for him to stagger toward the nearby police station, trailing blood. Two policemen with tommy guns on their shoulders stare through and past him, unmoving. The O.A.S. men, realizing that they have botched their jobs, return and empty a magazine into the body of the dying Moslem, who falls at the feet of the policemen.

The plague had come to the land of Camus, even as he had described it in his novel. It was not only the hideous death in the streets, the blood in the gutters and the smell of gunpowder and plastic in the

dry spring air; it was also the moral massacre, the decay of civilized
principle on both sides, the total indifference to horror, brutality and
pain. The security forces were no less infected than were the *pieds
noirs,* the O.A.S. and the Moslems; they even saw advantages in this
moral anarchy. Captured O.A.S. men would be driven by *barbouzes*
into the heart of the Casbah and left to try and make their way out of
that maze of death. The police had a confidential list of some two
thousand Europeans suspected of O.A.S. sympathies, that is to say,
people whom the authorities knew perfectly well were behind the
O.A.S. activities, either financing or hiding them, but against whom
the evidence was insufficient for arrest. This list was passed confiden-
tially to Si Azzedine, chief of the F.L.N. in Algiers. The rash of kid-
nappings of Europeans occasioned shocked front-page stories in the
French press, and General Gardy in Oran asked Algiers for a report.
He received a memorandum from an O.A.S. captain, which said in
part:

> The kidnapping of Europeans really began in November
> last year at the same time as the *barbouzes* started to ar-
> rive. About a hundred persons have disappeared between
> then and the end of March, and they are almost always
> persons who are known to sympathize with the cause of
> French Algeria. In my subsector alone I have found sixteen
> of these missing people, 10 bodies thrown up by the sea
> between Saint Eugène and Guyotville, two bodies tied up
> in sacks and abandoned in Saint Eugène, two in plywood
> boxes in the village of Dély-Ibrahim. All these bodies
> showed signs of torture, burns and cuts. In addition we
> found two Europeans still alive but barely in the garage
> of a villa at El Biar. We have evidence of collusion between
> the F.L.N. and the *barbouzes* in two instances, the kid-
> napping at Guyotville, and the recent plastic-bombing of
> European restaurants in Bab-el-Oued.

Meanwhile a lunatic orgy of wishful thinking was sweeping the
O.A.S. itself. Just as Hitler, in his bunker, had moved imaginary
German armies to relieve Berlin, the O.A.S. imagined reinforcements
of its own. General Massu had disappeared from his headquarters at
Metz, it was rumored, and was on his way to assume command of the
O.A.S. in Algiers. Robert Lacoste and Max Lejeune, two favorites of
the *pieds noirs,* had joined the C.N.R. Gardy was constantly bringing

out the Foreign Legion. Now it would have to join, said the *pieds noirs*. If it didn't it would be disbanded, and all those S.S. men would have to face trial in Germany for war crimes; the *pieds noirs* said these things of their former heroes with a certain relish, as though such fates would serve them right.

On May 2 a truck carrying explosives was rolled into the port of Algiers and ignited, killing 62 Moslem shipyard workers and wounding more than a hundred. These men were unloading supplies for the European Establishment. It was hardly surprising that the next day no one put in an appearance and the cargoes rotted on the quays, but the *pieds noirs* were too far gone in their hate and fear to question this economic *felo-de-se*.

"The O.A.S. strikes when it wants, where it wants and against whom it wants," said the signs on the walls of Algiers, but one was reminded more of Meursault, the Algerian hero of Camus' *The Stranger*, who, after killing a Moslem for no reason, could explain, "I know I had shattered the equilibrium of the day, the spacious calm of this beach where I was happy."

Banks were robbed more and more frequently, but less and less of the loot went into the official O.A.S. exchequer. The O.A.S. was disintegrating into a rabble. But as discipline sagged, two themes of rather greater logic were discussed, two last throws of the dice left to the Organization. One was to blow up the military camp at Rocher Noir, into which the Algerian Provisional Government was already moving under the chairmanship of Mr. Abderrahman Farès. The other was to assassinate General de Gaulle, a course against which General Salan had always been obdurate.

But, without Roger Degueldre, the O.A.S. lacked organizers capable of carrying out the former course; and, when the latter was attempted shortly afterward, it was without the knowledge or aid of the O.A.S. in Algeria. The fact was that the arrest of Salan had broken the O.A.S. as a monolithic force, and it had become little more than a collection of petty chieftains running individual gangs of bravos. Gardy and Dufour controlled a still-disciplined team in Oran. Vaudrey ran the crumbling forces in Algiers, and Château-Jobert commanded effectively a small, tough group in Constantine. Gardes, since the disaster of the Ouarsenis, was a used-up force.

As for Dr. Perez, he had been, since the capture of Degueldre, the sole head of O.R.O., the bureau of direct action, which should

have made him the most powerful man in the O.A.S. But O.R.O. itself had disintegrated, and Perez was in hiding from some of the
cadres of the O.A.S., who believed rightly or wrongly that he was
holding hundreds of thousands of O.A.S. dollars.

Susini was still making his plans to negotiate with the Algerian
Provisional Government, and he knew how bitterly he would be re-
viled, especially in Oran, where political moves were less well understood. He explained his position to a friend: "We must understand
the weakness of our resources. Since the setback in the Ouarsenis,
and the lamentable affair at Bab-el-Oued our troops have panicked,
squads have vanished into thin air. Those that I have under my control
are utterly demoralized. The arrest of Degueldre hit them harder than
the arrest of Salan. We are in a worse position now than we were just
after the Putsch, without the manpower, the material or the morale
we had then. Today there are not in Algiers more than twenty effective Deltas. Our stocks of explosives are almost exhausted. Much of
what we have left we cannot get our hands on because the only officers who know where they are are either in prison or have vanished.
I have a thousand kilos of plastic in Ghardaïa, but I have no one that
can tell me where it is. If I have decided to play the card of negotia-
tion, it is not because I have any illusion about its value—it is the only
one I have left in the pack."

On May 18 Susini, with the grudging consent of Godard, put out
his first feelers to Farès; the response of the rest of the O.A.S. was one
of murderous resentment and rage. Château-Jobert sent abusive messages from Constantine, and Gardy and Dufour in Oran formally
condemned Susini to death. Argoud sent word from Vienna that he
was against any attempt at rapprochement. Too much spilled blood
separated the two communities, he said. The gulf was beyond bridg-
ing. It was easy for Argoud to be so bellicose from his comfortable
vantage point. Argoud considered Susini's project so serious that two
days later he appointed himself Commander in Chief of O.A.S.-
Mètropole and announced that Captain Pierre Sergent would thenceforth be his Chief of Staff. The order was signed by both Argoud and
Sergent, but Argoud was still prudent enough to avoid setting foot in
France.

When the furore over Susini's "treachery" died away, it was clear
that the only colonels to back him were Vaudrey, Gardes and Broizat.

Farès accepted the offer of a meeting with alacrity, and the two opposing sides met at a house in the village of Alma, near Rocher Noir. Farès came with several advisers, Susini flanked by Gardes and Broizat. The first explorations were unexpectedly cordial. Farès wanted the O.A.S. to prevent a mass exodus of *pieds noirs,* whose presence he considered vital to the future conduct of Algerian affairs. Susini wanted the establishment of a European security force, commanded by O.A.S. officers, to protect the *pieds noirs* who remained. It was a ridiculous suggestion, but the meeting ended amicably with cigars, and Farès went so far as to describe it as "historic." The effect of this adjective on Susini's ego proved to be disastrous.

The news of the negotiations set off a stampede of *pieds noirs* to leave the country. Previously they had remained reasonably obedient to the O.A.S. In order to leave the country, they had to apply to the O.A.S. for exit visas, without which many airline officials refused to issue tickets. But all that routine was forgotten in the panic created by the negotiations; the Europeans flocked to the airports and docks like soapsuds being sucked down a drain.

"Susini is bargaining away French Algeria against the possibility that the Europeans can take their refrigerators with them," said some.

"Why did they ask us to kill so many people in the first place?" said others. "We could have stayed home and made our peace with the Moslems. Now it's too late."

General Jouhaud wrote a letter from prison to General Salan:

> Independence is now practically an accomplished fact. It revolts us and it tolls the bell on our hopes, but it has to be considered realistically. Today, with death in my heart, I ask everyone who has obeyed me not to continue fighting. We must stop the blind attacks against Moslems. Among those who are falling to the haphazard shooting are some who perhaps were former comrades in arms, perhaps our friends.

Jouhaud begged Salan to countersign the message. Salan refused.

In the unaccustomed silence of the truce, the O.A.S. men discussed their future. One urged Axel Nicol to go with him and join O.A.S.-Métro under Pierre Sergent. Sergent, perennially calm and loyal, had become the man everyone wanted to touch, in case a little of his *baraka* might rub off. The most wanted man in France had seen many of his friends and colleagues arrested only a few hours after leaving him. He had lost de Blignières, blinded by a tear-gas grenade. He had lost Robin, Vincent, Castille, Godot. Yet he himself remained invulnerable, and in the disintegrating climate of Algiers he even symbolized a kind of security.

Nicol declined the suggestion. "If Roger were still with us I would go," he said. "Now I am finished, empty."

On June 17, at about 8:00 in the evening, the new City Hall of Algiers went up in an explosion of an intensity never before heard in Algeria. A modern white building facing the sea was turned in that ear-splitting moment into a blackened shell. The truce was over. At the same time, the citizens of Bab-el-Oued burned their marketplace. Men, women and children threw tables and chairs into the flames— or bottles of gasoline, which exploded. If they had to leave their possessions behind, they were determined that the Moslems would not enjoy them. They laughed, sang or broke down and sobbed hysterically, and when their frenzy was spent they went home to pack what they could carry.

It was the last of the violence, in Algiers at any rate. Susini came to an agreement to end all warfare, and the agreement was given formal approval by Jouhaud and Salan.

Events in the dying moments of French Algeria were not unlike some of those in Germany at the end of the war. Susini's self-appointed role as O.A.S. emissary had gone to his head, and, flattered by the cordiality he had been accorded, he actually offered his services to the new republic, suggesting himself as Minister of Agriculture. The offer was turned down with courteous regrets. Susini then issued an official statement praising "the ardent patriotism of the Algerians." General Salan pleaded with the *pieds noirs* to stay in Algeria and work to help the new régime.

Dr. Perez, packed and ready to go, addressed a letter to Bidault, Soustelle, Argoud and two others, in which he wrote incoherently of plots, thefts and murder:

> On the morning of June 2 four operations were taken by the Gardes Mobiles against my four command posts. It is not difficult to guess their origin. I was given away. Not only that but it has been stated that I was a party to it and had lifted a considerable amount of money from our exchequer. Susini, who would never have the guts to try something like that on his own initiative, is now ready to offer my head in a basket at his wedding to the Algerian Pro-

visional Government. My special squads advised me to break with Susini or else order them to kill Susini, Godard, the financier* with the 1,200 million, Caruana,† and eight others. It would have been a real night of the long knives. But we needed the financier "on the hoof" for the wretched pocket money of my squads. This being June 8, I am taking the decision to leave Algeria and I have ordered my men to disengage. I have heard for several days now rumors that were, in truth, predictable. Godard, who never really commanded anything, Cimeterre,‡ who spent his time playing the busybody and depositing cash that others went to find for him, Susini, who would give anything to be a Minister in the Algerian Republic, are allowed to state that I am leaving with 250,000,000 francs, which is false. If I had access to that kind of money I would have been smarter than to leave it in Algeria. I would have taken it with me for the revolutionary war we will keep on fighting.

Such was the Canossa of the O.A.S.

Once more Algiers and the Forum were scenes of wild excitement, but this time the demonstrators were all Moslems. Young Moslems in stolen cars carrying the green and white flag of the Algerian Republic drove down the Rue Michelet (which would soon, of course, be called something else), tooting horns in the same ti-ti-ti ta-ta rhythm that had once meant *Algérie française* and later *L'O.A.S. vaincra;* now, directed at the departing *pieds noirs,* it had a new significance of unsubtle but understandable sadism: *F.L.N. Yah! Yah!*

"The last time I saw the Mussulmans so excited," said one *pied noir* who drove through mobs hammering fists on his car, "was on the 13th of May."

A slight figure in priest's habit boarded a plane at Algiers Airport bound for Rome. Jean-Jacques Susini, who would have enjoyed being Minister of Agriculture in the Republic of Algeria, was making his exit. As had Perez before him, he carried enough of the O.A.S. exchequer to keep the wolf from more doors than one. That meant he had to change the door often.

* The financier was not identified.
† Major Caruana, a Delta commander and former aide-de-camp to Degueldre.
‡ "Cimeterre" was the pseudonym of General Gorel, official treasurer of the O.A.S.

21
ORAN
May–July 1962

✦✦✦

An everyday conversation in Oran, 1962:
   "Good morning Madame Lopez. Is your son Jean-Paul at home?"
   "No he isn't. He's out plasticating [*au plastic*]."
   "Thank you Madam Lopez."

✦✦✦

In Oran the shock felt at Susini's decision to negotiate was indescribable. For a year the O.A.S. had controlled the city. But the
O.A.S. in Oran was quite unlike the O.A.S. in Algiers. It had formed
itself before the Algiers O.A.S. It contained more brothers and more
cousins, more Jews, fewer Legionnaires and no Moslems. It did not
involve itself in useless dialectic on whether or not Algeria could remain French. It never doubted its ultimate victory or suspected that
the F.L.N. would ever be anything more than a fugitive rebel force.
The *Écho d'Oran,* owned and edited by Pierre Laffont, although
more liberal than the *Écho d'Alger,* was unquestioningly confident.
Even if Algiers, with its intellectual remoteness, were lost, Oran
could withdraw into itself, a bastion with outposts at Mostaganem and
Sidi-bel-Abbès. The Department of Oran was not self-supporting,
but Oran was a prosperous mercantile city, and its linchpin was the
great naval fortress at Mers-el-Kébir five miles away. By the Évian
agreement, the fortress was to remain under French control for fifteen

years. To the Europeans of Oran Mers-el-Kébir was France's Gibraltar, and to the Jews the Department of Oran was France's Israel. Both Gibraltar and Israel had shown signs of surviving forever. British Gibraltar was, indeed, seventeen years older than French Algeria. As far as the citizens of Oran were concerned, the *pieds noirs* of Constantine and Algiers who wished to remain in their native land could move into the Oran compound. They themselves did not intend to budge.

The boldness of the O.A.S. in Oran was breathtaking. The headquarters was situated in a library not two blocks from the Grand Hotel, the principal hotel of the city, and there was almost no attempt at concealment. One of the commanders was an Amazon who weighed two hundred pounds; she had jet-black hair pulled back in a bun, a small and docile husband and two sons as big and as tough as their mother. In the ground-floor storage room, the tracts and pirate broadcasts were taped and roneoed, and documents were duplicated; in the upstairs reference library there was a minor arsenal.

Even the twin disasters of Bab-el-Oued and the Ouarsenis did not shake the confidence of Oran. For one thing, Colonel Henri Dufour had finally arrived to take over operational command of the O.A.S. The former commander of the 1st R.E.P. was as big a personality in Oran as General Massu would have been in Algiers, a talisman of victory to come, a laurel wreath to crown a victory already achieved.

The headquarters of the Paris-controlled administration was in the new fifteen-story Préfecture, a fortress from which, since the putsch, no one ventured without armored-car escort or entered without passing three rings of barbed wire and sandbagged barricades. The interior was a maze of locked and guarded doors and separate elevators. The Prefect lived in a guarded apartment on the top floor, but, despite precautions, it was twice wrecked by explosions, once by a bazooka from a neighboring building and once by a charge of plastic left on the floor below.

A few Europeans played both sides, but they were rarely locals. One was Pierre Amand,* a French businessman and health faddist, who maintained a tasteful apartment near the Grand Hotel and a beach bungalow on the waterfront. He gave the apartment to Colonel Dufour to use as his headquarters. The beach bungalow he gave to

---

* Pierre Amand is a fictitious name.

General Joseph Katz, Commander in Chief of the French Army at Oran, for swimming and relaxation.

We have encountered General Katz before. His were the tactics that the Army had followed so successfully during the uprising at Bab-el-Oued, and it was Katz who had arrested and humiliated General Jouhaud. Katz was also the man who had ordered the Army into the Ouarsenis to break up Colonel Gardes's venture. Katz, Katz, Katz. Whatever the O.A.S. tried, it was confronted by Katz. "Butcher Katz" they called him. No name aroused greater resentment, not even that of Debrosse.

Joseph Katz was an unusual man in many ways, especially in the higher ranks of the French Army. He had been a foundling, left at the door of a convent in Paris. He had gone through school on public funds, working in his spare time as a goatherd. He joined the Army and rose from the ranks. He fought with the Free French and subsequently in Algeria against the rebels. To borrow an expression from a later war, his "head count" of dead fellagha was the highest of any officer in the French Army. He was a small, stocky fellow, all muscle and common sense. When his enemy was the F.L.N., he fought the F.L.N. as efficiently and as dispassionately as he knew how. When his enemy became the O.A.S., he allowed no feelings of former comradeship or Army freemasonry to deter him.

It was this detachment that more than anything else made him the object of so much hatred in Oran. Colonel Debrosse in Algiers was at least a policeman, doing a policeman's job. Katz was a soldier and even brought the French Army for the first time into the fight against the O.A.S. by offering special leave to any soldier who, in the official orders "neutralized a terrorist." Katz's point of view was that he had been given a disagreeable job to do, that he disliked it, but that he did it. He had seen too much of war in the bled to believe in the efficiency of moving large forces aimlessly, and in his fight against the O.A.S. he recognized both his strength and his limitations. If he were to bring overwhelming forces into an area held in strength by the O.A.S., he knew that the O.A.S. would be tipped by sympathizers in his own headquarters and disappear before his men arrived. The O.A.S. had taps on all official telephones, including his own. Knowing that there could be no such showdown in Oran as there had been in Bab-el-Oued, he was concerned at the tactical level with keeping the O.A.S. worried and off balance. Early in June 1962, the O.A.S. occupied the central telephone exchange building. Katz was informed and asked for orders. "No orders," he said.

"Aren't you going to throw them out?"

"No," said Katz.

His staff officers were incredulous. "Why not?" they demanded.

"Because that is what they want me to do. They want to show the population how tough they are. You don't do what the enemy wants. You make him do what *you* want. They'll get bored in time and leave."

"And you?"

"I'm going swimming."

All day a powerful force of uniformed, helmeted O.A.S. commandos waited for Katz' big push. When night fell, they went home.

Discussions about how to kill Katz were endless, and attempts were frequent. Once a Jewish commando unit crept through the sewers until it was under Katz' office in the old Prèfecture in the Arab quarter. The men pushed twenty kilos of plastic through a protection grill and, when they were clear, detonated it. In their confined, uncomfortable position, however, they had packed it badly. Instead of shredding Katz, it only made an infernal bang and blew a hole in the floor.

On another, more bizarre occasion, the O.A.S. killed another general, thinking he was General Katz. The Organization had been advised that Katz was going to Baudens Hospital to pay his last respects to an officer, Colonel Mario, who had been fatally wounded by the O.A.S. the day before. At the last moment Katz asked General Philippe Ginestet to deputize for him. Ginestet, who had been in Algeria for only a month, was accompanied by Surgeon-Colonel Mabille, director of the hospital. As they left the hospital chapel, a solitary gunman sprang from behind a column and opened fire with a tommy gun. Mabille died instantly, Ginestet shortly afterward. What gave these new murders a diabolical irony was that Ginestet was believed to have strong O.A.S. sympathies, whereas Mabille was a *pied noir* and a secret member of the Organization.

The O.A.S. had the grace to be embarrassed. To cover its confusion, it spread word that Ginestet had actually been killed by Katz' men. Or that Katz had heard of the impending ambush and had deliberately sent Ginestet to his death. Anyway Katz, they said, was guilty of all sorts of other things too. The O.A.S. addressed an open letter to him:

General Katz; Nobody either in the Army or among the population is fooled. You are personally responsible for the murder of Colonel Mario first, General Ginestet and Colonel Mabille afterward. [This promising start, alas, could have qualified for *The New Yorker* as the most intriguing news story of the week, for afterward the letter completely changed the subject.] Nothing is beyond a man, and a general at that, who pointed a carbine at a fellow officer. This incident, certainly unique in the annals of the Army, took place last May 18. Your collaborators, your Adjutant-Colonel of the Gendarmerie, your Chief of Staff, your Corporal-orderly all heard your yells. If they were too cowardly to intervene against your demented behavior, they remain embarassing witnesses against you.

Remember, General Katz? On May 18 you called a fellow officer who was passing in the corridor. You asked his point of view of the situation in Oran. The officer had the honesty to tell you what he thought of the actions of your Red Guards. His frankness put you in a terrible rage. Passing from white to purple you chased your orderly from the office, you got up, you took from your cupboard a carbine fitted with a silencer, and you advanced on the officer until the gun was pressed into his stomach. The officer turned the barrel away, and you, shaking all over, collapsed on your desk screaming "Get out!"

You had this officer transferred to France, General Katz, and he fearing he might be murdered by your thugs, asked the O.A.S. for protection until his departure. It is to satisfy your sense of discipline that you approve the tortures and murders committed by your Red Guards. It is to terrorize the population that you fire on women and children. It is to reaffirm your discipline that you go as far as to murder your second-in-command, a doctor and a colonel with whom you recently had a violent argument. Officers, N.C.O.s and men; this is your chief! Are you going to continue to obey him? Do you want to be forever associated with his record of murder? Your honor and your conscience will make you rebel.

The letter was signed simply, "Captain B."

But, though the O.A.S. could not get Katz, neither could Katz do more than contain the O.A.S. He could not trust his conscripts, who were stopped and amiably disarmed by the O.A.S. whenever the latter was short of arms, and he had to hoard his good troops with care. It was the O.A.S. that patrolled the streets in uniform, the O.A.S. that searched passersby, the O.A.S. to which one applied for permits to travel. Captain Ferrandi has in his possession a note on embossed German Consulate stationery, signed by the Consul, asking O.A.S. permission to move his personal effects back to Germany.

One of the principal hazards for the forces of law was Molotov cocktails tossed from roofs and upstairs windows. It was Katz who inaugurated the policy, carried out so efficiently in Bab-el-Oued, of firing heavy machine guns into any open upstairs window. In Oran, the fact that innocent women and children died from this practice simply spurred on rather than deterred the bombers. It helped to intensify the hate.

Jewish commandos had a trick that rarely failed. They would penetrate the Moslem quarters in Arab disguise, which was easy for them, as Jews and Arabs are both Semitic and often almost indistinguishable. When a patrol of the Gardes Mobiles would enter the quarter, the Jews would open up on them with professionally expert cross fire. The police would conclude that they were from the F.L.N. and not merely random snipers; they would reply with 20-millimeter shells, which caused heavy casualties and damage. In the confusion of the shooting, the Jews would slip away, shed their jellabas and look in on some discothèque or other, where they would be greeted as heroes.

The discothèques played a curious part in this eerie war within a war. O.A.S. patrols assembled in them, went out on missions with machine guns and plastic, then returned; occasionally there were losses that had to be counted, as in "The Dawn Patrol." The girls of Oran loved the O.A.S. almost ritually, as Japanese girls had loved the kamikazes. With their Spanish blood and French emancipation, the girls of Oran were the most beautiful and exciting in Algeria. There were some who considered it their duty to sleep with any O.A.S. men who asked them but spurned all others. There were some who fought like cats for particular heroes. A girl without an O.A.S. boyfriend was regarded with contempt. "We were gods at seventeen," an O.A.S. veteran recalled some years later in his exile in Alicante. "We rarely knew our leaders, so we became our own leaders. We would receive instructions to attack such-and-such a place in 25 minutes. We would arm ourselves, kiss our girls and keep our rendezvous. We operated in commandos—or *collines* as we called them in Oran—of thirteen men. But after we had plasticated, and we heard the police sirens, we remembered that we still had guns in our pockets and tommy guns in the car and it seemed a waste not to fire them. If someone had told us to stop, we would have stopped. We did not know where we were going, really. I suppose that in Oran we believed to the end that the Legion would come out, and everything would be all right."

So when the news came that Susini had thrown in the towel and was prepared to negotiate with the F.L.N. as a spokesman not only for Algiers but also for the whole country, the reaction in Oran was one of flabbergasted incredulity. Dufour, Gardy and their lieutenants met in Dufour's apartment, and the atmosphere was such that had Susini shown himself at that moment he would have been torn to pieces. But rage was mixed with panic. Algiers had seen war in all its facets and had become reconciled to the possibility of defeat. Susini's decision merely solved the problem of whether to stay and see it through or to pack up and go. In Oran the *pieds noirs* had known only victory, and they had to face defeat suddenly, as though all at once they stood on the edge of a sheer precipice. The effect was sickening in its implications. How did one get out and where to? The local boys, never having been abroad, held no passports; the only country to which they could escape was France, where many would be put in prison. The Legionnaires were in an especially terrifying position. The Legion reserved its most brutal punishment for deserters, and, although O.A.S. deserters belonged to a special and more privileged category, the Legion since the Putsch had been remanned with officers who had none of the old Germanophile tradition of the professional Legion officers—and certainly no sympathy for the mystique of the former 1st R.E.P. Neither the locals nor the Legionnaires—and certainly not the Jews—could surrender to the F.L.N. Their backs were to the sea. Smething had to give somewhere; some Delphic solution was required in this desperate confusion.

Most great solutions are simple ones, however, and the problem was solved by a bearded Falstaffian figure who deserves better than the fictitious name given him here; but for reasons that will become obvious, it is necessary. "Pierre Dubois" had been acting for nearly a year as tacit but unofficial go-between for the O.A.S. and the besieged administration. This remarkable man, whose achievements will never be accorded a rosette in his lapel, had, on his arrival, impressed the O.A.S. by refusing to accept the state of siege in which most of the civil servants lived. Although his office was in the new Préfecture he walked in and out without a guard, drank champagne in the cocktail bar of the Grand Hotel and, as spokesman for the administration, gave press conferences to hostile *pied noir* journalists, most of whom were active in the O.A.S. In Oran, the city of murder, where a pause, a glance to right or left, a wrongly phrased sentence, even a wait to use a telephone or toilet brought the danger of a magazineful of bullets, his courage was as great as his resourcefulness.

Dubois, in order to avoid a bloodbath, now prevailed upon the authorities to accept an ingenious and thoroughly illegal and unethical solution. The O.A.S., he said, *had to be given passports.* If not, the men would fight on, and their ghastly deaths would be on Paris' hands. His arguments were so persuasive that blank passports were flown in in boxes and placed at his disposal. Dubois, who could visit Dufour and the O.A.S. cadres as easily as he could visit General Katz, informed the O.A.S. that passports were available and asked that the message be passed along to Algiers and Constantine. Furthermore, passports were available to Legionnaires, as well as to *pieds noirs.* Nor was that all. The O.A.S. men did not have to present themselves in person. They had merely to send Dubois passport photographs, in disguise or not, and slips of paper with their names, dates of birth and so on; any names, any reasonable plausible data would do. These documents Dubois passed on to his mistress, a Yugoslav ballet dancer, who prepared the passports in secret in one of the abandoned luxury bungalows by the sea. Thanks to Dubois, the lives of many O.A.S. men were saved.

But then there were the death commandos, who refused to accept defeat. Their leader was Colonel Dufour, who was making plans to level Oran and to leave only rubble for the F.L.N. Pierre Laffont, owner of the *Écho d'Oran,* came to Dufour's apartment to plead with him to spare the city. Dufour was never the most decisive of men. The episode when he stole the regimental colors of the 1st R.E.P. was sufficient evidence of that. He agreed with Laffont and even wept a little at the thought of the destruction of this lovely city. Nor was he insincere. But when he left, the commando chiefs came back, and Dufour's resolve hardened again.

Garage doors opened to spill out armored cars and even tanks.

Thousands of rounds of ammunition were loaded onto trucks, and the operation to destroy Oran proceeded with hideous efficiency. Rockets ripped into petrol tanks, igniting 4 million gallons, and the harbor went up in an explosion that sounded like an atom bomb; it broke windows three miles away. From the outskirts of the city Oran looked like the victim of nuclear war. The entire city was covered in an umbrella of black smoke, occasionally belching flame, which hid the sunshine and plunged the streets into reeking, suffocating darkness.

Even General Gardy was at the end of his tether. French journalist Robert Buchard found him in his apartment with his head in his hands. "I've lost everything," he groaned. "Degueldre has been condemned to death. My daughter was his mistress and has just had a baby by him. My wife is dying of cancer and my son-in-law is in prison. There's nothing left for me except to die in the ashes of Oran."

Was it all necessary? An objective though far from detached observer of this last agony of Oran was Paul Davis, an N.B.C. correspondent. Davis, a slight, bearded young man belonged to the new breed of television correspondents, who, even more than newspapermen, found it necessary to be at the heart of great events while they were happening; he had been wounded twice in the course of the Algerian war. He was party to one incident that, though undocumented and recountable only with concealed identities, still carries the authority of personal witness by an experienced American correspondent: Davis called in at the old Préfecture to say good-bye to one of the intelligence officers, who is still serving. He found the soldiers packing crates.

The officer said: "I want to show you something. I could have shown it to you a year ago, but a year ago was a different world. Then, it would have been just a captured document. Read it *now*."

He handed Davis the photostat of a letter. It was dated February 1961, two months before the Putsch; it was from Si Azzedine, F.L.N. commander in Algiers to Colonel Boumédienne, Commander in Chief of the Algerian Army in Tunisia, and had been taken from the body of a dead F.L.N. man. Davis did not copy it because it was irrelevant to his assignment, but he recalls that in essence it said:

We are desperate. We are finished. The French are everywhere. Their agents have infiltrated us and know everything we do. Supplies are not reaching us. We cannot communicate even within the cells of the Willayas [military sectors]. I suggest that we end the war and try to negotiate with the French in the hope of resuming the war some time in the future when we are stronger.

"The letter is genuine," said the officer. "I vouch for it. Do you realize what it means? General de Gaulle knew even before the Évian negotiations began that the F.L.N. was licked. But he did not care. Algeria was a caraway seed stuck in his teeth. All he wanted to do was to spit it out, and free himself to carry out his policies, and the hell with a million *pieds noirs,* the hell with the Army, the hell with the million or more pro-French Mussulmans, and the hell with Algeria."

❖❖❖

One of the saddest things about those last ghastly days of French Oran was the apparent disinterest shown by the French administration in the plight of either the Algerians or the *pieds noirs.* Just over a week before independence was scheduled to go into effect, a shipload of Algerians arrived in Oran from Marseilles. These men, mostly un-skilled laborers who had been working in France, had returned to celebrate. The French police and customs officials on the dock could have warned them of the homicidal mood of the city and directed them to the Moslem quarters by roads that would have evaded con-centrations of Europeans. They gave no such advice. The Algerians, laughing and cheering and waving their green flags, climbed to the Place du Gouvernement and into a row of O.A.S. *doucettes,* which mowed them down.

Oran was indeed becoming a redoubt, but only for those fleeing the rest of the country. Every day saw more and more packed buses, roofs piled with suitcases, carrying *pieds noirs* in from the rural countryside. The refugees reported that many interior towns had been completely abandoned by the European population. Banks ran out of cash and closed. Others were besieged by long lines of Europeans. *Pieds noirs* camped in tens of thousands at the airport without food and with almost no medical assistance. Even with Caravelles shuttling them to France all day, it was days and sometimes more than a week before they could leave. They were charged full fare and obliged to carry their own bags, as there were no Moslem porters. They were taking with them as many of their possessions as they could escape with, and there were many old women and children in arms. Nor was their ordeal over when they reached France. Reception facilities in Paris and Marseilles were almost nonexistent, and exhausted immigrants stood in lines for hours at customs and immigration.

On the docks the situation was, if anything, worse. One quay had a single toilet for two thousand people. At the period of maximum density there were thirty thousand people waiting at the airport and docks for transportation. Only a score of Red Cross workers was available to give assistance.

General Joseph Katz watched the chaos in Oran with a mixture of helplessness, compassion and satisfaction. He could not stamp out the flames, but he was watching the O.A.S. disintegrate before his eyes. Even in his most optimistic moments he had never conceived of so total a defeat. His war with the O.A.S. had dragged on for so long indecisively that it had become for him almost a way of life. Like the *pieds noirs* of Oran, he saw Oran as a last-ditch redoubt that could well remain French for all time. Even a week before, he had needed a powerful escort before he could venture out of his headquarters. Now the whole edifice had crumbled. Even in the sufferings and the depredations there were legitimate reasons for satisfaction, and Katz was determined that there should be no last-minute complications. He had passed the word to the O.A.S. leaders that they need fear no opposition from his men and that they were free to leave.

In those last hours the indefatigable Paul Davis drove back and forth, taking advantage of his comparative immunity as an American to help friends organize, pack and get out before the F.L.N. arrived to distribute the Kabylia smile, as the slit throat was called. On his way to Mers-el-Kébir he came upon a horrible sight. A heavy water cart was being drawn, not by horses, but by two men who were almost unrecognizable from dirt and beatings. They appeared to be Jews or Moslem collaborators. Their guards wore F.L.N. armbands and drove them along with whips and spittle. Davis stopped his car, but a tommy gun was pressed to his chest, and he obeyed the staccato order to keep moving.

At the docks he found thousands of harkis camped outside the entrance. They had erected their tents and sat with their families and children around little campfires cooking their food. Sanitation facilities were nonexistent, and the smell was abominable. Davis showed his credentials and was taken to the office of the commanding officer, a major in the Marine Commandos. The man was overworked and harassed. Davis mentioned the hordes of squatting harkis.

"We are taking Europeans first," the officer said. "Those are my orders."

Davis was outraged. "You can't!" he exclaimed. "I have been in this country for four years and so, probably, have you. You know what this means, Major. At least let the Moslems come inside the base where they will be under French protection. These people should get away *before* the French. The new Algerian Government will have to be circumspect in the way they treat the French, and they can leave later. But the harkis have sacrificed everything for French promises. You are condemning them to a horrible fate. If you are abandoning them why the hell did you promise them in the first place that Algeria would stay French?"

The exhausted officer leaped to his feet and with a shaking hand waved in the general direction of the city. "Have you seen the airport? Have you seen the docks? The *pieds noirs* are camping out too. If there is no room there is no room. I can't build ships and planes in this office with my typewriter. I'm only a major of Marines."

Davis made his way out again into the smoky, stinking sunlight. As he left, the scene grew even more poignant. Hundreds of dejected harkis were pulling carts with their families and possessions and heading back to their homes. They had given up hope of escaping to France and had decided to go into hiding until calm was restored. Hundreds of them were slaughtered on Independence Day and thousands more afterward. The French Government later estimated unofficially that between six and ten thousand harkis had been murdered. This statistic, horrifying though it is, has to be balanced against the fact that the harkis in the course of the war had killed many times ten thousand of their fellow Moslems.

And all the time the smoke lay on the city; around every street corner it seemed that a tommy gun chattered or a charge of plastic deafened the ears. Glass broke in showers of splinters. Public transport stopped, although private cars still darted through the acrid gloom, traveling very fast, with horns baying their owners' fears as

they ran the gauntlets of real or imagined death. Many telephone lines
had been cut, and all the restaurants were closed. Both the O.A.S.
and the F.L.N. had threatened to poison the water supply. Such
Europeans as were still left, the administrators and correspondents,
sat in their rooms eating tinned sardines and drinking whatever they
had been able to buy before the shutters slammed on the liquor
stores. Yet there is a limit to the horror that the human spirit can absorb, and one of the last scenes in French Oran was one of black
comedy. Nearly all the *pieds noirs* were leaving their cars behind. Any
kind of car left on the street could be stolen with impunity, for law
and order had broken down. The thieves were not so much Moslems
as European scavengers, the scatterlings of every holocaust, who
crawl out like roaches through the gaping holes of a collapsed civilization to rob the dead, ransack the stores, dress in stolen finery.

Colonel Dufour kept his pirate radio hidden in the trunk of his
Peugeot 403. As a transmitter of low power, it could be kept easily in
a confined space, and it was brought to his apartment only for broad-
casters to make their prerecorded tapes.

Dufour had finally agreed to the inevitable and had drafted a
cease-fire speech acknowledging the end of the war. But, coming
down in the elevator, he found that his car had been stolen. The
comic aspect of the situation was in the hair-raising terror that the
thief would experience when he opened the trunk and found the
transmitter. The O.A.S., although it was a finished force, was still
synonymous with instant death in Oran. If he were caught by the
O.A.S., he would be promptly exterminated; if he were caught by the
F.L.N., the captors would assume from the transmitter that he was an
O.A.S. man and kill him more slowly. Dufour's dilemma also had a
comic solution. He took a friend's car, drove to the French military
radio station, identified himself and conferred with the commanding
officer. They agreed on the necessity for the broadcast, but if it were
to be believed by the remaining O.A.S. forces it would have to sound
as if it were emanating from the pirate transmitter. The radio tech-
nicians were called in to advise, and Dufour went on the air to make
his speech.

"And a very good speech it was too, Colonel," said the officer after
it was finished.

"Very good of you to say so," Dufour murmured, gratified.

"Not at all."

"It's very convenient to broadcast through official channels," said Dufour shaking hands. "Pity we didn't think of it before."

Gardy and Dufour and a handful of others were among the last to leave Oran, boarding a trawler on July 5 and making their way to Spain. There the O.A.S. men assembled and looked around for Perez and Susini in order to receive their pay. They are still looking.

❖❖❖

Ahmed Ben Bella, head of the new government, arrived in Algeria from Morocco in an open presidential car lent him by the King. He was received by cheering crowds and two guards of honor, one presented by the French Army and another by the Algerian Army of National Liberation. General Katz represented the French Government. But before acknowledging Katz' salute, Ben Bella did a surprising thing. He took from his breast pocket a hand mirror and comb and combed his hair. Correspondents who observed the incident felt that the new chief's order of priorities did not augur particularly well for the new Algerian Republic.

22
INTERLUDE
May–July 1962

❖❖❖

To judge by the circumstances surrounding the trial of General Salan, no one would have thought that the O.A.S. was a shattered army. Around the Boulevard du Palais iron barricades had been set up to frustrate attempts at plastication. Military police with machine guns were stationed every few feet. Identity papers were scrutinized by armed guards, ladies' handbags were searched and men were frisked. The Mandarin was defended by France's inevitable spokesman for the extreme Right, Maître Jean-Louis Tixier-Vignancourt. "Tixier," often called "T.V.," which means the same thing in French as in English, was a short man with the shoulders of a boxer, brush-cut gray hair and a mouth like that of a hunting dog that has clamped onto a ferret. Tixier-Vignancourt stood so solidly on his feet as to seem immovable. He made his points in an even baritone voice and usually without a smile, although his great gray eyes would twinkle at a point well made, especially by himself. Tixier-Vignancourt, who campaigned three years later, not very successfully, for the Presidency of the Republic, was to the French Bar rather what Jean Gabin was to the French cinema—an institution, a star whom it was a pleasure to see and hear for his own sake, even in a bad film or a poor case, a man with whom one is happier to grow old. One had the impression that neither Gabin nor Tixier-Vignancourt would have the slightest difficulty in playing the other's part. The nearest personality to Tixier's in American law is that of Melvin Belli. Both relish decrying the paradox by which human frailty is judged by frail humans and the unwisdom of people in glass houses' throwing stones. Belli's denunciation of Texas justice was in the true Tixier-Vignancourt mold.

The trial before a high military tribunal lasted eight days, during most of which Salan sat slumped, dispirited and hollow-eyed while Tixier sprayed phrases as rich as perfume over the prosecution. His was a relaxed performance, that of a man already condemned, who knew he could offer nothing but virtuosity. Only one verdict was possible for the chief of the O.A.S., death by firing squad, the sentence Jouhaud had received earlier. Tixier told the court that, since June 18, 1940, all officers had learned the wisdom—he did not say "justice"—of disobeying orders that violated the promptings of conscience. He cast doubts on the competence of the tribunal and drew parallels between the trials of General Salan and of Marshal Ney. "Salan," he said, "was given only three days examination by the *juge d'instruction,*" compared with three months granted to Ney "who," he added, "was shot." The lawyer paused and added: "A Paris boulevard was named after Marshal Ney. The magistrate who condemned him did not even get his name on an alley wall."

Tixier-Vignancourt announced that Salan would make a statement and would refuse thereafter to open his mouth or reply to any questions. Salan's voice was unexpected. It was surprisingly gentle, and it warmed the cold air of the Paris courtroom with a distinct accent of the Midi. It was the wrong voice for the face. The voice belonged to thick black hair and brown eyes, not to the haggard face of Salan. Yet the sentences followed elegantly—for Salan was always stylish— the words ending with the gentle, almost subliminal "aw" of the Méridional: *Je suis-aw le chef-aw de l'O.A.S.-aw.*

> I am the chief of the O.A.S. My responsibility is therefore total. I acknowledge it, having no intention of changing a line of conduct I have maintained for over 42 years of command. I am not the chief of a gang, nor of a defeated army, but a French general representing a victorious army. The difference between you and him you ask permission to execute is this, that I have served most of my career outside France. I have fought to guard the Empire of Gallieni, Lyautey and Father de Foucauld. My body is covered with the scars of combat. I have helped to make the light of France shine overseas. I have commanded, I have secured, I have distributed, I have defied, but above all I have loved. . . .

He went on to recount events since the 13th of May as he saw them and concluded:

> I chose to bring de Gaulle back to power. If I misled the people of Algeria it was because I myself was misled. It is the French Government which, by denying its origins, is responsible for the blood that is flowing, and, more responsible than anyone else is the person to whom I myself gave power. I don't have to exonerate myself. I don't have to apologize for not wanting to see communism establish itself an hour away from Marseilles, and Paris within range of its short-range rockets. I do not have to exonerate myself for having defended the wealth that our young pioneers have given to France in the Sahara, assuring our independence in oil. If we, the Allies, had lost the war, the Germans would be demanding de Gaulle's head, just as the F.L.N. is demanding mine. You will have to seek the answer in your own consciences, but whatever your decision, it will not affect my honor. I owe no debt save to those who suffer and die for having believed in a word of honor disowned and in obligations betrayed. From now on I am silent.

One of the most effective witnesses against Salan was his former subordinate, General Ailleret, who gave a different picture of the O.A.S. and of Salan. He said:

> It is common knowledge that Salan was the chief of the O.A.S. I will add that he was the real chief of the O.A.S. not simply the nominal chief. That we know because we have had directives and instructions signed "Salan" fall into our hands. . . . One has seen in the course of history numerous forms of terrorism; there are certain aspects of sport about it. The O.A.S. is a terrorism which we might call bureaucratic insofar as the principal goal is the safety of the terrorist himself. I have never heard of anyone killed by the O.A.S. who was killed in combat, or hardly anyone. . . . A burst of gunfire from a passing car on defenseless victims, or a mortar fired and then the squad disappears immediately. That is the style of this kind of terrorism. . . .

In French law the lawyers do not cross-examine. They put the questions to the judge, who decides whether or not to transmit them.

In this case the prosecutor asked and was given permission to question Salan, despite Salan's statement that he did not intend to utter another word. "Are not your heart and spirit shaken by the facts that have been recalled, and of which you stand accused?" he asked. Salan did not reply, disproving the old maxim that a silly question demands a silly answer. He folded his arms and looked into space. The prosecutor let the silence pour slowly over the court and said: "No answer. Do you consider that your crimes were made legitimate by your intentions? By what claim do you find absolution and reason?" Salan gave an invisible sigh, waiting for the monologue to end. "No answer," said the prosecutor. "Do you consider that, lacking excuses, these crimes are attenuated by your reasons for committing them? Obstinate silence. I am not going to comment on all this. There are no replies for us to comment on. We cannot comment on silence."

It was good theater, but it was Salan who emerged from the one-sided encounter as the more sympathetic figure. After all, it was he—the most decorated soldier in the French Army, a man who had abandoned everything for a cause, misguided or not—who was going to die. Death rhetoric is not a comfortable thing to listen to, and even the prosecutor himself seemed to sense doom, for he could not bring himself to call it "death." He called it "irreversible judgment."

On the eighth day Tixier-Vignancourt allowed himself to climax his own rhetoric: "The Parliamentary commission met yesterday to discuss the amnesty bill," he said quietly. His voice rose: "Think, gentlemen, of your consciences, if, one week after General Salan has fallen before a French firing squad, an amnesty law is passed. For the rest of your lives you will not be able to extinguish your remorse."

The tribunal retired for two hours and a half, then returned to declare that it had found "extenuating circumstances." For a brief moment there was an incredulous silence. *What* extenuating circumstances? The dead were dead. The O.A.S. had killed them. Salan had commanded the O.A.S. No extenuating circumstances had been found for General Jouhaud, who had been sentenced to death after a year spent lounging in the cafés of Oran.

There was pandemonium in the court. The presiding judge could scarcely be heard condemning Salan to prison for life, as the packed courtroom burst into hysterical cheers and shouts of *Algérie française*. Even Tixier-Vignancourt's iron aplomb was momentarily shaken. With tears in his eyes, he held his arms out to the judges and cried: "Thank you! Oh, thank you!" and turned to embrace Salan, who seemed too overwhelmed to know what to say but merely smiled blinking. In the corridors outside the courtroom one could hear the cry taken up and voices singing *Le Chant des Africains* and the *Marseillaise*.

General de Gaulle made no attempt to conceal his anger at the verdict, and two days later he dissolved the Tribunal.

Next it was the turn of Roger Degueldre. Once more Tixier-Vignancourt was the defending attorney, but he was not in his usual devastating form. Possibly he was overconfident, or possibly he was constrained by his very success. If he could save Salan, he should have been able to save Degueldre. Precedent had given him a formidable weapon. But pleading a hopeless case is often easier than pleading one that is merely difficult. His premise was unarguable, but then he became too clever and fumbled.

"Go and tell the world," he exhorted the judges, "Go and tell the world that in France you condemn to death the *pied noir,* Piegts, the sergeant, Dovecar, the lieutenant, Degueldre, but from the rank of general up—no! It seems that to preserve one's existence today one must write theses. What do you want? That Degueldre approve the Treaty of Brest-Litovsk? It might have been better if 'President' Susini had asked 'President' Farès to put Degueldre at his service, then all would have been simple. 'President' Farès would have written to Monsieur Joxe who would have written to Monsieur Gerthoffer [one of the judges] and it would have been in the bag. You could have stayed home."

It actually sounded better than it reads. His reference to Brest-Litovsk, as he slowly turned and plaintively indicated Degueldre, as mournful as Disney's Pluto in the dock, was as funny as it was cruel and made the court both laugh and wince at the gallows wit and Tixier-Vignancourt's bad taste.

Degueldre was condemned to death. "He could expect nothing else," said Axel Nicol. "Somebody had to take the rap seeing that Salan had only been imprisoned."

Yet even in his condemned cell, Degueldre held a moral domination over his captors. Two warders stood outside his door day and night, and the cell on either side of him was kept empty as if anyone but Degueldre could free him. He was told of the execution of his friends Bobby Dovecar and Claude Piegts in the Trou d'Enfer (Hell-hole) outside Paris. The verdict on Dovecar was inevitable, but on Piegts it seemed unnecessarily harsh. Piegts had handed Dovecar the key to Commissioner Gavoury's apartment, and he was later arrested on the Riviera while raising money for the O.A.S. But life had become too unreal for Degueldre to grieve, and he amused himself with fantasies, removing himself in spirit from his own body and observing himself dispassionately as a stranger, someone quite different, a fellow called "Jules." He wrote:

> After a certain trial Degueldre Roger has been transferred to his condemned cell. That is what those fellows say, I who knew D.R. for 37 years. The man imprisoned at Fresnes is called Jules (at least that is the name I have given him). Jules is very different from poor Roger. Since his arrival he had done nothing but sleep, read, drink and eat. Everybody is being very pleasant to him. One would have said that he is an important person who has just escaped death after a long illness. He is convalescing but has to be carefully looked after for fear of a relapse. It is also important that he lacks for nothing, and they open the door often to make sure whether he needs anything. Rich and abundant food is necessary for this great invalid, and they do not hesitate in giving it to him. At night it is necessary to keep watch on poor Jules, and they leave on a blue light to check his sleep without hurting his eyes. In the morning they bring him coffee in bed, they help him take a little promenade, always under the careful surveillance of one, two, or three guardians. These are always armed, and that is one of the reasons I say that it is not Degueldre Roger because Jules does not get the same treatment.
>
> The head of the house sometimes comes to see him and give him medicine. The chaplain came to see him yesterday. Very gentle and very understanding, but Jules is suspicious about these fellows. In so far as that goes he does resemble D.R.
>
> Everyone in Jules' everyday life gives him a sad smile, full of understanding. Jules replies with a big smile and a friendly word, and it seems that each time he smiles he hears a sigh of relief. The sigh seems to say, "Ah! He's getting better." And Jules is quite content with this farce he is playing. Sometimes but not often a blue funk instills

itself into Jules, and it is quickly rejected because this
funk is destined for D.R., and Jules wants none of it. This
is another reason why I say it is not D.R., but Jules, who is
here.

Jules is quite detached from the world and isn't interested in anything. All day long the radio talks of a certain
Tour de France which it seems is interesting all France,
but Jules pays no attention to these guys who sweat away
the kilometers when a car or a plane would do it so much
more quickly and restfully.

Jules' room is yellow, clean and neat, but the door and
window are barred and always closed. The devil with it,
one never knows what goes on in the head of a great in-
valid! Jules doesn't give a wild damn and thinks only to
stretch himself on the bed, not too comfortable because
it's too soft, and smoke, eat, read, drink and sleep. Every
day after the walk, they make him shower, always under
attentive and close guard. He enjoys it and it amuses him
to ask one of the guards to switch the water from hot to
cold and they obey him to his instant satisfaction. When
Jules leaves his room everyone who is not a guard is ordered
to his own room and hidden away. No one has the right
to look at Jules, because he is such an important person. I
think by now I have said everything there is to say about
Jules and his calm and gentle life. And Degueldre Roger,
you say, where is he then? What is he doing? What is he
thinking? Ah, that is a secret I know well, but only I
know it.

On the evening of July 1, the word spread through the Santé:
"Degueldre dies tomorrow at dawn." A terrible din broke out, com-
pounded of tin plates clattering against bars, banging feet, yells of
Algérie française and "assassins" and the chant of "De-gueldre!
De-gueldre! De-gueldre!"

Degueldre knew nothing of it. He was sleeping in his cell at
Fresnes. The following morning before it was light he put on his
uniform and decorations, which included the Legion of Honor and
the Military Medal. He courteously declined the services of a priest.
Guarded by twenty *motards* against a possible O.A.S. attempt to
rescue him, he was taken from Fresnes to Fort d'Ivry. His hands were
tied behind his back at the execution post. He refused the blindfold

and was permitted a few last words. He thought for a moment and said: "I want to say to all my fellow officers that I am proud to go to the end and die for having held to the oath I made that every fighting officer has sworn to at least once, not to deliver Algeria to the F.L.N. I am going to join my chief, Colonel Jeanpierre, who was my inspiration. . . ."

He hesitated for a moment, and the young officer commanding the firing squad looked to see if he had finished. Degueldre, gathering last thoughts as the seconds faded away, went on, "And please tell General Salan and General Jouhaud that I am proud to have fought under their orders."

"Is that all?" the officer asked. Degueldre nodded.

It is relevant, even as Degueldre stands before the firing squad, to interrupt and explain something of the workings of a firing squad. The author of this book witnessed several executions in the Cabaña Prison of Havana in the weeks following Fidel Castro's accession to power. The captain of the fort's *pelotón* was an American named Herman Marks, sometimes known as "Herman the Hangman"; he was later imprisoned in the United States. Marks told the writer that, in his experience, out of a *pelotón* of six rifles, on an average only three bullets reached their mark and never more than four. The misses he attributed to religious conscience on the part of one, superstition on the part of a second and nervousness on the part of a third, although he could never decide which of the six was which. To correct the inefficiency of his charges, he switched personnel and put them through repeated exercises with straw-filled dummies, which were invariably hit by six bullets. But no matter how often he exercised his troops, when the target was human flesh, the same odds prevailed. Being a man of limited philosophy, he settled for what he had and relied on the unerring marksmanship, no complimentary pun intended, of his own coup de grace.

Tixier-Vignancourt was present at the execution, and, although the Army later issued a statement that his version of what happened was "inexact," several witnesses corroborated it. The *peloton* was composed of twelve Army conscripts, their guns visibly shaking in their hands. At the order, *"Peloton! Attention!"* Degueldre began to sing the *Marseillaise*. As he reached the words *le jour de gloire* the order was given, "Fire!" The song ended with the crash of guns, and, as the echo died away, one saw through the gunsmoke Degueldre staring ahead, with glazed eyes blinking, like a boxer who has taken a hard punch. Only one bullet had hit him and that through the side. He was in no pain. In such a situation pain does not exist, either in the body or in the mind. Degueldre was numb and swaying; his hands tied behind the execution post stopped him from falling. One of the soldiers in the firing squad began to sob. The officer, as appalled as the rest at Degueldre's hideous devotion to life, drew his revolver from his shoulder, aimed tremulously at Degueldre's head and hit him in the shoulder. Degueldre leaped a little but apart from that scarcely moved. A second bullet went clumsily through his ear, and he slumped forward wheezing loudly. Six coups de grace were needed to dispatch him, which was not in itself unusual. Even Marks, the professional, on at least one occasion needed four.

At any rate *le grand Roger* had been given the gratification, even as he joined his colonel, of knowing that he was a better killer than his killers. When his uniform was removed, a small French tricolor was found against his heart. The soldiers had missed it. Degueldre died as he had lived, an innocent. Even as he did so, his superior officer in the Foreign Legion and his prospective father-in-law, General Gardy, who had devoted so much thought to the best use of Degueldre's killer's talents, was installing himself comfortably in San Sebastian, Spain, with his daughter and grandson, Degueldre's child. There he was in no danger; he wrote away to the Argentine for employment. It was a trail well worn by the Nazis in 1945, and Father Grasset would have no trouble in furnishing him with contacts. In the meantime, he could walk his dog in the cool of the evening and acknowledge the hats tipped by the locals in deference to his age and rank.

23
INTERLUDE
August 1962

✦✦✦

One does not often ascribe the word "beautiful" to a man, but this young man could be called "beautiful." His hair was thick and brown, his eyes under heavy brows poetic. It was a face that the French themselves might have selected by consensus to represent the nobility and spirit of Frenchmen. "Is it not true, Father," he asked, "that the Church will pardon tyrannicide if the conditions are such that society would benefit from it?"

It is obviously a question not often asked, but the priest acknowledged that he believed it was so. "What tyrant do you have in mind?" he asked.

"General de Gaulle," said the young man. "I believe that his betrayal of French Algeria merits his death."

This singular exchange took place at Dinard in France in the summer of 1962 while Susini was negotiating with the Provisional Government in Algiers and while Degueldre was writing funny notes to himself in his cell in Fresnes. The priest's ultimate opinion is locked in the secrecy of the confessional, but the young man walked out into the summer night refreshed with the conviction that he had a holy mandate to do what he planned to do. He was the kind of man who, had he been advised otherwise by the Church, would not have persisted.

His name was Jean-Marie Bastien-Thiry; he was 35 years old and a graduate of the École Polytechnique, the school of Argoud and Lacheroy. Once more this remarkable institution figured in the history of the O.A.S. The Polytechnique, a creation of the French Revolution, stands near the Panthéon and expresses the martial spirit of Napoleon. It's motto is "For Country, Science, and Glory." To be a Polytechnician is to follow such men as Jules Henri Poincaré, the mathematician; Auguste Comte, the philosopher, and two French Presidents, Carnot and Lebrun. In the First World War the Polytechnique had produced four marshals of France, including Joffre and Foch. Another product of the Polytechnique was Roger Wybot, head of the French Secret Service, who for years seemed as invulnerable as J. Edgar Hoover does—until General de Gaulle discovered that Wybot had "bugged" his conversations during his years of retirement at Colombey-les-Deux-Églises and fired him. Whatever reasons Bastien-Thiry had for wanting to kill the President, it was not lack of privilege.

After leaving the priest's house, Bastien-Thiry walked through the empty streets of Dinard to his hotel and aroused the telephone operator to make a long-distance call. Although it was past midnight, the telephone was picked up at the first ring, and the voice that answered was alert. Bastien-Thiry said "This is the Colonel" and hung up.

At 8:10 on the evening of August 22, the Presidential Citroën left the Élysée Palace and, with a security Citroen and two *motards* close behind, drove through Paris toward Villacoublay Airport, where an airplane was waiting to take de Gaulle to Colombey-les-Deux-Églises. De Gaulle sat in the back, with Madame de Gaulle by his side. His son-in-law, Alain de Boissieu, sat in front with Henry Marroux, the chauffeur (Boissieu was a cousin of the Boissieu who had insulted Debré at the Barricades and had later conveyed Challe's surrender to Paris after the Putsch).

At the village of Petit Clamart, the small convoy slowed at a traffic circle. A man jumped from the rear of a Renault truck and opened fire with a machine gun. Bullets streamed through the car, which swerved and caromed off the edge of the pavement. Boissieu, ignoring his own danger, pushed the General and his wife to the floor and ordered the driver to accelerate. One hundred yards farther on, the car was spun around by cross fire from a Citroën.

Bullets continued to hit the chassis, smashing the windows and blowing two of the supposedly puncture-proof tires. The car narrowly missed hitting a parked truck and limped away down the highway in a cloud of black smoke, swerving like a sandcrab at a breakneck hobble.

At the airport, General de Gaulle, unflappable, stepped out and examined the wreckage of the car. "Those fellows really cannot shoot straight," he said. General de Gaulle was yet again being less than fair to his critics. He had missed death literally by inches. To be precise, he had missed death by exactly two inches. Six bullets had penetrated the rear part of the car where he had been sitting. Four had hit the security car. One hundred and fifty shell cases were picked up at the scene of the ambush. Had it not been for the courage of Alain de Boissieu, far beyond any son-in-law's duty, General de Gaulle would certainly have been dead.

It was the second major attempt on De Gaulle's life since May 13, 1958. The other had been crude and amateurish. This one had been planned with precision by experts. The purpose of the first burst of fire was to force the car to swerve into the cross fire, which it did.

One of the would-be assassins' vehicles was quickly found abandoned about half a mile away from the scene outside a bar called the Green Carpet. In it were found two automatic rifles, five magazines, a phosphorous grenade, two smoke bombs and two pounds of plastic explosive, but no fingerprints and no real clues as to who the men were.

Now the story of the O.A.S. becomes, briefly, a detective story. The case, with all its enormous international implications, was given to one of France's best detectives, Commissioner Bouvier of the Paris Sûreté. Bouvier was 42 years old, quite young to have risen so high in the police service. He was a pipe smoker, like so many fictional detectives, and something of an athlete. For more than a year he had been in charge of police operations against the O.A.S. in Paris. The would-be assassins had made a clean getaway, leaving behind not even a rough description; Bouvier was obliged to start from scratch. Road-blocks had been set up along every road leading from Petit Clamart, causing traffic chaos, for it was August, when every Frenchman not at his favorite holiday resort is either on his way there or on his way back. More than 1 million automobiles were stopped and questioned without result. The very mass of traffic covered the attackers' escape.

A check was made on every known O.A.S. sympathizer in the country and on the *pieds noirs* clustered in their thousands in the Midi and at Port Vendres, the port of entry from Algeria. Ironically it was the collapse of the O.A.S. in Algeria that saved the skins of the leaders of O.A.S.-Métro. Pierre Sergent and Jean-Marie Curutchet had already fled to Belgium. Traces of Sergent were found in all sorts of places, and he would certainly have been gobbled up in the investigation had the assassination been attempted two months earlier, when the O.A.S. organization was still intact.

The hard work began, the unbelievably hard, unrewarding work that policemen undertake on such occasions. The Citroën from which the attackers had fired the second burst was identified. As expected, it had been rented by a man who called himself "Jean Murat." The famous name was, of course, false, and the girl who rented the car to him had only the vaguest recollection of his face, for he had worn his hat down over his eyes and dark glasses. From her vague description, the police assembled an identikit face and circulated thousands of copies to police stations all over the country.

One detective was assigned to the area where "Jean Murat" had rented the car, showing the identikit and asking questions. Another was given the task of combing every single café along the President's route to Petit Clamart, to learn if any telephone call had been made as de Gaulle passed.

Among the thousands of reports turned in, one proved to be of the highest significance, although the police could not know it at the time; a man had gone into a bar and had told the *patronne* that his name was Perrin and that he was awaiting an incoming call.

After that Bouvier found himself against a blank wall. The attack had taken place so suddenly that even the police escort could offer no clue to the identities of the assailants.

Ten days after the attempt there seemed to be a break. Police moving from apartment house to apartment house along the Presidential route found that a small flat in the town of Meudon had been rented shortly before to a girl called Monique Bertin, who had been active in the French Algeria cause. Monique's brother, Pascal, nicknamed "the Pickle," also a sympathizer but with no known association with the O.A.S., visited her frequently with friends. Descriptions of these friends were taken from Monique's neighbors. One, more easily identifiable than the others, was an ugly lame man in his forties.

At the Quai des Orfèvres, dossiers were examined for a man who was lame, in his forties, ugly and identified with French Algeria.

The man they came up with was Georges Wattin, known as "Clubfoot," a *pied noir,* an O.A.S. man, a crony of Jésus Giner and a veteran of the Barricades. He was traced and arrested with Monique Bertin, but their alibis held, and a search of their homes revealed nothing. Once more the police were at a dead end. The suspects were released, but their movements were watched.

Bouvier was not a temperamental man. A detective cannot afford the luxury of despair or even of pessimism. He had no alternative but to persist in his investigations, start all over again if need be and hope for the best. So far all he had to show for the massive endeavor and expense was the shadowy identikit of a man who had given himself the alias of one of Napoleon's marshals and a group of people with O.A.S. or French Algeria backgrounds visiting an apartment in Meudon. Perrin's waiting for a telephone call was buried among thousands of reports and was not even considered a clue at all. Intuition suggested to Bouvier that Monique Bertin and Clubfoot Wattin *were* involved in the plot; but there were too many people in France with vested interests in de Gaulle's death, and all were prepared to perjure themselves and offer false alibis to frustrate the police. What Bouvier needed at that stage of his investigation was *baraka*. On September 3, eleven days after the attack, it arrived.

A spectacular robbery was committed in Marseilles, and the robbers escaped in a Dauphine car. Police set up roadblocks around the city to check all Dauphines. One man, stopped at Tain, was recognized by an alert detective as Pierre Magade, a young gangster from Montmartre. His nickname was "Pierre le Globule," probably because he was slightly cross-eyed.

Magade had been driving all day, and he was tired and hungry. A traveler's anticipation of a good meal and a rest are a great boon to any detective when he wishes to elicit information. Magade, instead of dining, found himself in a drab and uncomfortable police station being questioned about a robbery he knew nothing about—and then about the incident at Petit Clamart, about which, it so happened, he knew a great deal. The detective, certainly an able man, was pursuing a hunch. Marseilles, traditional hangout of the Corsican Mafia, had also become the refuge of the *pieds noirs,* just as Miami, Florida, had become the capital of the exiled Cubans. The French had urged and even bribed *pieds noirs* to move north, but every *pied noir* who could find a job on the Mediterranean settled in the familiar atmosphere of warm sunshine. The question that exercised the detective was, What was a Paris criminal with no Corsican connections doing in Marseilles unless he was on business, honest or otherwise, with the *pieds noirs?*

For several hours, while he grew steadily hungrier and more weary, the Globule denied any knowledge of the attempt on de Gaulle's life, but all at once he broke down. Yes, he said, he *was* at Petit Clamart, and once a man starts to talk he does not stop. He had been one of the drivers, he said, not a gunman. Wattin the Clubfoot had been there too. Monique Bertin's alibi was false. Monique's brother, the Pickle under the false name of "Perrin," had been assigned to wait in a bar for a telephone call and then to pass the word that de Gaulle was on his way. According to the Globule there was another gunman he knew at the scene, as well as several whom he did not know. The one he knew was Alexis *le Barbu*, an Army deserter, whose father, a retired general, lived in the Rue Vaugirard in Paris.

Then, at a certain point, the torrent of confession ceased.

"Who was the leader of the plot?"

Magade replied: "I don't know. We know him only as 'the Colonel.' "

He could not be shaken. Finally he was given food and left to sleep in a cell, not quite the conditions he had anticipated while driving, but not altogether unfamiliar. Certainly they were better than interrogation.

This was the major breakthrough that Bouvier had sought. With his tremendous police machine, it was no difficult task to winkle out a deserter, and Alexis *le Barbu* was found hiding in a farmhouse on the Riviera. Bouvier ordered that he was not to be questioned until he was brought to the Quai des Orfèvres. In the meantime, Alexis' father's telephone was tapped, and it too yielded evidence.

The listeners heard an outside caller talking to the maid. "I would like to speak to Alexis," said the voice. "Tell him it is the Pickle."

Bertin the Pickle, alias "Perrin," was speaking from the restaurant of the Samaritaine department store in Paris, a short walk from the Quai des Orfèvres. Within minutes it was ringed by police. The restaurant of the Samaritaine is the kind of rendezvous where women meet to gossip. It is not a man's place, and so it was easy to close in on Bertin sitting alone. He looked up from the brandy he was sipping into the barrels of police automatics, and his hands went up.

At the Quai des Orfèvres, Bertin admitted his part in the affair. He named other men involved in the plot, and they proved to constitute a weird fallout from every crisis that had convulsed Algeria from May 13 to the Ouarsenis. They included a veteran officer and deserter from the 1st R.E.P. named Captain Bougrenet de la Tocnaye, who had been captured but had escaped from prison the previous January; three Hungarians who had joined the Legion after the Hungarian revolution; Jean-Jacques Prévost, who had been wounded at Dien Bien Phu, had been arrested at the Barricades, had survived the disaster of the Ouarsenis and had become one of the last O.A.S. men to leave Algeria. Others were young enthusiasts of French Algeria, students and former members of the movement of Robert Martel. Yet none appeared to know the identity of the man who had planned the operation.

"All we know," said Bertin, "is that we call him 'the Colonel.' "

He claimed that he could not describe him because he had never met him, nor did he know anyone who had. The other prisoners told the same story. Nobody had ever seen "the Colonel." Worse, the police had no clue to his identity. They knew all the pseudonyms of the O.A.S. from "Albatross" (Argoud) to "Yazid" (Jouhaud). There were colonels aplenty, but the only "Colonel" on the list was André Canal, who had been caught six months earlier and was in prison.

All the men identified were arrested. One of the Hungarian deserters, a man named Laszlo Vargas, was found in the apartment of an eccentric countess who had been known to support O.A.S. causes, but all told the same story. Bouvier, however, was at last able to piece the entire plot together. The attack had been meticulously planned, both the ambush itself and the smooth getaway into the countryside on buses and passing trains. The first burst of gunfire from the Renault truck was the work of Bougrenet de la Tocnaye, known to the gang as "Max," who was field commander of the operation. Three subordinates were waiting to drive him clear without even waiting to see the result of the second burst. Prévost had fired the second burst. Wattin had been at the wheel of one of the cars.

Bouvier had evidence enough to show that the "Colonel" was a man of first-rate intelligence. With the expert assistance of Colonel Debrosse, who had been transferred to Metropolitan France, he was able to narrow down the list of possibilities. The "Colonel" had either known Roger Degueldre or was familiar with his methods; the whole operation had the Degueldre touch. The O.A.S. colonels were discussed and eliminated in turn. Godard was incapable of it. Gardes might have done it, but so far as they knew he had not left Spain. Broizat had the intelligence but lacked the ruthlessness. Château-Jobert was capable of it, but he had been losing his mind in recent

months, and his concentration span would be too low. It was too
imaginative for Dufour. The only colonel left with both the organizing ability and the technical intelligence, was Antoine Argoud. It
was the characteristic essay of a man who had gone through the
Polytechnique. Bouvier's thoughts had returned frequently in the
course of the investigation to the great Écoles.

One of the missing links in the case was "Jean Murat," who had
rented the car. If "Murat" and the "Colonel" were the same person,
a major link was established.

All the time the grinding house-to-house inquiry went on all over
France. At the Hôtel de la Poste in Dinard, a telephone operator
looked at the identikit of "Murat" and thought it looked "familiar";
it had looked familiar to thousands of other people, but the police
neglected no clue. The telephone operator, evidently a young lady
with unusual capacities of recall, thought more about the picture
until it became identified in her mind with a guest of the hotel who
had made a long-distance telephone call, but she could not remember the destination. The Post Office was called to check long-distance
calls made from the Hôtel de la Poste in Dinard before, during and
after the attack.

This step led to another break in the case. In the town of Brive-la-
Gaillarde, one of those on the list of calls from Dinard, the police
discovered a local notary who permitted his home to be used as a
mailing address and for telephone calls. Most of the letters, he said,
were addressed simply to nicknames and were picked up periodically
by different people. One of the nicknames was "Max." Some, he
added, were quite amusing, "like Pickle. And Clubfoot. And Globule . . ."

Bouvier and the whole force of the Sûreté descended on Brive-la-
Gaillarde. The remarkable telephone operator had been right. "Jean
Murat" and the "Colonel" were the same. Bouvier questioned the
notary himself. Yes, he had heard of the "Colonel." He had even
seen him once, briefly. Someone had told him he was a Polytechnician.

Bouvier had been right all along. But the description, which was
confirmed by the telephone operator, completely killed the Argoud
theory. The "Colonel" was tall, exceptionally handsome, with thick
hair, and about 35 years old. Argoud was small, good-looking yes,
but with thin hair and in his late forties. Bouvier sent the message

back to Paris; trace a Polytechnician that fits the description and resembles the identikit picture.

Then he addressed himself to the good citizen of Brive-la-Gaillarde who apparently did not mind his telephone ringing for strangers late at night. Bouvier said: "You mentioned that 'someone' told you that Colonel was a Polytechnician. Who was that 'someone'?"

"Major Niaux," was the reply.

Major Henri Niaux, a retired officer living at Lauzun, was a deceptively weak-looking man in his forties, with an anxious face and a nervous tic. He immediately confessed to his part in organizing the affair at Petit Clamart, but his confession went further than the police expected. "I was in charge," Niaux declared. "I planned the assassination, and I am sorry only that it failed. I am the Colonel."

But it so happened that Bouvier already knew better. A dossier had been placed on his desk. It was a lifetime report, with photographs, on Jean-Marie Bastien-Thiry, born in Lunéville, Moselle, October 10, 1927. It would be difficult to find in France a family that had rendered the nation more illustrious service than had the Bastien-Thirys. The family included two generals and two chief magistrates. The father of Bastien-Thiry was a distinguished science professor at Lunéville. The son had maintained the family tradiion. He held the rank of lieutenant colonel in the Air Force, in which he had served as a test pilot, and he was a man of great physical courage. He currently held an important post as engineer with the Technical Industrial Direction of the Air, a leading government agency dealing with flight research.

One of the pictures showed Bastien-Thiry wearing his cocked hat and sword on parade at the Polytechnique. He was really a beautiful young man. He had entered the Polytechnique in 1947, the dossier said, and had studied nuclear physics. One picture showed him on his wedding day. He had three small daughters and was said to be deeply and devoutly Catholic. In the Air Force he had served in the Sahara, but that seemed to be his only connection with French Algeria.

"You were saying?" Bouvier said to Niaux, looking up from his dossier.

"I planned everything," said Niaux again. "I am the Colonel. You need look no further."

Bouver lifted one of the photographs of Bastien-Thiry and held it in front of him. "Do you know who this is?"

Bouvier was pleased with the reaction he received but admired Niaux's courage. "I have never seen him before," Niaux said, and Bouvier knew that he was lying. At last he had before him a man who knew the "Colonel." He left further questioning of Niaux to his subordinates. Niaux was grilled far into the night, but, despite his appearance, he was a tough man, and stuck to his story until the detectives were as exhausted as he. After they had gone, Niaux, in his cell, tore his sheet into strips and hanged himself. The one man who could identify the "Colonel" was dead.

Bastien-Thiry was kept under close observation and was given no indication of the closing net. The important arrests had been kept from the press. Now Bouvier ordered him to be brought to the Quai des Orfèvres for questioning, and the two men met. Bouvier was subsequently quoted as saying how strange it was "that the working-class son of working-class parents had to defend the French Republic and its President against a man whom France had given every privilege she had to offer."

Bastien-Thiry's alibi was unshakable. He had been home with his father and some friends when the attempt on General de Gaulle's life was made. He even added a touch that Bouvier expected of him; he said that one of the friends concerned was the local chief of police.

Bouvier was stalled. The evidence against Bastien-Thiry was far too slight. The three people who might have identified him were summoned. Neither the dignitary from Brive-la-Gaillarde nor the girl who had rented him the car was certain. The telephone operator *was* certain "because he was so good-looking," but that was scarcely sufficient for a court of law. Then the final breakthrough came. In one of Bastien-Thiry's chests of drawers a policeman found a telephone number. It had been scribbled on a scrap of newspaper, and the scrap had been torn off and preserved. Bouvier ordered the number to be called, and it proved to be that of the bar in which the Pickle had waited for a call on the day of the attack. The newspaper itself was traced. It was torn from *France-Soir* dated August 22.

The case was effectively solved. Apart from those already accused, many aristocratic families were implicated by the police and

was too cold in the winter, and the Castilian plateau affected their breathing. Many settled along the Costa del Sol and opened restaurants. The colony in Alicante grew large enough for a French school to be opened, and a weekly newspaper, *Courrier de Soleil,* to be published; it was staffed exclusively by former O.A.S. men. The *pieds noirs* are no more popular in Spain than anywhere else. In Madrid they are resented by the French and Anglo-Saxons because the children of the wealthier *pied noir* families have left no room in the Lycée Français, and in Alicante the *pieds noirs* are too numerous for comfort. "Neither French, nor Spanish, nor Arab—nothing" is a popular local point of view.

The last great rally of the O.A.S.-C.N.R. took place in Lisbon in November 1962. Among those present were Bidault, Soustelle, Argoud, Gardy, Godard, Gardes, Dufour and Vaudrey. Gardy, a titular head of the O.A.S. gave his support to the C.N.R. as constituted under Bidault and handed over $400,000 from the O.A.S.-Oran treasury. Bidault and Soustelle were both exiles; Soustelle had gone into hiding, and Bidault had been stripped of his parliamentary immunity since the previous July. Most of the colonels present refused to have anything to do with Soustelle, who they felt had not pulled his weight. Château-Jobert refused to have anything to do with anybody or even to attend.

Bidault and Argoud then based themselves on Munich and became friendly with the press there. Bidault gave interviews and was even persuaded to fly to London, where he was interviewed by the B.B.C. for television and photographed having a beer in a pub by the *Daily Express.* Argoud had grown a small pointed beard, which gave him a somewhat puckish appearance, like the toy red devils that some motorists hang in the rear windows of their cars. He permitted himself to be photographed smiling over a copy of *France-Soir* that had splashed in its largest headlines, Ex-COLONEL ARGOUD ARRESTED IN BELGIUM.

The announcement was premature, but this sudden avidity for spectacular publicity had a kind of torero's bravado that seemed imprudent, to say the least. Although Argoud had announced himself head of the O.A.S.-Métropole, he was careful not to visit France. But his peripatetics—his habit of escaping, then of fading away, then reappearing in unexpected places—was good copy, and the irritated police wanted him more than any other. They could not appeal to Interpol, for Interpol shuns political matters; other agencies had to be called upon.

One evening near the end of February 1963, Argoud arrived in Munich by plane under the name of Gilbert Marchal and took a taxi to the Eden Wolff Hotel. The end of February is a groggy time in Munich, midway in the pre-Lenten *Fasching*; the city was gay with costumes. Three hours after Argoud had registered, two men came into the crowded lobby; pushed their way to the desk through the crowds of Columbines, Pierrots and ancient Romans, and asked for "Monsieur Marchal." Argoud emerged from the elevator and spoke to the visitors, who showed him a card. The three walked towards the swinging doors, but Argoud suddenly changed his mind and began to resist. The two men seized him, punched him in the face, threw him into a car and drove away. The Columbines and Pierrots looked startled for a moment, then shrugged the incident off as a *Fasching* brawl and thought no more about it.

The next afternoon, a man, recalled as thickset and wearing a dark suit, entered the Café Esmeralda across the square from Notre Dame Cathedral in Paris and asked for a telephone token. He left the door of the telephone box open, and several people in the cafe heard the following extraordinary conversation: "This is the O.A.S. I repeat. This is the O.A.S. We are giving you Argoud. He betrayed us, bungled all the jobs he was supposed to do, particularly the affair at Petit Clamart. You can take delivery of him immediately. He is in a blue truck in the alley opposite Notre Dame."

The man hung up and left, apparently indifferent to the incredulous stares that followed him. Police headquarters on the Quai des Orfévres is only a few minutes walk from Notre Dame, and the police were there at once in scores, scurrying like blue ants all over the square. They found a small delivery truck parked in an alley and inside it a gagged, trussed and blindfolded figure, moving feebly. Detectives lifted the blindfold and stared into a face that reminded one of a poached egg and another of a crushed raspberry. The gag was removed; Argoud was conscious. His spirit was far from broken, and his first words were of indignation, of outraged *amour propre*. "Just see for yourself what the police have done to a French officer," he said. He was formally identified by Commissioner Bouvier.

Throughout his trial he maintained complete silence. Tixier-Vignancourt's defense was that Argoud "was not there." He was legally in Germany. Tixier had all his knives out for General de Gaulle. He recalled that Napoleon Bonaparte had arranged for the Duke of Enghien to be kidnapped from Baden-Baden and shot. "Bonaparte at least admitted what he had done," he said. "He had the courage to say 'I did it.'"

Argoud was sentenced to life imprisonment. The incident was significant, in that it showed how profoundly the Algerian war had corroded the ethics of a great nation. By any standards the kidnapping of a man by secret policemen from a friendly foreign country is inexcusable. The car in which Argoud had been spirited across the border was spared customs and immigration investigation because it carried French military plates. The diplomatic exchanges that followed showed the French authorities to be impenitent and brilliantly shifty.

It was stated by the prosecution that the West German Government had not asked Paris to return Argoud. The relevant passage read, "The Foreign Minister has today given formal assurance through the Prosecution that he has received no note from the West German Government requesting the return of ex-Colonel Argoud to the German authorities. . . ."

But on the same day, a Bonn Foreign Office spokesman said that the German Government had indeed addressed that very request to the French Ambassador in the form of what is known in diplomatic usage as a "verbal note," a note that is written but not signed; it is an old diplomatic trick, which leaves the recipient free to take notice of it or not, as he wishes.

When Bonn saw that Paris preferred not to accept the note, it sent a proper note to the German Ambassador in Paris, who handed it to the Quai d'Orsay. If the signed note had been received by the French Foreign Office in time, that is to say, before the trial, Foreign Minister Maurice Couve de Murville would have been obliged to define his attitude formally, and the Court would have had to take that attitude into consideration. But it arrived while the trial was in process, and the course of law could not be influenced. Both the reputation of Bonn and the honor of Couve de Murville were thus satisfied, and Argoud was the loser.

No one believed that Argoud had been captured by the O.A.S. One cannot help thinking that the *barbouzes* had been restive in their silent role, for that is human nature. Every man needs a certain recognition for his accomplishments. For two years the O.A.S. had dominated the publicity while the *barbouzes* could not even admit their own existence. Here was a coup they could not resist.

There is one further point of interest in the Argoud kidnapping: When the Munich police examined his bags, they found the considerable sum of $11,000 in various European currencies.

Less spectacular but in a way nastier and more disquieting was the abduction of Jean-Marie Curutchet, the officer who had joined the O.A.S. the day he was promoted to captain. He was not kidnapped; he was "intercepted." He had escaped from Algeria to Rome and had made arrangements to take a job in South America. At the end of 1962 the French Embassy in Rome issued him a passport and even gave him the money for the tickets. Curutchet had every reason to believe that all was in order. But the plane was to make a stop at Dakar, and the Paris police, hearing of Curutchet's intentions, informed the Dakar police, who boarded the plane and arrested him. He was flown back to Paris and prison.

With the capture of Argoud and Curutchet the serious decline of the O.A.S. began. Bidault understandably lost his appetite for publicity. He asked for and was given asylum in Bavaria; he moved to Madrid but was ordered on his way and departed for Brazil. In the summer of 1967 he was allowed to settle in Belgium. Soustelle was allowed to remain in Italy, on the condition that he take no further part in politics. In March, Colonel Gardes was ordered out of Spain and flew with his family to Argentina. General Gardy rallied the remains of the movement and proposed that leadership of the O.A.S.-C.N.R. be given to the organization's leading uncaptured hero, Pierre Sergent. Sergent announced in the press that the name of the organization would be changed to *Comité Nationale de la Révolution,* and little more was heard of it or him.

Only in the prisons did one find density and camaraderie of O.A.S. friends, the newcomers being duly briefed by the old-timers. Jouhaud was at Fresnes, his death sentence having been commuted to life imprisonment. When Robert Martel, the mystic of the Mitidja, was arrested, several prisoners went on a work strike against having him for a cellmate; as he had been sentenced to only a few months, he was reminded at length of his celebrated maxim to distrust "those whom the régime regilds by liberating them too quickly from prison." Maurice Gingembre imparted to new arrivals something of the prison philosophy. The worst time, he said, was the period between the twelfth and eighteenth months. For the first year one was still living with the outside world. One was conscious of being in prison, but one felt and thought as a free man. After eighteen months, one had accepted one's fate and had accustomed oneself to prison life. But from the twelfth to the eighteenth months, prison seemed a nightmarish limbo between the fading past of a free man and a future one dared not contemplate.

In the years 1962–1963, when the O.A.S. was putting its greatest strain on French prison facilities, there were more than 3,000 prisoners, of whom some 560 could be considered leaders. They included 49 officers, 43 N.C.O.s and 111 enlisted men, 62 workmen, 50 white-collar workers, 44 artisans, 40 students, 18 shopkeepers, 15 engineers, 7 men of letters, 5 professors and a few of miscellaneous calling. The 3,000 included some 50 Moslems.

The O.A.S. members refused to consider themselves convicts, insisting that they were prisoners of war, whose duty it was not only to preserve high morale but also when possible to escape. Many were offered amnesty if they would write public letters of apology to the President of the Republic, but almost to a man they refused. As political prisoners they were granted more liberties than ordinary criminals. They distilled their own alcohol from crushed potatoes flavored with oranges and discussed the product like gourmets.

"A little green as yet."

"It was better with pear."

They discussed on a high intellectual level, the B-grade western movie shown in prison, as if they were highbrow critics discussing Fellini. Every year they made a point of observing a minute of silence on each anniversary of the executions of Dovecar, Piegts, Degueldre and Bastien-Thiry, but as the minutes and the years multiplied time weighed heavily.

Escapes were frequent, at least at first, in the days of fresh memories and high morale. On May 3, 1964, Marc Robin escaped from the prison hospital at La Rochelle; he has never been caught. He reached Brazil, from where he writes to his old comrades and tells them he is doing "very well." Lieutenant Daniel Godot had a try but was caught. "A soldier is made to fight, not rot in prison," he told the police.

Gradually, most were amnestied, but many continued to languish. Then in November 1967, the O.A.S. burst briefly into the headlines with something like its old panache. Claude Tenne, one of the four killers of Commissioner Gavoury, was serving a life sentence on the Ile de Ré, a remote island off the Charente Maritime. Two other prisoners, one of them Laszlo Vargas, the Hungarian Legionnaire who took part at Petit Clamart, helped him escape in a trunk. Police stations ordered "Plan Rex"—maximum urgency—and once again traffic jams piled up at anti-O.A.S. roadblocks from Paris to the Riviera. Tenne reached Belgium and disappeared completely. With Dovercar, Danglade and Petri, Tenne launched the O.A.S.'s year of violence. Today the scorecard reads, Dovecar executed, Tenne escaped, Danglade never apprehended, Petri still in prison.

The O.A.S. leaders are dispersed today on two continents. Colonel Gardes is one of the more successful. He runs a shop in Buenos Aires and makes a hare pâté from a recipe of his mother's; the pâté can be bought in the luxury food stores in Paris. Pierre Lagaillarde and his wife Babette are schoolteachers in the new French school in Alicante. Lagaillarde is a lonely man who finds little stimulation in either society or business, and he is still too young to have carried so much history on his shoulders. Jean-Jacques Susini lurks—one cannot resist the word—in Rome. Although the French police have long since lost interest in him, he still finds it natural to be secretive and suspicious and carefully covers his traces with false names, confidential addresses and letter drops.

Pierre Montagnon, O.A.S. commander in the Ouarsenis, married Bernadette Pujol, but they were subsequently divorced. Geneviéve Salasc lives in an elegant apartment overlooking the Mediterranean at Marseilles, where her husband is in practice. Her enthusiasm is undimmed, and her driving is, if anything, more maniacal than ever. She has never forgiven Susini for negotiating with the Algerian Provisional Government. When asked what alternative he had, she takes both hands off the wheel of her car and exclaims, "We should have fought to the end." Her counterpart in feminine courage, Djamila Boupacha, married an officer in the Algerian Army, has visited England to study British education methods for the Algerian Government, and now lives quietly in Algiers.

Maurice Gingembre owns a publishing house in Paris. Jésus Giner, the pocket terror of Bab-el-Oued is a construction worker at

Alicante Airport, where his wife runs a small restaurant for the local *pied noir* workers. He is as friendly and as gregarious as he was in his bold bad days, although his liking for anisette occasionally leads him into barroom brawls. He is usually extricated by the police and persuaded to cool off for a night in Alicante jail.

Michel Fechoz still makes the rounds of the Madrid nightclubs and can be seen most evenings in the Borbón Street and the Whiskey Jazz. In 1966, two Frenchmen arrested in New York for carrying heroin cited him as the ringleader. Colonel Dufour lives in San Sebastián, Spain. General Gardy, his daughter Nicole and the son she bore by Roger Degueldre moved to the Argentine and live in the interior, in a colony of *pieds noirs*. On Majorca Château-Jobert writes mystical tracts and corresponds with Father Grasset. Colonel Lacheroy directs a real-estate agency and teaches science in his spare time. Joseph and Andrée Ortiz own a café.

Colonel Godard disappeared. Being without family ties it was easier for him to fade from the public eye, and as recently as 1966 many of his old colleagues believed him to be helping the Americans in Vietnam. His adventures were not that romantic. Early in 1967 he was discovered living with a pretty Frenchwoman called Solange Weiss in an apartment with double doors over a grocery in a North Brussels suburb. He was allowed by the police to remain in Belgium.

His old adversary, Yacef Saadi, continued to acknowledge the chivalry with which Godard treated him after the Battle of Algiers. Saadi was one of the producers and advisers of the film *The Battle of Algiers* which won much acclaim and many international awards. The character of Godard (called Mathieu in the film) is sympathetically presented.

General Katz went on to hold several commands in Metropolitan France and was retired with the rank of General of the Army. The Bachaga Boualem, with a few score of his harkis, was given a wild stretch of land at Mas Thibert in the Camargue, near Arles. Friends in the French Air Force flew a few of his Arab horses from Algeria, but they are his only luxury. He lives as simply as do his men in a cold, gloomy house almost empty of furniture. His son Mohammed, one of the leaders of the Ouarsenis operation, is with him, but sixteen members of his immediate family have been murdered in Algeria.

The mistral blows hard and frequently in this part of France, tearing at nerves and snapping tempers. The former Vice-President of the National Assembly greets visitors courteously and contains as best he can his bitterness against General de Gaulle, but when the wind blows it is not always easy. Colonel Broizat and his wife live in Rome and are almost destitute. The Benedictine who turned Protestant, then Communist, then religious mystic did achieve at least one of his goals: He enrolled in the Salvation Army. Pierre Sergent lives in Lausanne and occasionally visits France on business. The police know about it, but they leave him in peace. Colonel de Blignières served his sentence and lives in Paris with his wife, daughters and memories. Captain Ferrandi married after his release from prison and now directs a chain of hotels in Paris and the Caribbean. He is a wealthy man. Colonel Argoud, in prison, applied to the courts for divorce. His wife, who has an independent income, lives with her daughters in Vincennes. The daughters visit their father in prison, the wife never. Some former prison friends believe that Argoud will take holy orders after his release. Dr. Perez lives in Venezuela in fear of assassination by some of his former colleagues. He is still believed to hold a great deal of O.A.S. money.

The *barbouzes* have not been disbanded. The kidnapping of Ben Barka in October 1965 was a typical botched *barbouze* exercise. One of the key figures in the affair was Georges Figon, who told the press that he and three others had guarded Ben Barka before his death. Figon was an ex-convict and was also described as "a secret agent." A warrant was issued for his arrest, but, when the police broke into his apartment, he was found dead with a bullet through his head and an automatic by his side. The official version was "suicide," but his death came as a relief to many. Georges Figon was, in 1961, a *barbouze* marked on the O.A.S. lists for assassination. The news of the Ben Barka affair deeply agitated Antoine Argoud in prison, as its methods, and even some of the people in the case, were painfully familiar to him.

All the O.A.S. leaders have one characteristic in common, an air of defenselessness. Their contacts with one another are too indirect and too infrequent, and, since their single year of comradeship, they have had many years to ponder and brood, to wonder, to ask themselves questions, and then to find all too many reasons, real and imaginary, for resentment. Lagaillarde especially has broken from

almost every tie with the others. He is intensely suspicious, and hates
Ortiz almost hysterically. Oddly enough he has little resentment
for Susini, the man who outmaneuvered him for leadership in the
O.A.S., perhaps because in this struggle between the two former
students of Algiers it was Lagaillarde and not Susini who emerged
the winner. Susini, by leaving Lagaillarde stranded in Madrid, did him
a service in the end. The O.A.S. lost the war. Lagaillarde, being
such a splendid and handsome figure of a man, would have found
disguise a difficult business, and he may well have been captured,
like Salan, in which case he would be languishing in prison to this
day. Lagaillarde at least lives openly, and still has many admirers.
Alicante, in climate and even in atmosphere, is in some ways like a
small Algiers. So, while Lagaillarde tans himself golden in the
sunshine, Susini skulks around Europe, in hiding even from such old
O.A.S. comrades who feel no ill-will toward him. Lagaillarde, the
man of the day, and Susini, the man of the night, have both found
their true levels and natural backgrounds. Lagaillarde is still ready to
communicate as a human being with anyone who wishes to acknowledge himself as such, and the same can be said for most. But
not for Susini.

25
CONCLUSION
(1968)

✛✛✛

Of the original equation mentioned in this book: that the O.A.S. equaled the French Army plus Algeria plus de Gaulle—one factor, Algeria, is gone. De Gaulle will go sooner or later. The French Army found itself in 1962 without a war on its hands for the first time in more than twenty years. It had abandoned its empire, and joined the nuclear Establishment; it is unlikely that any French soldier will ever point a gun at an enemy again. Where does that leave the O.A.S.?

Nowhere. It is an episode in history, important only to those who fought in it. There is no more O.A.S. today, except as a kind of fraternity of old comrades who meet to recall the days of great adventure. There are no secret calls, no plans for future action. It is a memory. Among the members, Roger Degueldre is a legend, a kind of Robin Hood. Only a few years after his death he has already divided the O.A.S. into two classes, those who knew him personally and those who did not. Those who did know Degueldre enjoy a special aura and a shade of extra glamor in the O.A.S. hierarchy. In time a cult will grow around his son. One problem in Degueldre worship, however, is that, in death as in life, he continues to be haunted by his alter ego, Roger Deguelle; even today newspaper reports frequently refer to him as a Belgian and an S.S. man.

The O.A.S. succeeded in confirming General de Gaulle's place in one of the niches of history. To acknowledge that he was wrong, as de Gaulle did about Algeria, requires great courage, something that the General's bitterest critics would never deny him. He sensed that

Metropolitan France was sick of Algeria, and he bowed to the will of the people. But to turn his own coat and then to denounce as blackguards and renegades the people who followed him loyally up to the moment of change are something else. As in the Second World War, de Gaulle showed over Algeria that, whatever his political wisdom, he is less than generous in his human relationships. The colonels pleading at the Barricades, the desperate lieutenants in the bled, General Challe in his bloodless and half-hearted revolt, Soustelle with all his years of Gaullist loyalty behind him, Bidault broken by long and thankless service to the Fourth Republic, Salan whose judges gave the wrong verdict, Bastien-Thiry who fired and missed —all these men gave General de Gaulle opportunities to show magnanimity, and he declined to accept one of them. They may all have been wrong, but they were not all rogues. Some observers, among them James Reston, in *The New York Times* on June 6, 1967, went so far as to suggest that de Gaulle's stand in the most recent Arab-Israeli war was partly influenced by continued resentment at Israeli agents' infiltration of the O.A.S.—scarcely motive enough for such a radical and controversial change of policy.

The O.A.S. could not have succeeded but it could have been more effective. Its failure was not idealogical, but tactical. It could not coordinate its various arms. May 13 proved that revolt in Algeria could succeed only when every group—*pied noir,* Moslem and soldier—worked together. At the Barricades only the *pieds noirs* moved, at the Putsch only the Army. Too much was attempted too late and in too short a time; then the attempt was abandoned too quickly. The Organization had all sorts of major enemies to eliminate, from General de Gaulle to General Allaire, General Katz and Colonel Debrosse, but its final score was only a few police commissioners and a few hundred *barbouzes.* At the Barricades, Challe, Broizat and Dufour all supported the revolt in principle but, in fact, suppressed it. Challe could have persevered with the Putsch but abandoned it without even informing his fellow generals. Salan did not want to see de Gaulle assassinated. Oran could have been used as a redoubt to force concessions from the F.L.N., but it wasn't. Lagaillarde, who at least had energy and panache, played scarcely any role at all. Bastien-Thiry came closest to success, but he was not in the O.A.S. at all, and he acted far too late, when the issues were resolved and the game over. As was said of the Habsburgs:

It is the curse of our proud dynasty
To move half-heartedly, stop half way,
And adopt half-measures, hesitatingly.

Few men in the O.A.S. were bought with money. Some acted
from revenge, some for self-preservation, some because they were
oppressed and frightened and saw the future as a matter of killing
or being killed. Whatever divided them politically and ethically, it
was fair to say that every one was an idealist, however warped. There
were brutes among them, like the loveable little brute Dovecar; there
were sadists and bores, and even cowards, but every one was prepared
to sacrifice rank, family, pension, reputation. All were ready to risk
disgrace, imprisonment and death in most disagreeable forms. Success, even if success had been possible, would have brought rewards
to no one.

One cannot say that these men did not hesitate. A huge majority
did hesitate. They sat on the fence, spoke sympathetically and waited
to see which way the wind would blow. Even the colonels hesitated.
General Challe said at his trial, "If we had not accepted the command, the colonels would not have moved." Those who hesitated
were not cowards; in fact, they were some of the most determined of
the officers, men like Massu and Bigeard. Colonel Gouraud hesitated
in Constantine at the time of the Putsch, finally declined to join it
but still received a seven-year prison sentence for his pains. It was a
very small band of men and women who refused to hesitate, who
plunged in, fought, suffered and murdered; it was they who put the
story of the O.A.S. on the books.

The rising up of such a large group of officers, students and
civilians was one of the most bizarre episodes of post war history.
The revolt could be explained in many ways. It was caused partly
by frustration at a politically sterile, neo-Salazarist atmosphere that
the Fifth Republic had imposed on a temperamental and high-spirited
people. It was partly caused by a resurgence of political romanticism
in some, of old-fashioned French nationalism in others and of the
bourgeois fear of communism in still others. It appealed to no one
class or philosophy. It derived inspiration from many sources—from
the Cagoulards, from the Resistance, from Mao Tse-tung and Ho
Chi Minh, from the Congo mercenaries—with a few touches here
and there from Nazi Germany. If it had any cement at all it was

hatred for General de Gaulle, and even that hatred varied in intensity. Some of the Legionnaires had scarcely heard of him.

The O.A.S. was, in fact, inevitable. Young Frenchmen who had grown up to expect a certain national destiny had to revolt against a political orientation that changed it completely. As Jean Laréguy wrote in *The Centurions*, "Algeria is the ball and chain attaching France to her great-power role and forcing her to behave with more greatness and generosity than a Switzerland of today, a nation of merchants and fat bourgeois." The O.A.S. men had to resist the ultimate result: namely that, according to de Gaulle in his 1966 press conference, "France now lives without drama." It was impossible to expect that an all-powerful European minority would abandon its privileges without a fight, impossible to expect soldiers who had been suffering frustrations ever since 1940 to go on accepting frustration for ever. The French had an expression for the professional officer in Algeria. He was *le soldat perdu*. Those lost soldiers had to find themselves somewhere, and they found themselves in the O.A.S. They did horrible things and said ridiculous things about "international communism," of which they understood nothing, and "our Moslem brothers," whose numbers they so spectacularly reduced. But there will always be men who believe that some tasks must be attempted, even though they know in advance that they are bound to fail, as D'Annunzio knew at Fiume. Such men do not have to be philosophers, and if one has to sacrifice everything, including one's life, it is essential that the cause be made to look not merely just but also simple.

BIBLIOGRAPHY AND NOTES
ON SOURCES

❖❖❖

It will be clear to every reader who has reached this far that I have drawn widely on personal observation and confidential reminiscences, as well as on notes and diaries of people who figure in the history of the O.A.S. Many of these people now lead normal lives in France. Some have served prison sentences. Others are still in exile abroad under their own or fictitious names. Still others are in hiding. Whether they remain in touch with their old comrades or remain completely apart, they are all interlinked by memories in which the words of one affect all. In such a situation there can be no question of naming sources without betraying confidence. This has even led occasionally to my using fictitious names. The man I call Danglade, for example, is wanted by the French police for murder. He lives openly abroad with a wife and family under his own name, and I do not consider my responsibility as author extends to exposing him to the authorities of the country in which he has found asylum. I can say, however that I am deeply indebted to M. Georges Ras and M. Georges Bousquet, who observed the O.A.S. from the inside, from the beginning to the end, and gave me unsparingly of their expert knowledge, while divorcing themselves from any points of view I have expressed. I am indebted also to Mr. Paul Davis for his eyewitness accounts of the last hours of French Oran.

A major source of information on the O.A.S. is the testimony at the trials of the various participants. Another is *L'O.A.S. Parle*, a collection of O.A.S. documents published by Julliard and edited by

Pierre Nora, in 1964. Use has been made of these documents throughout the book.

Part One. The Origin.

Beauvoir, Simone de, and Gisèle Halimi. *Djamila Boupacha.* Gallimard, 1962. Illustrations by Pablo Picasso.

Bidault, Georges. *Resistance: The Autobiography of Georges Bidault.* Weidenfeld, & Nicolson, 1967. Published in France in 1965 as *D'Une Résistance à l'Autre.*

Bromberger, Merry and Serge, *Les Complots du 13 Mai.* Fayard, 1959.

Bromberger, Merry and Serge, Georgette Elgey and J. F. Chauvel. *Barricades et Colonels.* Fayard, 1960.

Bromberger, Serge. *Les Rebelles Algériens.* Plon, 1958.

Brune, Jean. *Cette Haine Qui Ressemble à l'Amour.* Table Ronde, 1961. A novel.

Chevalier, Jacques. *Nous Algériens.* Calmann-Lévy, 1958. Chevalier is former Mayor of Algiers.

Clark, Michael. *Algeria in Turmoil.* Thames & Hudson, 1957.

Delarue, Louis. *Avec les Paras des 1e R.E.P. et 2e R.P.I.Ma.* Nouvelles Éditions Latines, 1961.

Fall, Bernard. *Hell in a Very Small Place: The Story of Dien Bien Phu.* Lippincott, 1967.

Fauvet, Jacques, and Jean Planchais. *La Fronde des Généreaux.* Arthaud, 1961. Describes the Putsch.

Feller, Jean. *Le Dossier de l'Armée. Française: 1914–1962.* Perrin, 1967.

Gorce, Paul Marie de la. *The French Army.* Braziller, 1963.

Hora, Karel. *Mon Tour du Monde en 80 Barouds.* Éditions de la Pensée Moderne, 1961.

Juin, Maréchal. *Le Maghreb en Feu.* Plon, 1957.

Lentin, A. P. *L'Algérie des Colonels.* Petite Bibliothèque Républicaine, 1958.

Morland-Barange-Martinez. *Histoire de l'Organisation de l'Armée Secréte.* Julliard, 1964. (The authors are three police officers writing under pseudonyms without Christian names.)

Paxton, Robert O. *Parades and Politics at Vichy.* Princeton University Press, 1966.

Phillips, John. *Odd World.* Simon & Schuster, 1959.

Planchais, Jean. *Où en Est l'Armée?* Chastel, 1960.

Roy, Jules. *Dien Bien Phu.* Julliard, 1963.

————. *La Guerre d'Algérie.* Julliard, 1960.

Serigny, Alain de. *La Révolution du 13 Mai.* Plon, 1958. Serigny was publisher of *Écho d'Alger.*

Servan Schreiber, Jean-Jacques. *Lieutenant en Algérie.*

Ysquierdo, Antoine. *Une Guerre Pour Rien.* Table Ronde, 1966. Describes the 1st R.E.P. five years later.

Part Two. The Happening.

Abro, Ben. *Assassination.* Morrow, 1963. A fascinating novel about the *barbouzes* by a Jewish *barbouze* writing under a pseudonym.

Buchard, Robert. *Organisation Armée Secréte,* Vol. 1. Michel, 1963.

Laroche, Fabrice. *Salan Devant L'Opinion.* Saint-Just, 1963.

Laroche, Fabrice, and Françoise d'Orcival. *Le Courage Est Leur Patrie.* Collection Action, 1963. Collection Action is the publishing firm founded by Maurice Gingembre after his release from prison.

Montagnon, Pierre. *Pas Même un Caillou.* Collection Action, 1965.

Nicol, Axel. *La Bataille de l'O.A.S.* Sept Couleurs, Axel Nicol is a pseudonym.

Susini, Jean-Jacques. *Histoire de l'O.A.S.* Table Ronde, 1963. An editor's note says that the obvious cuts were made at the behest neither of the author, the publisher, nor the printer but because the book was seized on the day of publication.

Vivie, Francois de. *O.A.S. L'Inévitable Rébellion,* Historia (special edition), January 1967.

Part Three. The Frenzy.

Buchard, Robert. *Organisation Armée Secrète,* Vol. 2. Michel, 1963.

"Interview with General Gardy," *Topic* (now defunct), June 27, 1962.

Lentin, Albert-Paul. *Le Dernier Quart d'Heure.* Julliard, 1963.

Présence de Bastien-Thiry. Fuseau, 1966.

Reimbold, Jean. *Pour Avoir Dit Non.* Table Ronde, 1966.

Welles, Benjamin. "Interview with Roger Degueldre," *The New York Times,* March 18–21, 1962. A series of four articles.

INDEX

✦✦✦

DATE DUE

GAYLORD			PRINTED IN U.S A.